1-16   £2-69

GW00808648

What's Left?

What's Left?

Labour Britain and the Socialist Tradition

David Powell

PETER OWEN

LONDON AND CHESTER SPRINGS

PETER OWEN PUBLISHERS
73 Kenway Road London SW5 ORE

Peter Owen books are distributed in the USA by
Dufour Editions Inc. Chester Springs PA 19425-0007

First published in Great Britain 1998
© David Powell 1998

ISBN 0 7206 1041 9

A catalogue record for this book is available from the British Library

Printed and made in Great Britain by Hillman Printers (Frome) Ltd.

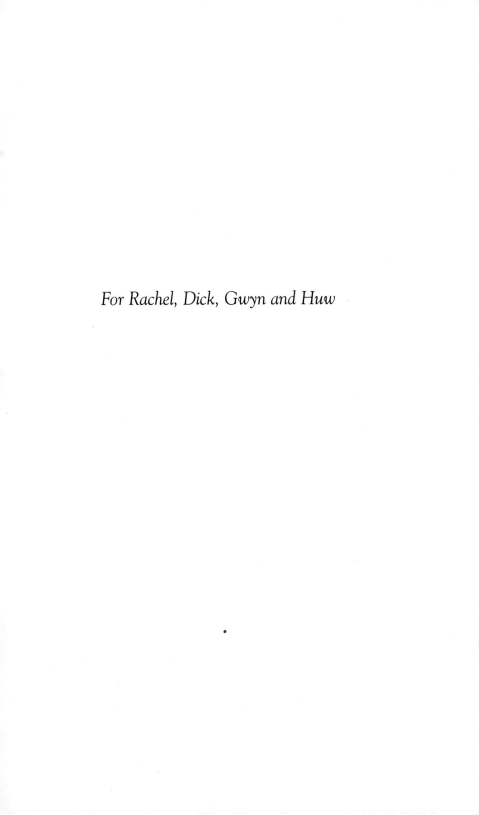

For Rachel, Dick, Gwyn and Huw

Foreword
Rt Hon. Tony Benn, MP

This is a book that everyone who is interested in British politics should read, for it provides a far better account of the underlying debate that is going on in this country than can be found in the mass media reporting of public affairs. Parliamentary democracy, for which the Chartists and the Suffragettes worked so hard, has degenerated into a new form of feudalism where the King and his courtiers receive endless coverage, while issues are sidelined and philosophical arguments and moral choices are virtually ignored.

The Labour Party founded at the beginning of the century was the product of hundreds of years of human effort and analysis. This is therefore a good time to assess its record and its prospects for the future – a time when socialism has been written out of the scene by a wildly over-confident global capitalist establishment that is forever celebrating its power and apparent invulnerability to any challenge.

In writing the history of socialist ideas David Powell takes us back to the very beginning and shows the permanent relevance of the arguments that have always gone on between the rich and the powerful and the people with their aspirations for social justice, democracy and peace. When Keir Hardie founded the party he drew on this rich inheritance and identified the trade union movement as the most powerful force for social improvement, working with socialist and progressive Christians.

Since its foundation Labour has had its turn in office and has made some formidable improvements in the conditions of the people. We have seen the creation of the modern Welfare State, the National Health Service, full employment after the war and full trade union rights. But there have also been periods when it looked as if the party might be destroyed, as when Ramsay Mac-Donald joined with the Tories and the Liberals to reform a national government in 1931.

More recently, in 1976 Labour gave way to the International Monetary Fund and the cuts it demanded, which triggered the Winter of Discontent and paved the way for the Thatcher years when the Social Democratic Party formed to weaken us further still. Now 'New Labour' has taken over the party and moved it to the right by formally abandoning socialism, distancing itself from the trade unions and sidelining its annual conference and democratic traditions.

But still the movement carries on and keeps reasserting its faith in the face of establishment hostility, drawing on the resources that this book describes so vividly. Everyone learns best from their own experience and nowhere is this more true than for socialists, who now have a hundred years in which their ideas have been tried out, here and worldwide.

The Russian revolution of 1917 marked a turning point when the first attempt was made to build a new society against a background of bitter hostility from the West. The war of intervention, the fascist counter-attack and the Cold War were all launched to destroy this experiment, which failed because it never managed to develop the democratic traditions that were needed to make it durable. But the Social Democrats failed too, because they finally capitulated to the pressures of market forces and became apologists for capitalism themselves.

Now we can see what unreconstructed capitalism is doing to the world, and the demand for social justice, peace, democracy, development and international cooperation is growing again everywhere. Therein lies the importance of this scholarly, well-documented and immensely readable work, which is more than a history, although it is that too. It is really a map for us to use in the future, drawing on the successes and failures of the past. Certainly, it fills me with optimism as we move into a new century, and this is how I believe it should be read.

Tony Benn
London

Contents

Introduction

'We are all socialists now-a-days.' – The Prince of Wales, 1895

The Labour Party is founded on a contradiction. Basically, how can a party rooted in dissent ever become the party of government? This is the central dilemma of socialism, which has racked the party since its foundation at the turn of the century. As often as not Labour has settled for the expedient solution of forgoing its radicalism in order to convince the electorate that it is, indeed, fit to govern. Reflecting as much on the party's confidence in its principles as on its faith in the electorate, the formula may have proved fitfully successful. None the less it raises the further question: power at what cost?

Or are power and socialism incompatible and compromise an essential agent of power? The answers are as difficult to come by as the definition of socialism is elusive. The word came into general use only in the second half of the nineteenth century, since when it has become an ideological shibboleth, claimed as the exclusive property of both the right and the left of the movement, the one modestly asserting that it consists solely in 'the organization of the material economic forces of society and their control by human forces', the other militantly proclaiming that it is to secure for the workers 'the full fruits of their labour, thereby seeking to change the system of Society from Capitalist to Socialist'.

For all the subtleties of interpretation subsequently placed on the definitions, the dichotomy at the heart of socialism has remained unchanged since Ramsay MacDonald and Tom Mann spelled out their political agendas in the early 1900s. And if their differences have survived the century, so have the disputes that have divided the party over the means for realizing its goals, pragmatists dismissing the militants' programme as 'impossibilist' and maintaining that there was no realistic alternative to 'the inevitability of gradualism'.

Recognizing that there have been opposing strands in the party's theory and practice is not to play the game of alternative histories. It is legitimate to consider whether the hopes that Bernard Shaw vested in his Fabian vision of socialism, 'which could be adopted either as a whole or by instalments by any ordinary, respectable citizen without committing himself to revolutionary attachments', have been realized or whether William Morris was not more percipient when he admonished the party-in-embryo more than a century ago: 'I want to know . . . whether the Society of Inequality might not accept the quasi-socialist machinery [of gradualism] and not work it for the purpose of upholding that society in a somewhat shorn condition, but a safe one.'

A century on it is still possible to catch an echo of Shaw's prudence in New Labour's vision of a stakeholding economy and of Morris's scepticism in Old Labour's denunciation of revisionism. And if the spirit of Shaw can take comfort in the achievements of gradualism, then the shades of Morris will take consolation in the knowledge that the spirit of the freeborn Englishman is alive and well, if temporarily living in reduced circumstances. For it was not only *A Dream of John Ball* with its wounded cry of

> When Adam delved and Eve span
> Who was then the gentleman?

that inspired him but also the long history of British dissent – of the Leveller Rainborough's challenge of 1647: 'I think that the poorest he in England has a life to lead as the greatest he'; of Wilkes's defiant demand at his trial of 1765 'whether English liberty be reality or shadow'; of Tom Paine's charge that 'Man has no property in man; neither any generation a property in the generations that are to follow.'

But if this was the genesis of socialism, Hazlitt had already noted a falling-off in the headstrong spirit, at least among the aristocracy of dissent on the opposition benches of the 1820s: 'In their dread of exciting the hostility of the lords of the earth, they are like the man who silences the appeal of his companion to the Gods: "Call not so loud or they will hear us.'" Half a century separated Hazlitt's contempt for the Whig opposition from Morris's concern for the future of socialism, yet both diagnosed a common con dition: the supposed reluctance of radical leaders – Whig or social ist – to call too loudly for fear that the Society of Inequality might hear. That the rank and file of the labour movement harboured no such fears appeared to be of little account. All too often it seemed that the party leaders, like armchair generals, were blowing the call to advance to cover their own retreat from socialism.

At times it may have been realistic for the leadership to order a withdrawal to new positions in order to regroup. Equally, however, and not least during prolonged periods of social and economic crisis (the period of the Great Unrest before the First World War, the depression of the inter-war years, the trauma of the Thatcher experiment of the 1980s), there were moments when, suffering from a loss of political nerve, the Labour establishment compromised its socialist principles and, by demonizing the enemy within, undermined the confidence of large sections of the labour movement in its own political integrity.

Maybe the alternatives on offer were 'impossibilist' and would have compounded the problems they were meant to resolve. It is none the less arguable that in their pursuit of political correctness the party leadership not only sacrificed much of their own credibility but sapped the *raison d'être* of the party itself. For dissent is as much the legacy as the life force of socialism, and unless it acknowledges the right to challenge received opinions as well as to advance alternative strategies Labour is in danger of losing both its character and its ideological dynamism. This is not to minimize the difficulties involved in imposing order upon dissent or the need to impose some unity of purpose on the party if it is to have any chance of winning office. Both realism and dissent are the prerequisites of an effective Labour Party. Unfortunately each has been savaged in the bitter internecine disputes that have accompanied the party's ideological controversies since that February day of 1900 when the Labour Representation Committee was formed. For the history of Labour has been as much about the makers of the party as the policies they have pursued – and if the one has been divisive, the other has been abrasive.

It is said that on hearing a comrade remark that Herbert Morrison was his own worst enemy, Ernest Bevin retorted, 'Not while I'm around.' True or not, the remark is symptomatic of the personal differences that have racked Labour since Wells ridiculed the Fabian project as 'some little odd jobbing about water and gas'; differences that caused Richard Crossman to wonder half a century later: 'Why is it that this person is Left and that person Right? What is it that binds the group together?'

The answer may lie in the pursuit of power. Yet, as Crossman's diaries reveal, even office did little to moderate the intense rivalries – as much personal as ideological – that have continually riven the party. Perhaps this too was inevitable. It took hard, implacable men and women to survive in the cockpit of left-wing politics, committed not simply to their own vision of the future but equally to their own means of attaining their goal. While there could be no question that their New Jerusalem was out there somewhere, there was little agreement either as to its nature or how it was to be reached.

In *The Soul of Man Under Socialism*, published in 1891, Oscar Wilde wrote: 'Socialism itself will be of value simply because it will lead to Individualism.' A century on he would have appreciated the irony that it was precisely this, the sheer bloody-minded individualism of the men and women who have attempted to shape the party and its policies in their own image, which has so often divided the party against itself. And yet it is this, too, that has provided Labour with its vitality: the freedom it has allowed its makers to contend for their own vision of the future, 'the one country', as Wilde remarked, 'at which humanity is always landing'.

The paradox is inescapable: for a century a party committed to fraternity has been involved in a most uncivil war with itself. For the purists there could be no compromising with capitalism; for the pragmatists there could be no alternative to compromise. And for neither could there be any compromise with the other. Thus the vendettas and bloodlettings, the witch hunts and purges that have bedevilled Labour on its road to the New Jerusalem. Indeed, the miracle is that the party has survived its own turbulent past. Notwithstanding the jibe that the people's flag is the deepest red from having so often been dipped in the blood of the comrades, the party has shaped the British political agenda ever since Keir Hardie first asserted that 'the socialist revolution represents the will of the people' – although even then the Webbs disagreed. 'Hardie . . . knows little and cares less for any constructive thought or action.'

And so the dialogue has continued, as personally bruising as it has been politically stimulating. For a time Harold Wilson felt confident enough to maintain that Labour was the natural party of government, but his hopes proved illusory; the return of the Thatcher government revealed how easily the socialist project could be overturned. In reaction, New Labour was quick to jettison Clause IV along with what Peter Mandelson described as 'the party's accumulated political baggage', yet the old tensions remained, and traditionalists wondered aloud whether the party leadership understood what socialism was really about – an echo of the time at the turn of the century when militants such as Tom Mann asserted that Ramsay MacDonald had exchanged his socialist principles for membership of 'the finest club in Europe'.

Plus ça change, plus c'est la même chose. In his speech at London's Mansion House in 1895, the Prince of Wales declared: 'We are all socialists now-a-days.' That no one, least of all his *gros bourgeois* audience, could define precisely what he meant was of no consequence. It was clear that a new spirit was abroad in British politics, and ever since then the contest for the hearts and minds of socialism has provided a political theatre of a high order – frequently bloody, occasionally comical but never dull. The principles at stake have been too high, and the players involved too charismatic for things to be otherwise.

For all the ideological controversies that have racked the party, however, the fundamental questions remain unresolved. How can socialism best be defined and, once defined, how can it best be achieved? Is it possible to build a New Jerusalem on an instalment plan, as Shaw envisaged, or will the Society of Inequality simply mock the conceit, as Morris feared? The debate continues, its terms of reference irrevocably conditioned by the history of the Labour Party itself. As the party prepares to commemorate its centenary, therefore, what better place to take stock of its future than in its discordant past, which is where the present work begins. As far as much of New Labour is concerned, the past may be another country, but for all the dexterity of the party's spin-doctors it will not be expunged.

In this attempt to retrace something of the history and pre-history of socialism, I am indebted to all the help and encouragement I have received from Nick Bagnall, Arthur Butler, Audrey Coppard, Michael Cornish, Greg Elliott, David Freeman, Chris Freeman, Tony Heather, Joe McCarney, Sarah Mallen, Liz Mandeville and Alan Shelley. I hope that the book will repay their commitment. In addition, I would like to thank Lord Healey, Lord Shore, Ann Clwyd, Michael Foot, Giles Radice, Alan Simpson, Dennis Skinner and Tony Wright for assisting me in my attempt to locate 'the radical centre' that is now the Grail of New Labour. Finally, to Rachel my thanks, once again, for being so tolerant with this 'absent guest' over the past couple of years.

1
Nothing But Force Can Keep the People Under

'Undiluted Atheism, theft and immorality . . . I know of no language sufficiently potent to express my absolute detestation of
what I believe to be the most poisonous doctrine ever put forward,
namely Socialism.' – The Duke of Rutland, 1897

The word 'socialism' may be a relative newcomer to the language,
but the socialist ideal is deeply engrained in the English consciousness. The Commonwealth grandees of the mid-seventeenth
century had every right to be concerned when they 'raised those
spirits they could not lay', for it was a dangerous game that they
played. In invoking the rights of freeborn Englishmen they stirred
memories of a restive past reaching back to the time when the
recusant priest John Ball called on God to intercede in the name
of the peasantry, for 'My good people, things cannot go well in
England, nor ever will, until all goods are held in common . . . and
we shall all be equal.'

For his audacity in leading the Peasants' Revolt, Ball was hung,
drawn and quartered at St Albans in 1381, but if his mortal
remains were summarily disposed of, his heresy in challenging the
powers spiritual and secular was not so easily expunged. Folk
memory was too resilient for that; his life evoked the inchoate
dream of a commonwealth that was to serve as a catalyst for the
English Revolution. Energized by the thrusting spirit of Puri-
tanism, the troopers of Cromwell's New Model Army may have
sworn allegiance to a god alien to that worshipped by John Ball,
but as with Ball they called upon God to realize their vision: 'Was
the earth made to preserve a few proud and covetous men to live
at ease . . . or was it made to preserve all her children?' The
answer was as clear to the ultra-libertarians of the Civil War as its
implications were odious to Commonwealth grandees such as the

Earl of Essex: 'Is this the liberty we claim to vindicate by shedding our blood? This will be the reward of all our labours, and our posterity will say that to deliver them from the yoke of the King we have subjected them to that of the common people.'

In the immediate aftermath of the Civil War, the hopes of the common people were not to be easily dismissed, however. For the libertarians, the execution of Charles I was an apocalyptic event. The King was down, and now was the time to build a new kingdom in the name of reason, and yet the poverty of people's daily lives continued to deny the efficacy of their secular godhead: 'Such is our miserie that after the expense of much precious time, of blood and treasure and the ruine of so many honest families in recovering our Liberties, wee still finde this nation oppressed with grievances of the same destructive nature as formerly.'

The bitterness was pervasive, and with the Restoration of 1660 it seemed that the restless spirits that had raised England had finally been laid. The grandees were to ensure that they were not resurrected when James II was sent on his travels three decades later. The Whig power-brokers recalled only too well where their previous flirtation with democracy had led, and there was little either revolutionary or glorious about their Glorious Revolution of 1688. The consolidation of oligarchic authority was its sole purpose, justified by the dictum of their philosophical mentor John Locke that 'The great and chief end of men uniting into Commonwealths, and putting themselves under government, is the preservation of their property.'

Concerned solely with 'the dominion of property', and contemptuous of 'men capable only of labour', the Whigs subordinated all else to it – constitution, church, law. In the first half of the eighteenth century alone, some 2 million acres of common land were enclosed, for Oliver Goldsmith to write in *The Traveller*:

> Each wanton judge new penal statutes draws.
> Laws grind the poor, and rich men rule the laws.

There was no suppressing dissent, however, and when in 1763 'that devil Wilkes' rose to defend himself against the charge of being the author of 'a seditious and treasonable paper' for having asserted that George III's ministers were 'the tools of despotism and corruption', it fused the militancy of the London 'mobocracy'. Wilkes's defence only intensified their anger:

> My Lords, the liberty of all peers and gentlemen, and what touches me more sensibly, that of all the middling and inferior set of people who stand in most need of protection, is in my case this day to be finally decided upon, a question of such importance at to determine at once whether *English liberty* shall be a reality or a shadow.

When a verdict of not guilty was returned, the new slogan of militant radicalism – 'Wilkes and Liberty' – was heard for the first time. Always latent, the radical spirit was stirring again, to gather momentum again following the fall of the Bastille in 1789. Momentarily it appeared as if the world was being born anew, but while Wordsworth was rhapsodizing 'Bliss was it that dawn to be alive./But to be young was very heaven', and the maverick aristocrat Charles James Fox was toasting 'Our Sovereign Lord, the People', Edmund Burke was already writing his *Reflections on the Revolution in France*. Haunted by 'that nameless thing across the Channel', Burke's polemic was to become the handbook of counter-revolution. Although its early sales were phenomenal, they were soon outstripped by the reply penned by a former companion of Burke's, Thomas Paine.

A lapsed Quaker and one-time stay-maker, Paine published the first part of *The Rights of Man* in 1791 to refute 'the horrid principles' that Burke had advanced in the *Reflections*, not least the hereditary right, enshrined in the political settlement of 1688, of a privileged minority 'to bind us, our heirs and posterity, to them, their heirs and posterity, to the end of time'. In demolishing the myth of the freeborn Englishman (only 4 per cent of the adult population had the vote), Paine invented the new rhetoric of radical egalitarianism. Within a year of publication more than 200,000 copies of the first part of *Rights of Man* had been sold or distributed through a burgeoning network of Corresponding and Constitutional Societies, to the growing alarm of the government. In private, Pitt the Younger mused: 'Paine is right, but what am I to do?' In public, his answer was to introduce an increasingly punitive series of measures to stamp out all traces of dissent.

As conditions in France degenerated, so reaction in Britain intensified. In the name of liberty both nations employed coercion, the point and counter-point of revolution. Within six years of Louis XVI's execution in 1793, and reinforced by the declaration of war with France, Habeas Corpus had been suspended, the Corresponding Societies outlawed, the Treason and Seditious Meetings Bill enacted and a series of Combination Acts placed on the statute book prohibiting any combination of working men. For all the repression, however, dissent was not to be suborned. Burke's 'swinish multitude' may have been cowed by the draconian legislation enacted by Pitt's ministry, but there was no denying them the hopes they vested in the Rights of Man.

It was the industrial rather than the French revolution that transformed British politics in the nineteenth century. While the revolution of 1789 concentrated the mind of radicals on what Paine called 'the puppet show' of the English constitution, it was the take-off of industrialization in the last quarter of the eighteenth century that provided the reagent for political debate in Britain in the century that followed, even though at the outset the two issues – political and economic – were closely linked. Indeed, it was the expedient alliance between an industrial bourgeoisie and a new industrial working class that was to provide the groundwork for the passage of the Reform Bill of 1832.

The triumphalism with which the bourgeoisie celebrated winning the vote was matched only by their elation at the seemingly inexorable progress of the factory system they managed. Macaulay wrote that 'Nowhere does man exercise so much dominion over matter' – or over mankind, for the enfranchisement of the new men of property was mirrored by the growing impoverishment of their still disenfranchised 'hands', a term that reflected the bourgeois attitude to labour that had developed in the previous half-century. As yet no one has fixed an exact date for the birth of industrialization. Much like Topsy, it just grew in a series of piecemeal developments that revolutionized the economy first of Britain, then the world – a revolution its devotees held would subordinate nature itself to the power of man.

As the new industries expanded, so the demand for hands to work the new machines grew. The eighteenth-century population explosion (between 1700 and 1800 Britain's population doubled to 10 million) supplied a part answer to the problem, which was supplemented by a growing army of labour dispossessed by the passage of some 2,400 enclosure acts that engulfed almost 5 million acres in the second half of the century. Deprived of what little property they had and defeated by a system over which they had no control, this new army of landless workers fed industry, to be fed, in their turn, by the agent of their own distress: agricultural improvement. The arrangement was elegant in its simplicity, and those who doubted its merits could always quote Adam Smith. As Locke had provided the constitutional sanction for the Whig grandees of the Glorious Revolution, so Smith conferred economic legitimacy upon a new generation of industrial entrepreneurs.

Scornful of the injunction expressed in Smith's *Theory of Moral Sentiments* that 'to restrain our selfish and indulge our benevolent affections, constitutes the perfection of human nature', the bourgeoisie preferred the model of his *Wealth of Nations*, first published in 1776. A celebration of 'economic man', whose 'self-love' powered industry, the book effectively demoralized the economy, providing the *nouveau riche* with a doctrine, *laissez-faire*, that they were happy to exploit. And as their wealth increased, so the condition of the poor deteriorated, with Alexis de Tocqueville writing of Manchester in 1835: 'From this foul drain the greatest stream of human industry flows out to fertilize the whole world. From this filthy sewer pure gold flows. Here humanity attains its most complete development, and its most brutish, here civilization works its miracles and civilized man is turned almost into a savage.'

The bitter truth was that the growth of 'labour-saving' technology was multiplying rather than reducing toil. As the radical William Godwin pointed out, rather than machines becoming the servants of men, men were becoming the slaves of machines. The father of Mary Shelley, it seemed to Godwin that society – like Frankenstein – was creating a monster that would eventually destroy its creator or destroy its creation. In January 1813 eighteen men were executed at York for machine-breaking. Only ten months had passed since the government had driven through legislation to make the practice a capital offence, prompting Byron to protest in the House of Lords: 'When a proposal is made to emancipate or relieve, you hesitate, you deliberate for years . . . but a death Bill must be passed off hand, without a thought of the consequences.'

Careless of sentiment, the Lords ignored Byron's appeal, sharing Sir Walter Scott's conviction that 'nothing but force can keep the people under'; the government deployed an army comparable in size to the one that had served under Wellington during his Peninsula campaign to enforce its punitive legislative programme. Where all else failed, there was always Methodism, the ultimate refinement of the Protestant work ethic, to convince the wayward that the path to God lay through labour. The exact role that Wesley's church played in ensuring Britain's quiescence during the early years of the industrial revolution remains an open question. All that is certain is the paradox that as Methodism laid claim to nonconformity, it anathematized dissent, for if Wesley's spiritual maxim was 'You have nothing to do but save your souls', his secular doctrine was equally explicit: 'unfeigned loyalty to the King and sincere attachment to the constitution' and 'subordination and industry in the lower orders of society'.

In deferring more immediate expectations, the redeeming power of the cross served the new order admirably, with Robert Peel writing in 1787: 'I have left most of my works in Lancashire under the management of Methodists, and they serve me excellently well'. As for those who broke step with Wesley's discipline, the 'spiritual police' of Methodism, as Robert Southey termed them, were quick to detect and punish backsliders, expelling them from the brotherhood of man in this world and the community of grace in the next. Neither spiritual intimation nor political force were capable of curbing dissent indefinitely, however, for as industrialization advanced radicalism burgeoned.

Although proscribed under the Combination Acts, the embryonic union movement had learned the essentials of organization from the trade clubs that had flourished in the eighteenth century, and where the movement lacked a coherent political agenda this was supplied by a new generation of critics, not least 'the great questioner of things established', Jeremy Bentham. Where formerly he had venerated the constitution, by 1810 Bentham had come to believe that political reform was a precondition for achieving 'the greatest happiness of the greatest number'. In pursuit of his Utilitarian goal, Bentham demanded a comprehensive reform of the constitution, advocating household franchise, annual parliaments and equal electoral districts.

While Bentham promulgated his theories, Robert Owen pioneered cooperation. As manager of a Lancashire mill he had had firsthand experience of 'the cogs tyrannical' of industrialization, and in 1800 he moved north to become the owner of a mill in New Lanark. Concerned as much to create a model society as a model manufactory, Owen built new homes and shops for his work people, abolished all forms of punishment in the workplace and startled his partners by refusing to employ any child under the age of ten years in his mills, proposing to provide schooling for all children of New Lanark aged twelve years. His partners were captious – 'They objected to the building of the schools, and said they were . . . commercial men carrying on business for profit' – but despite them New Lanark was soon to become a Mecca for social reformers, a vision of what might be achieved by cooperation rather than the principles of competition so dear to orthodox economists.

The political brew that Bentham and Owen mixed was a potent one, although they disavowed all forms of militancy, holding that constitutional reform was a prerequisite for social amelioration and subscribing to William Cobbett's view that it was 'from this [the middle class] . . . that whatever of good may be obtained must proceed'. Ultra-radicals such as Thomas Spence were sceptical. It was the old, old story that they had heard so often before – of lending themselves to a cause that, once realized, was only too quick to default on its pledges. In the summer of 1816, at the height of the post-war distress, the so-called Spencean Philanthropists called a meeting in London to demand land nationalization and invited the leading radical speaker of the day, Orator Hunt, to address them. He refused, agreeing instead to address a counter-demonstration in favour of the orthodox radical programme that demanded parliamentary reform. In the end the two meetings were held at the same place on the same day. The Spencean leaders were arrested and charged with high treason, while Hunt and his colleagues were left to toast the quality of moderation.

For all their political circumspection, however, the moderates were to become inextricably involved in the rising tide of agitation that their own works had helped to foster. At the end of 1817 a series of major strikes swept the Lancashire cotton industry, led by the weavers and spinners who had succeeded in creating unions of delegates from various mill towns in defiance of the Combination Acts, and the following year an attempt was made to organize a 'Union of all Trades' committed primarily to economic reform. That small band of pioneer unionists can hardly have realized that in laying emphasis on economic rather than constitutional issues they were to open a debate that was to become central to radical politics. On 10 August 1819 a correspondent of the *Manchester Mercury* wrote: 'As to the present distress, you and your kidney say it's all owing to bad markets . . . The root of the evil, in my judgement, lies deeper in a long way. We are unsound in the vitals – the Constitution's become rotten to the core . . . and what's the remedy, then? Why reform – a radical complete Constitutional reform.'

Six days later the cavalry delivered the government's reply. Called to press for reform, 60,000 Lancastrians had gathered in St Peter's Field to hear Orator Hunt speak. Within minutes the yeomanry appeared, sabres drawn, and 'In ten minutes the field was an open and almost deserted space'. Eleven died while a further 421 were injured, and the 'Peterloo massacre' entered the mythology of the emergent radical movement. The government was unmoved by the loss of life, however, writing to congratulate the Manchester magistrates on their 'prompt, decisive, and efficient measures for the preservation of the public peace' and tabling new legislation to crush further evidence of dissent.

Once loose, however, the restless spirit was not to be coerced. Indeed, the sheer ferocity of the government's measures proved counter-productive, focusing the mind of workers not only on their own distress but on the establishment's determination to deprive them of redress. *The Times* might regard them as 'deluded people', but there could be no delusions about the conditions of their lives or the fate of the young agitator Andrew Hardie, who went to the gallows at Stirling Castle in 1820 declaring: 'I die a martyr to the cause of liberty, truth and justice.' Fifty years later Keir Hardie was to take up his ancestor's cause – fifty years during which dissent was broken, then revived, to be broken and revived again.

Momentarily, however, the government succeeded in stifling the nascent radical movement, leaving Shelley to write the epitaph for Peterloo:

> To suffer woes which Hope thinks infinite;
> To forgive wrongs darker than death or night;

> To defy Power, which seems omnipotent;
> To love and bear; to hope till Hope creates
> From its own wreck the thing it contemplates.

From these wrecked hopes radicalism was to re-emerge little more than a decade later, although with a significantly new combination of forces. Where, until recently, the bourgeois had been wholehearted in their support of the repressive regime orchestrated by the Tories, by the mid-1820s they were becoming disillusioned with the economic policies pursued by their former allies, and with the return of the Whigs to government in 1828 they shifted their allegiance to support Lord Grey's ministry. Once a vehement critic of reform as much as of radicals, Grey was quick to temper his policies to the public mood. Although he agreed with the Tories that democracy was dangerous and objectionable, and that 'a stake in the country' was a prerequisite of power, Grey was Whig enough to recall Locke's injunction and to recognize that reform of the property franchise was now essential to protect the Whig interest.

In June 1831 Grey tabled his Reform Bill. Its contents startled even his own back-benchers, proposing, among other things, to create 106 new constituencies mainly in the previously unrepresented urban centres and to open the vote in the boroughs to every £10 householder. Once again property was to be the touchstone of reform for, as the Lord Chancellor, Brougham, remarked, 'We don't live in the days of the Barons, thank God. We live in the days of Leeds, of Bradford, of Halifax, of Huddersfield. We live in the days when men are industrious and desire to be free.' The Tories were aghast, the bourgeoisie delighted and the radicals naive. Confident that a vote for reform would lead to social and economic 'improvement' (a catch-all phrase of theirs), they neglected to ask Brougham: freedom for whom?

A handful of extremists had the answer – the Bill was 'a damnable delusion, giving us as many tyrants as there are shopkeepers'. Their jeremiads went unheeded, however. Whigs and radicals alike were in a bullish frame of mind, but their triumphalism was premature. Over the next year the Whigs were to table their Bill three times, for it to be thrown out three times by the Tories on the advice of their leader Wellington: 'A hard pounding this, gentlemen, let's see who pounds longest.' And as the pounding continued, tempers flared to the point where, fearful as much of a run on the bank as the possibility of widespread insurrection, Wellington finally advised George IV to recall Grey to accept reform to avert the crisis he had helped precipitate. On 4 June 1832 the Reform Bill became law.

The first reformed Parliament met in February 1833, only for one disillusioned radical to comment that the King's speech could just as well have been delivered by the Great Bonze of China, so far removed was it from the everyday life of the people. The Jeremiahs had been right. Reform had proved to be the 'delusive, time-serving, specious and partial measure' that the *Poor Man's Guardian* had suspected. The new middle classes had talked up 'improvement' simply to further its own ends. Ironically, it was Bertrand Russell, a grandson of Lord John Russell, one of the architects of the Bill, who was to write of its passage a century later:

> Continuity represents no real need of national safety, but merely a closing up of the ranks of the governing classes against their common enemy, the people. Ever since 1832, the upper classes of England have been faced with retaining as much as possible of the substance of power while abandoning their forms to the clamour of democrats.

As with their forebears, it was the people that the grandees of 1832 feared, and who were soon to learn the exact meaning of reform, for it was the reformed Parliament that condemned 471 agricultural labourers to transportation for their part in the riots of 1830 and that legislated the new Poor Law of 1834. Two centuries had passed since the leveller Gerrard Winstanley had damned the betrayal of the Commonwealth. Now the people's trust had been betrayed again, provoking the Irish radical 'Bronterre' O'Brien to write: 'the middle orders were supposed to have some community of feeling with the labourers. That delusion has passed away . . . No working man will ever again expect justice, morals or mercy at the hands of a profit-mongering legislature.' In the years ahead, however, O'Brien's own faith in the workers proved to have been misplaced, betrayed, in part, by the vehicle in which he had placed his trust: the emergent union movement.

In 1824, during a brief lull in the storm that had racked Britain in the previous decade, the Combination Acts were repealed, enabling the long-standing trades clubs to link up with a burgeoning nationwide union movement. The titles of the new unions expressed their exclusivity – the Steam Engine Makers' Union, the Friendly Society of Carpenters and Joiners, the Builders' Union, the Potters' Union, the Spinners' Union. Associations of skilled craftsmen, they were as jealous of their mysteries as they were suspicious of more general unions such as the National Association for the Protection of Labour, founded by the Owenite John Doherty in 1830. Unlike the leaders of the craft associations, Doherty was convinced that the unification of the working class into a powerful and inclusive society was essential if there was to be any real hope of changing the existing social and economic order

In this respect Doherty's initiative anticipated the foundation of the Labour Party and reflected a growing consciousness of the need for an economic as much as a political reformation. The *Voice of the People* declared roundly on New Year's Day 1831: 'Labour is the source of all wealth; the working men are the support of the middle and upper classes; they are the nerves and soul of the process of production, and therefore of the nation.'

Karl Marx was thirteen years of age, and the *Communist Manifesto* lay seventeen years into the future, yet the *Voice of the People*'s message anticipated the essence of the man and his work.

It was labour that manufactured wealth, and it was wealth 'that divided people into classes'. Rough hewn as it was, this declaration marked a revolution in working-class consciousness: the recognition not only that their identity and consequently their interests were quite distinct from those of the upper and middle classes but also that the poverty of their lives was rooted as much in economic as political exploitation.

If anything was to confirm the suspicion of radicals such as O'Brien that 'Without a change in the constitution, no improvement [in the workers' conditions] can take place' it was the Reform Bill. But if the Bill generated bitterness among working men and women on discovering that they had been gulled in everyone's interest but their own, the realization was to generate its own reaction. Within twelve months of the passage of the Bill the craft unions were claiming to have recruited some 800,000 members, while in February 1834 Robert Owen established the Grand National Consolidated Trade Union.

While Owen spoke of 'the imminent emancipation of the workers' by peaceful means, an altogether more militant note was being struck by radicals who believed that although 'The day of redemption draweth nigh' its arrival would require some assistance. The class war may have been joined, but the working class was already at war with itself. Even as the *Poor Man's Guardian* was applauding the 'spirit of combination' that was growing up among the workers, a London shoemaker, Thomas Benbow, was putting the finishing touches to his pamphlet, *Grand National Holiday and Congress of the Productive Classes*: 'Plundered Fellow Sufferers! I lay before you a plan of freedom; adopt it and you rid the world of inequality, misery and crime. A martyr in your cause, I am become the prophet of your salvation.'

Innocent sounding as it may have been, Benbow's plan for a Grand National Holiday disguised an altogether more radical programme for a general strike that would destabilize the economy and transfer political power to the workers:

There will not be insurrection, it will simply be passive resistance. The men may remain at leisure, there is and can be no law to compel them to work against their will, and what happens in consequence? Bills are dishonoured, capital is destroyed, the revenue system fails, the system of government falls into confusion, and every link in the chain which binds society together is broken in a moment by this inert conspiracy of the poor against the rich.

Benbow had devised in embryo what was to become the strategy of the syndicalist movement, to the alarm of Robert Owen. Preferring moral to physical force and confident that the revolution of which he dreamed would come 'like a thief in the night', Owen condemned all talk of militant action. Seven years had passed since he had coined the word 'socialism' (for the *Co-operative Magazine* of 1827, defining socialists as those 'Communionists' who held that capital should be held in common); seven years that had transformed the nature of dissent. By the 1830s even his own lieutenants were beginning to question the efficacy of his non-violent tactics, holding that only 'a long strike, a strong strike, and a strike altogether' would achieve the Grand Consolidated Trade Union's aims, and in June 1836 a handful of London radicals led by a one-time storekeeper of the London cooperative trading society, William Lovett, established the London Working Men's Association for Benefiting Politically Socially and Morally the Useful Classes.

Although the association's founders were committed to the 'moral force' precepts of their mentor Robert Owen, the association's seemingly innocuous title disguised its incendiary potential, its programme demanding the creation of equal electoral districts, the abolition of the property qualifications of MPs, universal manhood suffrage, vote by ballot and annual Parliaments. This was the People's Charter, of which a young German émigré, Frederick Engels, was later to write: 'Chartism is of an essentially social nature, a class movement. The Six Points which for the radical bourgeoisie are the end of the matter . . . are for the proletariat a mere means to further ends. "Political power our means, social happiness our end" is now the clearly formulated war-cry of the Chartists.'

The difference in intent that Engels identified was to polarize the new-born movement. What had begun in 1836 as a non-violent movement had, little more than eighteen months later, developed powerful revolutionary overtones, in the process decisively splitting the leadership. Where Lovett and his colleagues subscribed to moral force to achieve limited ends, 'Bronterre' O'Brien and his fellow Irishman Feargus O'Connor subscribed to the slogan 'Peaceably if we may – forcibly if we must' to secure a wider social and political settlement.

Ironically, it was a moderate MP, Thomas Atwood, who offered a compromise whose divisive potential he can hardly have appreciated. A Birmingham banker with radical sympathies, Atwood recommended launching a petition in support of the charter, which should be presented to the Commons by a convention (a menacing enough word in itself with its Jacobin overtones) elected by the association. If the word was ominous, Atwood's revival of Benbow's proposal to hold a month-long general strike – to be renamed a Sacred Month – should the petition fail was even more inflammatory. While the advocates of moral force welcomed the proposal for a petition, O'Brien and O'Connor regarded Atwood's programme as a sanction for their continuing militancy.

As canvassers collected signatures for the great petition, the differences between moral and physical force factions intensified, with extremists such as George Harney levelling the Jacobin charge '*Nous sommes trahis*' against moderates such as Lovett, prophesying that 'Before the end of the year, the people shall have universal suffrage or death.' Fearing that such revolutionary sentiments would provoke a government backlash, Lovett and his colleagues staked everything on the success of the petition, but the Whig ministry cared little for the weight of public opinion. When the petition, containing 1,280,000 signatures and weighing more than six hundredweight, was finally debated in the Commons on 31 July 1839 it was rejected by 235 votes to forty-six. The following day the convention opened a discussion on the possibility of staging a general strike, but not before the government had acted.

On 31 July the Home Secretary, Lord John Russell, issued an order to magistrates to take immediate action to stamp out all measures that were 'subversive to peace'. In August alone 130 Chartist leaders were arrested, moderates along with militants, in the first phase of a new purge of dissent that provoked the Commander of the Northern District of the Army, Sir Charles Napier, to question the policy that he was being ordered to pursue: 'Would that I had gone to Australia and thus been saved this work, produced by Tory injustice and Whig imbecility . . . the doctrine of slowly reforming when men are starving is of all things the most silly; famishing men cannot wait.'

Hunger and its causes were conditions about which the Whig and Tory power-brokers knew little and cared even less. Indeed, their political differences were secondary to the contempt they shared for the working class – and their fear of its bloody-mindedness. They had good grounds to be fearful, for within two years the Chartists had regrouped under O'Connor, who was released from prison in 1841. Fuelled by an economic crisis that had led to spiralling unemployment and savage wage cuts, the new-born movement spread like wildfire, and by early 1842 a revised petition had gathered more than 3,315,00 signatures. Unlike its predecessor, however, this was no longer a humble appeal for the redress of political grievances, rather a blunt rejection of the existing socio-economic order including demands for higher wages, shorter working hours and factory legislation. For a second time, however, the Commons would have no truck with the revised charter, Macaulay declaring that universal suffrage would be 'fatal to all purposes for which government exists and . . . utterly incompatible with civilisation'. Once again it seemed that Chartism had been crushed.

None the less it re-emerged for a final time in 1848, the Year of Revolution. On the surface the movement's revival had all the vitality of the previous campaigns. The appearance was deceptive, for even the resurrected O'Connor was forced to recognize that there was little hope of their new petition succeeding, although they had little idea of the débâcle that was to follow. On 10 May 1848 some 30,000 people gathered on Kennington Common in preparation for a march to Parliament. Under police pressure, however, the plan was abandoned. Instead the petition was delivered to the House by cab, where the clerks were quick to discover such signatories as Victoria Rex, the Duke of Wellington and Mr Punch. For a decade and more the Chartist movement had challenged the assumptions of power. At the last, it discredited itself.

In all probability, Chartism was doomed to fail from the outset, founded as it was on the belief that power would devolve itself. Half a century was to pass before the German syndicalist Robert Michels formulated the 'iron law of oligarchy', to reach the pessimistic conclusion that 'the majority of mankind, in a condition of eternal tutelage . . . must content itself with forming the pedestal for an oligarchy'. But for all the Chartists' failures – failures compounded by the bitter personal and ideological disputes that racked the movement – their successors could take heart from the epitaph that Thomas Carlyle was to write in Chartism's memory:

> It is the chimera of Chartism, not the reality, which has been put down . . . It is a new name for a thing which has had many names, which will yet have many. The matter of Chartism is weighty, deep rooted, far-extending; did not begin yesterday; will by no means end this day or tomorrow.

Karl Marx was not noted for his sense of humour, but there is certainly something ironic about the famous opening of *The Communist Manifesto* – 'A spectre is haunting Europe, the spectre of Communism' – when no such thing as a Communist Party existed

in 1848. The Year of Revolution produced a ferment of radicalism: the anarchist Bakunin took to the barricades at Dresden; the
nationalist Mazzini advocated the establishment of a republican
assembly in Milan; the Elector of Hesse was compelled to grant a
new constitution based on Chartist principles, but the *Manifesto*
was its most potent legacy. Although the first, German edition
went almost unnoticed, it was to become the handbook of revolutions to come.

Marx and his co-author Engels preferred the word 'Communist' to 'Socialist', because in their view the latter was already
compromised by a motley crew of: 'economists, philanthropists,
humanitarian improvers of the conditions of the working class,
organizers of charity, members of societies for the prevention of
cruelty to animals, temperance fanatics, hole-and-corner reformers of every imaginable kind'.

As contemptuous of those idealists who 'still dream of their
social Utopias . . . duodecimo editions of the New Jerusalem' as
they were of the bourgeoisie, they set out to redraw the ideological map of socialism on being invited to write a declaration of
principles for the London section of the Communist League late
in 1847. One of a scattering of such clubs, the league was certainly not a party in the accepted sense, lacking any unanimity of
purpose or programme of action. Yet what Marx produced – a
scintillating refinement of a first draft written by Engels during a
train journey from Manchester and London – was to become the
defining text of communism, a secular creed couched in messianic
terms that was to recover the world from capitalism.

Written in six weeks and running to little more than 12,000
words, the *Manifesto*'s arguments followed inexorably from the
first sentence: 'The history of all previous society is the history of
class struggles.' Scornful of the abstract concepts of liberty and
justice being peddled by his contemporaries, Marx catechized:
'Liberty for whom? You will never be able to liberate the worker
without restricting the liberty of the owner. Justice for whom?
Under capitalism it is the proletariat that get caught most often

and punished most severely.' As to the outcome of the titanic clash he foresaw, of 'two great classes directly facing each other: Bourgeoisie and Proletariat', Marx had no doubts: the proletariat had a world to win provided, always, that they heeded his injunction: 'Working men of all countries unite.'

Powerful as his thesis was, Marx was the first to recognize that Britain was an unlikely candidate for revolution. The restless spirit remained, but it had lost much of its vitality, in part as a result of the fragmentation of dissent itself. For Marx was not alone in prescribing for the future. While a hubbub of radicals engaged in ideological bloodletting on the continent, in Britain pragmatism was the order of the day – and it was pragmatism as much as ideology that inspired twenty-eight Rochdale pioneers to open a shop in Toad Lane in 1844. Half of them were Owenite socialists, committed to his belief in cooperation as a means of achieving his vision of the good life, and it was a strictly practical programme the pioneers formulated before opening their small store: an enterprise to be run on democratic principles, each member having one vote and one vote only in its administration, and all surplus income being paid to members in proportion to the amount of their purchases. Within twelve months the pioneers' numbers had tripled and their turnover had reached £710, on which they made a £22 profit. For all their success, however, they could hardly have imagined that their modest enterprise would not only help to transform the pattern of British retailing but would play a seminal role in shaping the character of British socialism.

Although he never elaborated on the cooperators' model, it might well have appealed to John Stuart Mill. A decade before the pioneers opened their doors to business, Mill had begun to refine the Utilitarian principles of his father's closest friend, Jeremy Bentham. Indeed, it was Mill who coined the term 'Utilitarian' to define Bentham's programme. Of much the same age as Marx, the two had a great deal in common. As a young man, Mill once described himself as 'a reasoning machine', an epithet that could equally well have applied to Marx, and in the same year that the *Manifesto* appeared Mill wrote: 'In the present state of human progress, when the ideas of equality are daily spreading among the poorer classes . . . it is not to be expected that the division of the human race into two hereditary classes, employers and employed, can be permanently maintained.'

So far the sentiment could have been Marx's, but there the similarities ended, for while Marx propounded class conflict Mill remained true to his Utilitarian principles: 'I regard utility as the ultimate appeal to all ethical questions, but it must be utility in the largest sense, grounded on the permanent interests of a man as a progressive being.' Even though lacking a coherent programme Mill's works exerted a powerful influence on the early Fabians. Reason in progress, progress within reason – it is possible to catch something of the Webbs' optimism in Mill's credo.

Beneath the carapace of pragmatism, however, altogether more metaphysical forces were at work. Indeed, there is a certain symmetry in the fact that, having read Mill's most famous work *On Liberty* at a single sitting, Charles Kingsley declared: 'It has made me a clearer-headed and braver-minded man on the spot.' An Anglican priest and author of such popular works as *Westward Ho!* and the *Water Babies*, Kingsley was a leading figure in the small but influential group of Christian Socialists led by the theologian Denison Maurice. The latter, a student of medieval philosophy, wrote in 1849: 'I think that they [the Owenites and Chartists] should be made to feel that communism, in whatever sense it is a principle of the New World, is a most important principle of the Old World . . . The idea of Christian communism has been a most vigorous, generative one in all ages.'

For their testament to 'muscular Christianity' Maurice and Kingsley were damned as seditious. Yet neither was a democrat. Maurice had no truck with the sovereignty of the people, while Kingsley excoriated the secular ambitions of the Chartists in *Alton Locke*, published in 1850: 'With those miserable, awful farce tragedies of April and June [1848], let old things pass away, and all things become new. Believe that your Kingdom is not of this world, but of One whose servants must not fight.'

Although the Christian Socialist movement foundered in 1854, its ethical principles and quietist practices had a long-term impact on the labour movement, Maurice's belief that 'Christian socialism in my mind is the assertion of God's will' finding its echo in many of Tony Blair's speeches 150 years later.

But if the spiritual was to ally with the secular in the contest for the soul of radicalism, it was Nonconformity that was to play the key role. The lesson that the elder Peel had learned in the 1780s was to be practised with varying degrees of success a century later, when Methodism numbered half a million members and the leaders of the Methodist Connection continued to preach Wesley's doctrines of humility and redemption. Faith, according to Voltaire, consists in believing when it is beyond the power of reason to believe, and there can be no question that the gospel of deferred expectation provided comfort to the poor throughout the nineteenth century. Equally, the 318,000 Sunday School teachers recorded in 1851 played a formidable role in helping to educate the working class, while the organizational skills required to administer an expanding ministry served as a nursery for a generation of trade union leaders.

The precise connection between the manifold Nonconformist sects, the craft unions and capital remains a subject for speculation, but by mid-century clear demarcation lines had been drawn between the 'respectable' and 'rough' elements of the labour movement. In 1864 the radical George Potter noted in *The Beehive*: 'The working classes are divided into two sections, one comprising the skilled artisan and mechanic, and the other . . . the roughs of all descriptions.' Employers were equally aware of the difference and happy to negotiate with the leaders of such unions as the Boilermakers to which, flattered by such attention, the leadership was happy to respond. Priding themselves on their exclusivity, the aristocracy of labour – joiners, pattern-makers, cotton spinners, shipwrights, masons – exploited the marketable value of their skills when it came to negotiating with their employers, often at the expense of their less favoured colleagues, 'the slow and unsteady ones' in the words of the Secretary of the Spinners' Union.

This was the cosy relationship that the Liberal Party was happy to exploit to its own advantage, William Gladstone taunting his Tory opponents in 1866 with the fact that there was little use in their fighting against social forces 'which move onward with their might and majesty and which are marshalled on our side'. And no one was better attuned to what Walter Bagehot called this 'spirit of quiet reasonableness' than the People's William. During his forty years in the inner circles of power, Gladstone played a five-finger exercise on the prejudices and ambitions of the aristocracy of labour, now bullying, now coaxing, now cosseting their vanity with the prospects of office. Union grandees such as Henry Broad-hurst and Thomas Burt might be listed in their constituencies as 'Labour candidatures' for general election purposes, but in prac-tice they were Gladstone's liegemen and, with rare exceptions, cast their votes for Liberalism.

Once embraced by the establishment they quickly succumbed to its blandishments. In 1884 Broadhurst wrote of a weekend spent as a guest of the Prince of Wales: 'I left Sandringham with the feeling of one who had spent a weekend with an old chum of his own rank in society rather than one who had been entertained by the Heir-Apparent and his Princess.' Embourgeoisement is nothing new. As the French radical Jean Jaurès was to say, and subsequent generations were to attest, you can get anywhere in socialism provided you get out of it. Gratifying as the arrangement was to the parties concerned, however, it generated mounting hostility among the rank and file of the labour movement. The Reform Acts of 1867 and 1884 certainly extended male suffrage, and the Liberal Education Bill of 1870 expanded the reach of the 'three Rs', but most working men continued to be excluded from a power structure that served everyone's interests but their own.

The gulf between the unskilled worker and the artisan was as wide as ever, and it was the ambition of a revived radical movement to bridge it. The attempt met with fierce opposition from the Liberal, Nonconformist establishment, as the leader of dock workers, Ben Tillett, found when he stood as an Independent Labour candidate for Bradford against the Liberal MP Alfred Illingworth in 1891. The very idea of his intervention, according to a correspondent writing for the *Bradford Observer*, was little short of sacrilege: 'for how could I see without sorrow, and I may say horror, the entrance of Mr Ben Tillett to fasten like a viper on his [Illingworth's] throat'. To the aristocracy of labour the emergence of men such as Tillett was an ominous development: the recrudescence of the restless spirit they feared. Thirty years had passed since the Chartists had regarded the reformation of politics as the cure-all for Britain's ills; thirty years during which dissent had become an ideological cockshy. As contumacious and contradictory as the constituencies they professed to represent, Marxists and anarchists, trade unionists and Christian Socialists, latter-day Owenites and Nonconformists of every persuasion peddled their political nostrums, each as jealous of their prescriptions as they were confident that, once accepted, their ambitions would be realized.

In 1900, the year of the foundation of the Labour Party, George Santayana wrote: 'And what is this ambition? Nothing less than to construct a picture of all reality . . . Is not the disproportion enormous? Are not confusions and profound contradictions to be looked for in an attempt to build so much out of so little?' He might well have been writing of the party in embryo.

2
Socialism!
Then Blow Us Up!

'Socialists, Communists and Nihilists . . . strive to uproot the foundations of civilised society.' – Pope Leo XIII, December 1878

Socialism has always been an ideology of enormous disproportions. So much is inevitable, for it is impossible to apportion ideals on a rational basis. Indeed, the very idea defies reason. Yet as they sung their socialist anthem ('Come, Comrades, Come') at the opening of a fraternal conference of socialists at the Labour Institute, Bradford, in January 1893 it was this just this that the 121 delegates were hoping to achieve – if not to rationalize the irrational and resolve 'the profound contradictions' that racked the labour movement, then to find a formula that would unite the warring factions in their contest with capitalism. Although their immediate hopes were stillborn, the formation of the Independent Labour Party on 14 January 1893 not only marked the the origin of the party but also the emergence of the man who was to shape its early history: Keir Hardie.

At the age of thirty-six Hardie was already worldly-wise in the ways of politics and had few illusions about the prospects for the conference. From the time he started work as a ten-year-old trapboy in the Lanarkshire coalfield he had been aware of the differences that rent the movement. Seemingly, they had always been there since the days when Scottish workers were regarded as no better than serfs: 'the property of their landlords, appurtenances to their estates, and transferable with them to any purchasers', and the pitmen of Kilmarnock had appealed to the colliers of Ayrshire to join them in their campaign 'to check several abuses that have gradually crept into the trade'.

It was for precisely this reason, to check the abuses of the manquellers, that Hardie's ancestor had been executed in 1820. But while memories of their turbulent past trenched deep into the consciousness, the Scottish miners remained proud of their independence. Hard, dour men, it often seemed that they preferred to wrangle among themselves rather than collaborate to defend their collective interests – a condition that the Liberal Party under Gladstone was adept at manipulating. It was a dilemma which, for fifteen years, was to set Hardie at odds with himself, and even when his work as a young trade union activist was to cost him and his two brothers their jobs in 1881 – 'We'll hae nae damned Hardies in this pit' – it appeared that his faith in the Lib–Lab concordat remained unshaken.

Yet all was not quite what it seemed. Appointed Secretary of the newly formed Ayrshire Miners' Association in 1886 on an annual salary of £75, he was to write in the preamble to their objectives: 'Those who own capital and land are the masters of those who toil. Thus Capital, which ought to be the servant of Labour, and which is created by Labour, has become the master of its creator.' Momentarily it appeared that Hardie's dilemma was resolved, and his conversion to socialism complete, the more so when the following year he voted for a resolution of the Ayrshire miners: 'That in the opinion of this meeting, the time has come for the formation of a Labour Party in the House of Commons, and we hereby agree to assist in returning one or more members to represent the miners of Scotland at the first available opportunity.'

The declaration was an historic one, marking the beginning of the end of the Lib–Lab pact. Yet Hardie continued to wrangle with himself. The words were all very well, but the reality was that, for all its failings, Liberalism seemed to provide the only practical answer to redressing the glaring inequalities of life. Some day, possibly, there would be a Labour Party to correct the abuses of power; some day, possibly, workers would march to the tune of William Morris's socialist hymn – 'Come, then, let us cast off fooling, and put by ease and rest/For the *cause* alone is worthy till the good days bring the best' – but meanwhile he continued to extol

Gladstone's name ('God bless him! May he be spared to accomplish the great work to which he has put his hand'), for it was pragmatism rather than romanticism that was needed to build a new world.

The photographs of the time capture something of Hardie's perplexity, thin-faced, full-bearded, with 'eyes that mirrored the pain of the world' – or, quite possibly, his own. Even in his late twenties he had still to decide precisely where his political future lay and, if he harboured growing doubts about his own political stance, those doubts were not enough. In the spring of 1887 he was actively being canvassed as the prospective Liberal candidate for the North Ayrshire constituency. The move failed; he was too radical a Liberal for the establishment's tastes, but within the year he was offering himself as the parliamentary candidate for the mid-Lanark constituency. The election captured the full ambivalence of Hardie's position. The local Liberals gave little credence to his protestations that he was 'a Radical of a somewhat advanced type' who had been a member of the Liberal Party all his adult life and chose a Welsh barrister to fight the seat in his place.

Hardie's response was immediate. He offered himself as an Independent Labour candidate, the first of his kind in British politics to receive support from, among others, the young Secretary of the Scottish Home Rule Association, Ramsay MacDonald:

> Dear Mr Hardie, I cannot refrain from wishing you God-speed in your election contest . . . The powers of darkness – Scottish newspapers with English editors, partisan wire pullers and other etceteras of political squabbles – are leagued against us. But let the consequences be what they may, do not withdraw. The cause of Labour and Scottish Nationality will suffer much thereby.

Although Hardie's candidature split the vote, the Liberals were returned with a comfortable majority. From that day on, however, there were to be no more deals in the name of expediency. His passage from Liberalism had been a long and tortuous one. Now there could be no going back.

Only three months later, in imitation of the Ayrshire miners' initiative, the Scottish Labour Party was formed, with Keir Hardie as its Secretary, and in 1892, in part as a result of the reputation he had won for his stand in the mid-Lanark election, he was returned as MP for West Ham. The election of Hardie, together with the dockers' leader John Burns for Battersea, were the first clear indications to the political establishment that new forces were in play and, while a London evening paper derided Hardie's appearance as 'the ideal dress of a Labour member – yellow tweed trousers, serge jacket and vest, and soft tweed cap', the arrival of 'the man in the cloth cap' marked the start of a new era in British politics.

Whatever Hardie's sense of elation that August day of 1892, however, it was quickly qualified by his own keen sense of realism. Labour's anxiety to free itself from its Liberal ties was to be welcomed, but, as ever, the movement lacked cohesion. In London the recently founded Fabian Society was at the throat of the Social Democratic Federation. In the industrial areas of Lancashire and Yorkshire a growing number of working men's clubs, encouraged by the appearance of the *Workmen's Times*, were pressing for independent Labour representation, while in the unions a contest was raging between the old guard, jealous of their privileged status, and a new generation of radical unionists. Such internecine disputes mocked their collective ambitions. The urgent need was to unify these disparate forces if socialism was to have a meaningful future. And the model for such collaboration was already to hand.

Since its formation in 1888 the Scottish Labour Party had established some thirty branches, all of which were affiliated to a Central Executive. It was an example to be imitated. In September 1892 the Trades Union Congress (TUC) voted in favour of independent Labour representation, and on 13 January 1893 a motley of delegates, each avowing their own brand of socialism, met at the Labour Institute, Bradford. As he took the chair at the opening session, Hardie may well have wondered as much at the differences that divided them as to what they might achieve.

In the forty years that were to pass between the first appearance of the *Communist Manifesto* and the publication of an English edition, Marx and Engels despaired of the English working class forming a revolutionary vanguard: 'the English proletariat are becoming more and more bourgeois, so that this most bourgeois of all nations is apparently aiming ultimately at the possession of a bourgeois aristocracy and a bourgeois proletariat *as well as* a bourgeoisie'. Occasionally, there were moments of hope, although all too often they were to be wasted by internecine feuding.

Seventeen years after the collapse of Chartism, the London Trades Council convened a meeting of international working men at St Martin's Hall, Covent Garden. The immediate outcome, as described by Marx, was as chaotic as the meeting itself: One of Garibaldi's lieutenants submitted a model constitution for the association ('evidently a compilation of Mazzini's'); an Owenite drafted an alternative programme ('of indescribable breadth and full of the most extreme confusion'), while an itinerant French music teacher 'read out an appallingly wordy, badly written and utterly undigested preamble, pretending to be a declaration of principles'.

Contemptuous of a farrago that offended his own keen sense of logic, it was left to Marx to redraft the founding articles of the International Working Men's Association. All-embracing in its ambitions, Marx's *Address to the Working Classes* was to generate as many differences as it resolved. Over the next eight years six congresses were held, but as the association's membership expanded to include more than a hundred organizations from Russia, Germany, France, Belgium and Switzerland, so the faction fighting intensified, to Marx's growing disillusionment. Like the Old Testament prophets he so much resembled, he had spent half his lifetime propagating his faith, for it to become if not the cat'spaw of schismatics then a plaything which 'Messrs Gladstone and Co. are bringing off in England even up to the present time'.

And while the International was racked by dissension the Democratic Federation was in an equally fissile state. A patrician eccentric in the Victorian tradition, Henry Mayers Hyndman first read *Das Kapital* in French on a business trip to the USA, and in 1880 he met Marx for the first time. Within the year Hyndman had convened the inaugural conference of the Democratic Federation, at which he handed out copies of his own recently published pamphlet *England for All*. Unashamedly based on Marx's texts, Hyndman's work none the less failed to mention Marx's name. It was an omission that was to cost him Marx's friendship ('Many evenings this fellow has pilfered from me, in order to take me out and learn in the easiest way'), but, whatever his shortcomings, Hyndman's initiative was a pioneering achievement, marking the establishment of the first modern socialist organization in Britain. Indeed, during the three decades during which the socialist movement had been virtually moribund, the connotation of the word itself had been transformed. Where, once, socialism had been synonymous with Owenism, by the early 1880s it had become a bogy-word, associated in the public's mind with anarchist outrages and nihilist bomb-plots, prompting the headmaster of Eton, Dr Warre, to declare: 'Socialism! Then blow us up! There's nothing left for it but that.'

Hyndman's achievement was to prove that there was, although the federation's first statement of intent was not significantly radical, rather a reprise of much that had been gone before, with the addition of a demand for land nationalization. All that was soon to change, however, and by 1883 the federation's agenda had come to include demands for free and universal education and free school meals, the abolition of private banking and the establishment of national banks, progressive taxation on all income above £300 and the nationalization of the railways and the land.

The platform was a powerful one, the more so because, although the federation's initial membership was small, its executive was influential, including Marx's daughter, Eleanor 'Tussy' Marx, an outstanding intellectual in her own right; Belfort Bax, a talented writer and polemicist; the ex-Etonian schoolmaster J. L. Joynes; and H. H. Champion, who had only recently resigned his commission with the Royal Artillery. A formidable combination of ideological as distinct from labour aristocrats, the federation's high command was to be reinforced in 1883 with the arrival of William Morris, a moment which, ever afterwards, he was to call his 'conversion'.

Seven years later Morris was to write of what he found on his first visit to the federation's basement headquarters opposite the House of Commons in Westminster Bridge Road. Lit by a couple of candles, it was precisely the sort of conspiratorial setting fearfully caricatured by the federation's critics, while as for the membership: 'Those who set out to make a revolution were a few working men, less successful even in the wretched life of labour than their fellows, a sprinkling of the intellectual proletariat . . . one or two outsiders in the game political; a few refugees from the bureaucratic tyranny of foreign governments; and here or there an unpractical, half-cracked artist or author.'

And dominating all the rest was Hyndman. A towering figure, the more so because he never could be separated from his top hat, he confidently believed that the millennium was close at hand, in preparation for which it was said that he always carried with him a list of the members of his first revolutionary council. The foible was in character and it was Hyndman's autocratic style that was to lead to the split in the federation. As intellectually talented as they were politically headstrong, Morris, Belfort Bax and Tussy Marx had been growing increasingly restless under Hyndman's diktat, and in 1884 they quit the federation to found the Socialist League, although it was soon left to Morris to manage its affairs.

Morris was arguably socialism's most notable convert, and his conversion had been a lifetime in the making. Indeed, since his time at Marlborough, when he had taken part in what later came

47

to be known as the Rebellion against conditions at the school, he had always been something of an anti-authoritarian. And his subsequent brilliant career as a poet and artist was to confirm his deep-rooted antipathy to the philistine culture of Victorian England:

> Think of it! Was it all to end in a counting house on the top of a cinder heap, with Podsnap's drawing room in the offing, and a Whig committee dealing out champagne to the rich and margarine to the poor in such convenient proportions as would make all men content together, though the pleasure of the eyes was gone from the world?

For Morris it was a hellish vision that inspired him to conduct his: 'holy warfare against the age'. And once committed there could be no trimming for the sake of political expediency, no compromising with the Podsnaps: 'No man can exist in society and be neutral, no-body can be mere looker on; one camp or another you have to join; you must either be a reactionary and crushed by the progress of the race . . . or you must join in the march of progress, trample down all opposition, and help it that way.'

In adopting militancy Morris rejected Hyndman's faith in the efficacy of Parliament, an institution he had come to regard as little better than a society for the preservation of vested interests:

> The real business of Socialists is to impress on the workers the fact that they are a class, whereas they ought to be Society; if we mix ourselves up with Parliament we shall confuse and dull this fact in people's minds . . . If by chance any good is to be got out of the legislation of the ruling classes, the necessary concessions are most more likely to be wrung out of them by fear of such a body [of Socialists] than they are to be wheedled and coaxed out of them by the continual life of compromise which 'Parliamentary Socialists' would be compelled to live.

This was the touchstone of Morris's political faith, for he had seen enough of where the 'continual life of compromise' had led men such as Broadhurst, as he had of the designs of the recently formed Fabian Society which was committed, as he believed, to 'substituting business like administration in the interests of the public for the old Whig muddle of *laissez-faire* backed up by coercion'. Fervent in his belief that, given the will, it would be possible to turn the world upside down, Morris stumped the country drumming up his vision of 'the New World Order', careless of the reality that if the British labour movement had little taste for revolutionary socialism it had even less for the tenets of Marxism. In fact, he might well have benefited from the advice of his radical contemporary Johnny Coe of Wibsey: 'We want no Karl Marx and labour values and that sort of stuff here. Make it plain and . . . when tha'rt coming t'finishing up tha' mun put a bit of "Come to Jesus" in.'

Instead of this, Morris stressed the secular, although in *A Dream of John Ball*, published in 1888, he was to capture something of the Lollards' vision of a Christian commonwealth. By then, however, the Socialist League was already riven by internal divisions provoked by the growing influence of an anarchist faction within its inner councils. In 1889 the anarchists consolidated their control of the league and replaced Morris as Editor of the journal *Commonweal* he had both founded and financed. The wound was deep, compounded by Morris's fears that the ends to which he aspired were being subordinated to the means. Morris the revolutionary idealist, however, was never to despair of his hopes for the future, modelled, as they were, on his romanticized 'dream' of the past: 'Go back and be happier for having seen us, for having added a little hope to your struggle. Go on living while you may, striving with whatsoever pain and labour needs must be, to build up little by little the new day of fellowship, and rest, and happiness' (*News from Nowhere*, 1891).

Only eighteen months had passed since he had written 'Fellowship is heaven, and lack of fellowship is hell.' In the last five years of his life Morris was left to consider the paradox of the hell that the fellowship of socialism had proved to be, leaving Hyndman and the renamed Social Democratic Federation (SDF) and the Fabians, led by Bernard Shaw, to contest the ideological high ground at the Bradford conference of 1893.

The minutes of the meeting of the Fabian Society of 16 May 1884 carry a scrawled footnote in the margin: 'This meeting was made memorable by the first appearance of Bernard Shaw.' The Shavian flourish is unmistakable. At the age of twenty-eight Shaw's ego was matched only by his talents, although there was some truth in his vainboasting, for there was certainly nothing immediately memorable about the nine founder members of the society.

Named after the Roman general Fabius Cunctator, one of the nine was to fabricate an historical association to sustain the choice of the names: 'For the right moment you must wait as Fabius did most patiently, when warring against Hannibal, but when the time comes you must strike hard, as Fabius did, or your waiting will be vain and fruitless.' The text, soon to be encapsulated in the axiom 'the inevitability of gradualism', established the political character of what was to become one of the most influential and and long-lived organizations in the tumultuous history of British socialism – even if at the outset the founder members were unsure as to exactly what they were about. All they knew was that they were not revolutionaries in the Social Democratic sense. Beyond that, however, they were not at all sure whether they were anarchists or communists or, quite possibly, a bit of both.

Shaw's arrival was to change all that. A self-proclaimed 'Socialist, Atheist, and Vegetarian' and author of the parody *An Unsocial Socialist* which had attracted William Morris's attention, Shaw had spent the early 1880s trying to find a political home for himself, speaking at various radical clubs and studying the works of Marx, of whom he was later to say: 'Marx was a revelation . . . He opened my eyes to the facts of history and civilisation, gave me an entirely fresh conception of the universe, provided me with a purpose and a mission in life.'

Early in 1884 Shaw became a 'candidate member' of the Social Democratic Federation, although not without reservations: 'I was in doubt about throwing in my lot with the SDF, not because of snobbery, but because I wanted to work with men of my own mental training.' The charge rings hollow considering the intellectual capacity of the federation's inner council – not least, of William Morris, whom Shaw revered. A born hero-worshipper, he found in Morris all that he admired: the social idealist or, conversely, the ideal socialist. As far as Shaw was concerned, in fact, only one thing was lacking in Morris's make-up – political acumen. While it did nothing to affect their friendship, it was to polarize their political attitudes and to mark a fault line in the labour movement which has been a feature of socialism for the past hundred years.

Indeed, it was not entirely coincidental that within six months of Shaw joining the Fabians in the summer of 1884 – a set of whom he was later to write that they 'met in middle-class drawing-rooms where a labourer would have been unbearably uncomfortable' – that Morris, Bax and Tussy Marx founded their breakaway Socialist League. Both Shaw and the dissidents were tired of Hyndman's autocratic ways, but the differences went deeper than that. While Morris was contemptuous of the Fabians' bourgeois pretensions, Shaw was as dismissive of Morris as a 'privileged eccentric and in no way an authority on socialist policy' as he was of the SDF.

If it had been possible for anyone but a humble satellite to work with Hyndman without a quarrel, the SDF would have enlisted and retained all the important recruits to Socialism . . . and there might have been no Fabian Society, no Socialist League, no Guild of St Matthew, no Christian Socialist Union, no Independent Labour Party . . . As it was, the Federation never federated anybody.

As with socialism, so with Shaw. He was divided against himself. Appointed a member of the Fabian executive within six months of joining the society, he none the less continued to contribute articles to Morris's *Commonweal* while cursorily rejecting an invitation addressed to Comrade Shaw to attend a meeting of the Socialist League: 'I am G. Bernard Shaw, of the Fabian Society, member of an individualist state, and therefore nobody's comrade.' It was only with the recruitment of Sidney Webb in the spring of 1885 that the Fabians began to develop a consistent political strategy and that Shaw was to find an individual who could complement his brilliant rhetorical skills.

The two men had been friends for more than five years, a friendship based as much on their differences in character as their common concern for the state of Britain. A clerk in the Colonial Office, who looked like a cross between a London tradesman and a German professor according to his wife-to-be, Beatrice, Webb was to become Shaw's political mentor: 'Sidney Webb. Quite the wisest thing I ever did was to force my friendship on him and to keep it; for from that time I was not merely a futile Shaw but a committee of Webb and Shaw.'

It was this committee that was to provide the Fabians with the intellectual rigour and literary dynamic that was to give the society its political momentum. Significantly, Webb's first publication for the Fabians, *Facts for Socialists*, concentrated exclusively on statistics. Convinced of the irrationality of capitalism, Webb none the less held that it was only by deploying irrefutable evidence of the 'the unequivocal division of the fruits of the combined labour of the working community that . . . divides us into two nations' that it would be possible to convince the opposition of the error of its ways. The approach was to become a feature of Fabian strategy, not least of its policy of permeating the opposition, of which Webb was later to write:

> We did not confine our propaganda to the slowly emerging Labour Party, or to those who were prepared to call themselves Socialists, or to the manual workers or any particular class. We put our proposals, one by one, as persuasively as possible, before all who would listen to them – Conservatives whenever we could gain access to them, the churches and chapels of all denominations, the various

Universities, the Liberals and Radicals, together with the other Socialist Societies . . . We realised, more vividly than most of our colleagues, that, at any rate in Britain, no political Party, however 'proletarian' its composition or sympathies, could ever carry far-reaching reforms in Parliament by the support merely of the members whom it enrolled, or even its sympathisers at elections.

The policy was to shape the strategy of the society, although not without a bitter internal wrangle as to who precisely should permeate whom, while a decision to pursue the parliamentary route to reform was agreed at a meeting open to all-comers at London's Anderton Hotel in September 1886 – but only after heated debate.

The issue before the meeting was clear – whether the society should opt for parliamentary or extra-parliamentary action – and it was the secularist Annie Besant, only recently elected to the Fabian executive, who seconded the motion 'That is is advisable that Socialists should organize themselves into a political party', to which William Morris added the rider 'whereas no Parliamentary Party can exist without compromise and concession . . . [thus] it would be a false step for Socialists to take part in the Parliamentary contest.'

The substantive motion was carried and Morris's rider voted down. This was to widen the breach between the militant and moderate wings of the labour movement. Half a century had passed since the issue of extra-parliamentary action had divided the Chartists, and in the quarter-century that lay ahead it was to divide the movement again, to generate intense hostility between the factions involved. In adopting a top-down approach to socialism, the Fabians, heavily influenced by Webb, who believed implicitly in the merits of British democratic institutions, tended to neglect the role of the working class in the contest for political power. While Marx had never idealized the proletariat, he had been quick to recognize its importance in advancing the socialist cause – a reality the Fabians accepted in principle but which its largely middle-class and innately paternalistic members tended to ignore in practice.

Their exclusivity did nothing to prevent their campaigning, however, and in the autumn of 1888, following the publication of Morris's *Signs of Change*, the society mounted a counter-attack on his position in the Fabian Journal *Today*. Although unsigned, the Shavian touch was unmistakable:

> Mr William Morris is about the only Socialist who can write with the pleasing certainty that his literary productions will be read; and, therefore, there lies upon him a weight of responsibility from which we ordinary scribblers are delightfully free. Unfortunately the burden sits but airily on his brawny shoulders, and his utterances on the platform are apt to smack too much of the 'hare-brained chatter of irresponsible frivolity' . . . Now we have no hesitation in saying that if the once hard-headed English workmen came to believe that these [insurrectionary] ideas of Mr Morris's were in any degree representative, the present by no means unbrilliant prospects of Socialism in England would vanish like a dream. Happily no such mistake is likely to be made for the rapid conversion of so many of our writers and lecturers to political methods has left Mr Morris almost alone in possession of his peculiar views.

The battle of words was joined. The Fabians had already launched their pamphleteering campaign, publishing a flood of papers as didatic in their contents as they were catholic in their concerns (*Why Are the Many Poor?*, *Capital and Land*, *A Plea for an Eight Hours Bill*, *Questions for London Vestrymen*, *What the Farm Labourer Wants*, *Socialism and Sailors*, *The Municipalisation of the Gas Supply*), but it was *the Fabian Essays in Socialism* of 1889 that was to provide the keystone of their programme. Edited by Shaw, and drawing heavily on the Utilitarianism of Bentham and Mill, it included pieces by Webb, Besant and the political scientist Graham Wallas.

The work's preface made clear both the authors' intentions

('The Essayists make no claim to be more than communicative learners') and their disdain for the existing socialist project: 'There are at present no authoritative teachers of Socialism.' If the latter reflected the essayists' self-esteem, the former not so much refuted Marxist economics as ignored them, preferring to pursue 'the greatest happiness of the greatest number' by gradualist means, of which Sidney Webb was to write in his customary, desiccated style:

> All students of society who are abreast of their time realise that important organic changes can only be (1) democratic and thus acceptable to a majority of the people . . . (2) gradual, and thus causing no dislocation . . . (3) not regarded as immoral by the mass of the people . . . and (4) in this country at any rate, constitutional and peaceful.

As gradual as it was inevitable, the formula Webb advanced was aimed at a distant goal of replacing private enterprise by the state, Shaw listing the full reach of such a statist society:

> In addition to births, marriages, deaths and electors, the State registers all solicitors, barristers, notaries, patent agents, brokers, newspaper proprietors, playing-card makers, brewers, bankers, seamen, captains, mates, doctors, cabmen, hawkers, pawnbrokers, tobacconists, distillers, plate dealers, game dealers; all insurance companies, friendly societies, endowed schools and charities, limited companies, lands, houses, deeds, bills of sale, compositions, ships, arms, dogs, cabs, omnibuses, books, plays, pamphlets, newspapers, raw cotton movements, trademarks and patents; lodging houses, public houses, refreshment-houses, theatres, music-halls, places of worship, elementary schools, and dancing rooms.

Seemingly, the inevitability of gradualism was limited only by Shaw's imagination – or the Fabians' capacity for what, sardonically, was to become known as 'the permeation of the Peers'.

Adopted as a core text by the society, the *Essays* were dismissed as, at best, ingenuous, at worst, subversive by Morris. As sceptical of Webb's leadership ('He seems to enjoy all the humiliations of opportunism, he revels in it . . .') as he was of the Essayists' belief in an 'irresistible glide into collectivist Socialism', he excoriated the Fabians' gradualist formula:

> The result is that the first clear exposition of Socialism, and the criticism of the present false state of society (which latter no one knows how to make more damaging than Mr Bernard Shaw) is set aside for the sake of pushing a theory of tactics . . . which if it could be, would still leave us in a position from which we should have to begin our attack on capitalism over again.

The Socialist League was disintegrating, but Morris had lost none of his idealism. Like a knight from out of one of his own medieval sagas, he tilted against the Fabian host, more especially Shaw's concept of socialism, 'which could be adopted either as a whole or by instalments by any ordinary, respectable citizen without committing himself to revolutionary attachments'. In one of his last lectures, delivered at Kelmscott House, Morris was to deliver a scathing riposte:

> For making a great many poor people somewhat more comfortable than they are now, somewhat less miserable, let us say, is not in itself a light good; yet it would be a heavy evil if it did anything towards dulling the efforts of the whole class of workers towards the winning of a real society of equals . . . For I want to know and to ask you to consider . . . whether in short the tremendous organisation of civilised commercial society is not playing cat and mouse games with us socialists. Whether the Society of Inequality might not accept the quasi-socialist machinery above mentioned, and work it for the purpose of upholding that society in a somewhat shorn condition, but a safe one.

Morris and Shaw's friendship survived their differences, yet in developing their respective positions they provided the clearest and most penetrating expression of the fundamental differences that were subsequently to rack British socialism – differences as much about the ends to be achieved as the means to achieve them.

For all his boundless energy Morris was tiring. At fifty-nine he had spent a decade engaging Fabian revisionism, and it may be significant that he was to close his Kelmscott House lecture with what amounted to an epitaph for the past and a plea to the future: 'So let us forgive the mistakes that others make, even if we make none ourselves, and be at peace amongst ourselves, that we may the better make War upon the monopolist' – significant in that his plea for reconciliation was delivered shortly after Keir Hardie chaired the inaugural Independent Labour Party (ILP) conference in Bradford.

Five years had passed since Hardie had launched his first attack on the faint-heartedness of the unions at the TUC conference of 1887, to open a major rift in the movement. In the years between the old guard had been forced on to the defensive. None the less they still commanded considerable influence in the inner councils of the unions; and justifiably so. Jealous of their exclusivity and opposed to militancy, the cat-and-mouse political games they played with the Liberals and Tories had led to the passage of the Trade Union Act of 1871, which had give the unions legal status, and to the repeal of the Criminal Law Amendment Act in 1875, which had extended the freedom of strike action and legalized the rights of picketing for the purpose of 'peaceful peruasion'.

Their successes only stimulated the taste for more – not least, among the majority of the labour movement which effectively had been disenfranchised by the elitism of the aristocracy of labour. It was all very well for the junta that dominated the unions to protest its concern for the general well-being of labour, when its chief concern was for the well-being of a minority of workers concentrated in the craft unions. The leadership was cautious of direct action ('Never surrender the right to strike, but be careful how you use a double-edge weapon'), preferring arbitration and conciliation, and wary of political commitments ('We do not wish to relax one iota of your efforts with reference to our social conditions . . . Nor do we wish to turn our trades societies into political organisations'). Nevertheless it found it impossible to ignore the need if not for parliamentary representation then for a parliamentary lobby.

Within three years of the first meeting of TUC in 1868, a Parliamentary Committee had been established. Sound Liberals as most of the movement's leaders were, they were not beyond a little political horse-trading. At the General Election of 1874, the unions issued a series of test questions to all candidates, advising members to back those respondents, Tory or Liberal, who provided the most satisfactory replies. The impact of this intervention may have been small; none the less Benjamin Disraeli kept his pledge to establish a Royal Commission on the Labour Laws on his return to power and within the year had enacted two major pieces of ameliorative leglislation. Flushed with success, the committee proposed its own abolition, its Secretary George Howell reporting that 'the legislation with respect to Trade Unions was then so perfect that the natural time had run for the existence of Trade Union Congresses so far as Parliamentary action was concerned'.

The Congress disagreed and on Howell's retirement appointed Henry Broadhurst in his place. Liberal by design but conservative by inclination, Broadhurst was to fight a bitter rearguard action not only against admitting women to union membership, fearing that 'under the influence of emotions they might vote for things they would regret in cooler moments', but also against providing any recognition for the emergent general as distinct from craft unions. Committed as much to Gladstonian policies as he was to union exclusivity, Broadhurst misread the situation as far as both the Liberal Party and the labour movement were concerned, for as the former was losing its political headway, the latter was gaining in momentum.

George Meredith captured something of the growing disenchantment with the Liberal project of untrammelled *laissez-faire* in his novel *Beauchamp's Career* published in 1876:

> The people are the Power to come. Oppressed, unprotected, abandoned; left to the ebb and flow of the tides of the market, now taken on work, now cast off to starve, committed to the shifting laws of demand and supply, slaves of Capital – the whited name for old accursed Mammon . . . They are, I say, the power, worth the seduction of by another Power not mighty in England now; and likely in time to set up yet another Power not existing in England now.

Meredith was right. Another power, as scornful of the posturing of the union leadership as it was contemptuous of its collusion with Liberalism, was already in the making. While the TUC might pretend that it represented British workers when it represented little more than 10 per cent of the work-force, and while its Parliamentary Committee might reject an invitation to attend an international trade union conference on the grounds that 'we are so far ahead of foreign workmen that little can be done until these are more on a level with the skilled workers of Britain', such pretensions were already being challenged by a new generation of politicized Young Turks – and the growing militancy of the labour movement.

As late as the 1880s, as the Webbs were to write later, there was no more affinity between the TUC establishment and the non-unionized and underpaid workers than there was between those workers and the House of Lords – which was precisely the situation that radicals such as Tom Mann and Ben Tillett were determined to rectify. As early as 1886, Mann was writing:

> How long, how long, will you [trade unionists] be content with the present half-hearted policy of your unions? . . . The true unionist

policy of aggression seems to be entirely lost sight of; in fact the average unionist of today is a man of fossilised intellect, either hopelessly apathetic or supporting a policy that plays directly into the hands of the capitalist exploiter.

In 1886 Tillett, who had already crammed a lifetime of experience as pit boy, circus hand, merchant seaman and dock labourer into his twenty-six years, failed in his attempt to organize the London dockers. Within eighteen months, however, a strike by the match girls at the East End factories of Bryant and May was to provide him with a new sense of purpose and a new model for labour activism. Inspired by Annie Besant, who published a series of articles on the horrific conditions in which the girls worked, public opinion was mobilized in support of their case, and within weeks the management had come to terms with their demands.

The lessons of their success were soon learned. In 1889 Tillett called a strike of London dockers in support of a wage claim that the employers had dismissed derisively. Within three days 10,000 men were out and the Port of London was at a standstill. Backed by Tom Mann and John Burns, both of whom had been members of the SDF and each of whom shared Tillett's contempt for the exclusive and non-militant policies of the TUC, the triumvirate were quick to exploit the methods pioneered by the match girls. For a month they stage-managed marches, organized mass meetings, cultivated the press and launched and administered a fighting fund to support the strikers' families. And for a month the port employees remained obdurate, before capitulating to the strikers' demands.

The aristocrats of labour might disapprove of their methods, but they were resisting the inevitable. General unions were no longer figmentary, rather a fact of life, although the 'old' and the 'new' were still easily distinguishable. John Burns wrote in 1890:

Physically the 'old' unionists were much bigger than the 'new' . . . A great number of them looked like respectable city gentlemen, wore very good coats, large watch chains and high hats and in many cases were of such splendid build and proportions that they presented an aldermanic, not to say a magisterial form of dignity. Among the new delegates, not a single one wore a tall hat. They looked like workmen, they were workmen.

And their politics were as different as their dress, for Mann and Tillett to write in the same month as Burns had remarked on their sartorial identities:

> In conclusion, we repeat that the differences between the 'new' and the 'old' is that those who belong to the latter and delight in being distinct from the policy endorsed by the 'new', do so because they do not recognise that it is the work of trade unionists to stamp out poverty in this land . . . Whilst we make no pretence to the possession of special values, we are prepared to work unceasingly for the economic emancipation of the workers. Our ideal is a Co-Operative Commonwealth.

If their ideal was entrenched in the past, their programme was to shape the future, although on taking the chair at Bradford in 1893 Keir Hardie can have had few illusions about how formidable the project would be. Six years had passed since he had first clashed with Broadhurst at a trade union conference over the question of increasing working-class representation to Parliament, for his interventions to be denounced by Broadhurst as 'these intolerable and un-English and lecturing attacks by Mr Hardie'; and it was four years since a Broadhurst acolyte and Congress delegate had savaged Hardie and his friends ('these ugly badgers, these stinking foxes . . . these anything but men'), yet there they were again, the men in the high hats, a minority maybe but still powerful none the less. As Tom Mann had remarked: 'Clannishness in trade matters must be superseded . . . brotherhoods must not be talked about but practised.' The trick was to realize such a goal.

Arguably the most notable achievement of Hardie's career was to win agreement from all the disparate factions involved in the Bradford conference – Fabians and Social Democrats, unionists 'old' and 'new' – to form an Independent Labour Party. Half a century on, Clement Attlee, leader of the rump that made-up the pre-war Labour Party, was to write:

> It was the emergence of the ILP which was the effective force in turning the Trade Union movement away from Liberalism, and Keir Hardie, its leader, is rightly considered its real founder. The great service he rendered was not in the realms of theory, but of practice. He had the prescience to see that a body of working men returned to Parliament, pledged to act with complete independence of either of the Capitalist parties, was bound in due course to adopt the Socialist faith.

And the essence of that faith? As the 121 delegates at the Labour Hall, Bradford, agreed that January day of 1893, it was to achieve 'the collective ownership and control of the means of production, distribution and exchange'. With modifications, Hardie's prescription was to remain the touchstone of socialism for the next hundred years.

3
A Little Cloud, No Bigger Than a Man's Hand

'The watchword of socialism is not class consciousness but community consciousness.' – Ramsay MacDonald, *Socialism and Society*, 1905

Seven years were to pass between the Bradford conference and the foundation of the Labour Representation Committee which effectively marked the birth of the Labour Party. It is widely thought that the one was the inevitable outcome of the other. Nothing could be further from the truth. In principle the delegates may have approved the formation of an Independent Labour Party, but that was their only concession to *realpolitik*. Even before the conference ended Shaw had determined that the Fabians would have no part of the venture, dismissing it as 'nothing but a new Social Democratic Federation', while Hyndman was as contemptuous of the initiative as he was of 'those mere palliatives, the unions' which, for their part, were as suspicious of the enterprise as they were of Hardie himself.

For two days the delegates argued the need for unity, but the old prejudices remained, as deep-rooted and corrosive as ever. Hardie's intentions may have been admirable, just as long as they did not trespass on the bailiwick of the parties involved – the Marxist credo of Hyndman and the SDF, the gradualist strategy of Webb, Shaw and the Fabians, the continuing exclusivity of certain unions. Each had staked out their political territories, and none of them were willing to forgo their individuality. Their obscurantist ways and internecine feuding did little to check the development of the ILP at grass-roots level, however. Within a year, 280 branches had been formed throughout the country, for Hardie to assert that while 'The business of the new Party is to do battle with Toryism' Liberalism remained 'the chief impediment' to realizing socialism.

As far as Engels was concerned, Hardie's ambition mocked the ideal; casting him as 'an over-cunning Scot whose demagogic artfulness one cannot trust'. While this was all they shared in common, Beatrice Webb concurred: 'Keir Hardie, who impressed me very unfavourably, deliberately chooses this policy [of social revolution] as the only one he can boss. His only chance of leadership lies in the creation of an organisation "agin" the Government; he knows little and cares less for any constructive thought or action.'

Caught in the ideological cross-fire, Hardie could not win for, if Engels regarded him as a crypto-Tory, then Webb suspected that his radical sympathies endangered the Fabian programme, of which she was already a leading exponent. Although only recently married to Sidney Webb, to the scorn of Shaw who maliciously maintained that 'She quite deliberately sampled the Fabians as possible husbands' before settling on Sidney, Beatrice had quickly established herself in the inner circles of the society. The thirty-six-year-old daughter of a *nouveau riche* railway promoter and, as her diaries reveal, an archetypical model of the Victorian *haute bourgeoisie*, she none the less embraced Fabianism with all the passion that she was rumoured to have denied her husband, a passion maliciously caricatured by H. G. Wells in *The New Machiavelli*:

> She had much of the vigour and handsomeness of a slender, impudent young man, and an unscrupulousness altogether unfeminine. She was one of those women who were wanting in – what is the word? – muliebrity . . . Yet you mustn't imagine she was an inelegant or unbeautiful woman, and she is inconceivable to me in high collars or any sort of masculine garment. But her soul was bony . . .

It was in their 'hard little house' in Westminster that Beatrice and Sidney Webb held court, permeating where they could – the airily fearless Arthur Balfour ('the intelligent Tory'), the young Herbert Asquith ('A shrewd and able lawyer; coarse grained and unimaginative'), the veteran trade unionist Henry Broadhurst ('a commonplace person; hard working no doubt, but a middle-class philistine'), the mercurial Tom Mann ('He is deteriorating . . . the perpetual excitement leads among other things to too much whiskey') – although their guest list reflected a strong Liberal bias. Indeed, Shaw's blunt statement at the ILP conference made his own and, by implication, the society's position clear, for as he reported: 'he himself was on the Executive of a Liberal Association, and he had taken some trouble to get the position in order to push the Labour interests there. He intended to stick to it . . . and found that there was a good deal to be gained thereby.'

The trouble was that the Liberals had already betrayed the trust that the Fabians had vested in them. In 1891 the party had published its Newcastle manifesto, a programme so radical that it unnerved the party itself. It included proposals for Irish Home Rule, 'the mending or ending' of the House of Lords and the payment of MPs, and the Liberals were to abandon virtually the entire programme in less time than it took them to lose office. It was a betrayal that inspired Shaw to write a scathing tract on *The Perfidy of Government* and compelled the Fabians to seek out new allies. As hostile to the SDF as they were suspicious of the ILP, they settled on the unions as the most likely candidates for permeation:

> On the whole, then, we may take it that representation of the working classes at the General Election will depend on the great national trade unions, and not on the Socialist societies. Neither the Fabian Society nor the Social Democratic Federation, nor the Society known as the Independent Labour Party, has the slightest prospect of mustering enough money to carry through three serious candidates, much less fifty. Their part will provide the agitation which will enable the trade union leaders to obtain the support of the rank and file in rising to the occasion.

The Fabians were right, as Hardie and Mann well knew, not that they were in any mood to compromise with what they regarded as if not opportunism then political casuistry of the Fabians. In February 1895 a dinner party at the Webbs broke up in disarray when Hardie accused his hosts of being the worst enemies of social revolution, which is what may have inspired Beatrice to declare that 'Labour men are babies in politics.' As careless of the Webbs' warning as they were of the reality that they had insufficient funds to mount an effective campaign, the ILP entered twenty-eight candidates for the election of 1895 all of whom, including Hardie, were defeated, to the delight of Beatrice Webb: 'From the General Election we held aloof, refusing to back either the ILP or support the Liberals. The rout of both, therefore, is no defeat to us. It leaves us free, indeed, to begin afresh on the old lines – on building a party on the basis of collectivism.'

However, it was not so much the aloofness of the Fabians who in the mid-1890s numbered fewer that a thousand members as the opposition of the unions that destroyed the ILP's electoral hopes, for the old guard of Lib–Lab persuasion still wielded considerable power at constituency level. Indeed, the more isolated they found themselves as a result of the emergence of new unionism, the more their hostility to the ILP, as the leader of the Gas Workers' and General Labourers' Union, Pete Curran, discovered when he stood in a by-election for the Barnsley constituency. Throughout the campaign, the miners' leader, Ben Pickard, canvassed tirelessly for the Liberals, Curran being mobbed by women and children and stoned by pitmen. But for all the hostility of men such as Broadhurst, who campaigned for the Liberals against Tom Mann at Halifax in 1897, the one-time aristocrats of labour were losing ground to an altogether more militant species of unionism.

And it was not only the Fabians who recognized its potential – in practical rather than theoretical terms. Long-standing union activists Hardie and Mann, respectively the chairman and secretary of the ILP, were well aware that the future of socialism, if it was to have a meaningful future, lay with the power-brokers of the

TUC, and in the last years of the century their efforts to build bridges with the movement were powerfully reinforced by the concerted assault of the courts against what the unions had come to regard as their rights. They were quickly disabused.

As a result of a series of legal decisions, culminating in the Taff Vale decision of 1900, the unions' freedom from collective responsibility was effectively nullified, while the right to picket peacefully, as provided for in the Trade Union Act of 1875, was eroded piecemeal. As the counter-attack against the unions intensified, so Hardie and the ILP intensified their efforts to persuade the TUC of the need for working-class representation in Parliament, the Scottish labour movement again providing the cutting edge for their campaign.

In 1897 a long-standing ally of Hardie's, Bob Smillie, demanded backing from the recently formed Scottish TUC for 'the working class socialist parties already in existence'. Eighteen months later a joint conference of Scottish trade unionists, socialists and delegates of the ILP was convened, and in 1899, at the third annual conference of the Scottish TUC, Hardie won support for trade unionists to campaign for parliamentary representation on an independent basis. Where the Scots led, however, the English unions lagged, ILP resolutions in favour of independent political representation receiving short shrift from the Parliamentary Committee of the TUC. For three years the diehards on the committee blocked any move that would attenuate their own authority, and for three years Hardie and the ILP attempted to undermine their position, finally succeeding in tabling a motion at the TUC conference of 1899 calling on the committee to collaborate with other socialist societies in holding a special conference to discuss the issue of labour representation.

Five months later, on 27 February 1900, 129 delegates representing sixty-five trade unions and three socialist societies (the ILP, the Fabians and the SDF) met at the Memorial Hall in Farringdon Street, London, in an attempt to resolve their past differences, and formulate a programme for the future. Solid, commonsensical men, as conscious of their responsibilities as of the difficulties they faced, they settled to the business in a matter-of-fact way, the chairman W.C. Steadman, MP for Stepney, setting the tone for the debate:

> I have been a member of the House of Commons but a short time, but I have been there sufficiently long to know that every interest is represented and protected in that House . . . but the interest of labour . . . .Whether we form a Labour Party or ally ourselves to other political parties in the State, let us be represented by men of character.

The delegates applauded the sentiment but disagreed, vehemently as to how it could best be achieved. Steadman had touched on part of the problem – labour's historic liaison with the Liberals – but that was only one element in the ideological mix. Thomas Ashton, Secretary of the Cotton Spinners' Union, scornfully dismissed a proposal to 'devise ways and means for securing an increased number of Labour Members in the next Parliament', declaring that 'not one trade unionist in ten thousand would give such a proposal a moment's consideration', while John Burns, the Independent Labour MP for Battersea, was equally contemptuous of the SDF proposal that future Labour MPs should form 'a distinct party with a party organisation separate from capitalist parties based upon the recognition of a class war'.

Burns had come far since being among the leaders of the London dock strike of 1889, and he had further still to go, becoming the first working man to achieve Cabinet rank in the Liberal administration of 1905, It was, however, already clear where his sympathies lay. Deriding the notion of a class-based party ('I am getting tired of working-class boots, working-class brains, working-class houses and working-class margarine'), he urged delegates to accept that parties and their policies were not necessarily determined on class lines. And as the day progressed, and the factions involved became more entrenched around their prejudices, the divisions were more apparent: one group demanding the election of working men and no others to Parliament; another supporting the election of candidates who were sympathetic to the aims of the labour movement whether they were working men or not; and a third pressing for the establishment of a class-based party committed to the socialization of the means of production, distribution and exchange.

Once again it seemed that the hopes of achieving some unity of purpose were to be proved stillborn, aborted as much by ideological differences as by the obstinacy of the ideologues who subscribed to them. It had happened not once but many times before, yet the conclusive fact was that what the delegates shared in common was greater than the issues that divided them. Committed to representing their own positions, they were realist enough to recognize what they were putting at risk, and it was Hardie who was to cobble together a formula on which they could agree:

> That this Conference is in favour of establishing a distinct Labour Group in Parliament who shall have their own Whips and agree upon their policy, which must embrace a readiness to co-operate with any party which, for the time being, may be engaged in promoting legislation in the direct interest of labour, and be equally ready to associate themselves with any party in opposing measures which have the opposite tendency.

Cannily crafted to establish the principle of independence, yet sufficiently vague to allay the fears of potential dissenters, Hardie's compromise – a foretaste of the composites that were to become a feature of party conferences – was carried unanimously. Another six years were to pass before the Labour Party was formally to adopt the title. It was the formation of the Labour Representation Committee in February 1900, however, that marked the party's birth, a correspondent of the socialist *Clarion* describing the event as 'a little cloud, no bigger than a man's hand, which may grow into a United Labour Party'. Percipient as he was, he was only half correct. It was a party, certainly, but united?

The euphoria following the Memorial Hall conference was short-lived. While Hardie was to write some days later: 'The Conference here has been most successful and promises well for the future', he was too much of a realist to suppose that the path was now open to socialism, however ambiguous the word's meaning. Momentarily, it may have appeared that his patchwork resolution had resolved the differences that rent the movement, but the appearance was deceptive. The differences remained. Indeed, it seemed that the only substantive achievement of the conference had been to commit the trade unions to taking independent political action – although all too soon even that assumption was open to question.

At the turn of the century Britain was in a bellicose mood, as the popular music-hall song declared: 'We don't want to fight, but by jingo if we do . . .' In October 1899 the Boer War had broken out, although the matter was not raised at the Memorial Hall four months later. It was too sensitive an issue for that, Beatrice Webb writing: 'The cleavage goes right through the Liberal Party into the Fabian Society.' While the SDF shared common ground with the ILP, both subscribing to Hardie's opinion that: 'modern imperialism is to the Socialist simply capitalism in its most predatory and militant phase', the unions remained indecisive, an anti-war motion being carried by a tiny majority at the TUC conference of 1900.

The coincidence was accidental, but within weeks the Tory administration went to the country, to expose the full extent of the split within the unions reflecting, as it did, the divide in the nation at large. Several ILP offices were attacked and stoned, and of the fifteen candidates entered by the Labour Representation Committee only two were returned, Keir Hardie for Merthyr Tydfil and Richard Bell for Derby, although even this result was deceptive, for Bell was much more a Liberal than a Labour man, as his subsequent career was to reveal. As for the rest, many had fallen victim to jingoism, among them Philip Snowden, George Lansbury and Beatrice Webb's 'brilliant young Scot', Ramsay MacDonald.

In the spring MacDonald resigned from the Fabians, together with seventeen other members, including Emmeline Pankhurst and Walter Crane, in protest at the belligerence of Shaw and the pro-war faction, and in October he stood on the Labour Representation Committee ticket to take on the Lib–Lab candidate, Henry Broadhurst, whose come-lately militancy in the name of patriotism had mobilized the union vote. Much later Churchill stated that no man could pack so many words into such a small space of thought as MacDonald, and his adoption address at Leicester was to provide a sample of the obscurantist skill of the future leader of the party. Quick to protest that 'It is too late to object to Socialism. You are living with it', he was equally quick to dissemble as to exactly what he meant, referring now to Charlemagne, now to the Liberal agenda; digressing now on the prospects for municipal enterprises, now on international relations, to close with the question: Was not Socialism the growth, the inevitable growth, of society?

What his audience made of the question is not recorded, although it provided a clue to the ambivalent character of MacDonald himself. The illegitimate son of a Scottish dressmaker and an itinerant farm hand, he was born in 1866 and left school at the age of eleven, although not before developing a passion for books, among them works by Dickens, Burns, Bunyan and 'the lightest burden I ever bore home, Orr's *Circle of the Sciences*'. An exposition of the evolutionary theory, the work clashed directly with the creationist teachings of the Free Kirk and, while MacDonald was to retain his reverence for 'the grand, crowned authority of life', he was equally impressed by Darwinism. An uncomfortable union, it was to make an enigma of the man.

At fifteen MacDonald left Scotland, moving south to Bristol where he joined the SDF. He wrote later: 'We had all the enthusiasm of early Christians in those days. We were few and the gospel [of Marxism] was new.' Like the young Hardie, MacDonald was a character in search of an identity, and during the next fifteen years he worked respectively as clerk for the Cyclists' Touring Club, as Honorary Secretary of the Scottish Home Rule Association and as a researcher for Leslie Stephen, Editor of the *Dictionary of National Biography*. Although he was a radical in the making, it was not until the early 1890s that MacDonald was to find his political niche, joining both the ILP and the Fabian Society. The dichotomy nevertheless remained, for him to protest in 1895: 'I ceased to trust the Liberal Party when I was convinced that they were not prepared to go on and courageously face . . . the problems of poverty, stunted lives, and the pauper-and-criminal-making conditions of labour.' Meanwhile he continued to subscribe to the Liberal sympathies of the Fabians.

It was not altogether surprising that in 1892 there was talk of appointing MacDonald Temporary Secretary of the society. Possibly, it was a combination of his proven administrative skills and his capacity as a speaker that recommended him for the post, or possibly it was that in MacDonald the society found a man whose belief in the inevitability of gradualism was buttressed by his appreciation of Darwinism, for, however distinct in practice, the one was the progeny of the other. A brand of Utopian socialism that defied exact definition, it was a formula that was to condition MacDonald's entire outlook and account not only for his equivocal reputation but also for the sheer opacity of his speeches as much as of his politics. Always elusive, MacDonald's interpretations of socialism were as enigmatic as they were gnomic:

> Socialism deals primarily with the evolution of economic relations and not with the moral nature of man . . . The watchword of Socialism is not class consciousness but community consciousness . . . The state is but one of the organs of the community, all which together form the organism of society . . . Socialism could not be better defined than as that stage of social organisation when the State organises for society an adequate nutritive system . . . Socialism is not merely mechanical perfection and social economy, it is life itself.'

It is ironic that MacDonald was later to complain that critics of socialism accused socialists of failing to define what they meant by the word, when he himself had done so much to confuse its meaning. But if Leicester was to provide an early example of his obscurantist skills, and if the outcome of the election was as disastrous as he anticipated – he came comfortably bottom of the poll – it none the less helped to reinforce his conviction that the only practical future for the Labour Representation Committee and, with it, the labour movement lay with the trade unions. As for the rest, they carried more ideological baggage than political clout. While the ILP played the mediator between the militants of the SDF and the gradualists of the Fabian Society, none had either the funds or the capacity to mobilize sufficient forces if the ambitions of the committee were to be realized.

Precisely what these ambitions were remained obscure, however. Admirable as it was, the general statement of intent agreed at the Memorial Hall was equally significant for what it lacked in detail. If it was clear that 'a Labour Group in Parliament' would no longer subscribe to the Liberal agenda, exactly what principles should it adopt, what programme should it follow? For twelve months the issue taxed the LRC executive. Consisting of one Fabian, two representatives apiece from the ILP and the SDF and seven trade unionists, the members of the executive shared little in common, and when the conference of 1901 again rejected the SDF proposal to form a 'a distinct party based on the recognition of the class war', the federation withdrew from the executive, its places being taken by two Lib–Lab trade unionists.

While the withdrawal of the SDF was to have long-term consequences, reflecting the divide at the heart of the labour movement, the appointment of the new members was to reflect the immediate confusion that dogged the LRC. Again, it had to be asked: What were the aims of the embryo party and how best could they be achieved? Keir Hardie had no doubts, to wean the unions away from their Liberal alliance, and on this the committee's Secretary, Ramsay MacDonald, agreed – while continuing to conduct secret negotiations with the Liberal Whips, intimating that the LRC would welcome an arrangement with the Liberals that would allow its candidates a straight fight with the Tories in more than twenty constituencies.

The entente, finally agreed at MacDonald's bedside in a Leicester isolation hospital in 1903, was based as much on Mac-Donald"s pragmatism as his continuing dalliance with Liberalism, the more so since the so-called New Liberals under their left-of-centre leader Henry Campbell-Bannerman appeared to have appropriated much of the radical programme, embracing a wide range of welfare measures. Beatrice Webb might despise the man, but it seemed that, as far as his party was concerned, the Fabians' policy of permeation was finally paying dividends. And nothing could suit MacDonald's chameleon-like nature better. A handsome, vain man, MacDonald was flattered by the attentions of the Fabian coterie, which regarded Hardie as an outsider and which, for his part, Hardie regarded with suspicion.

But for all his doubts about the so-called Rainbow Circle, and for all his misgivings about the Liberals' change of heart, Hardie was enough of a realist to recognize the LRC's need for some kind of electoral accommodation in pursuit of his ultimate goal: 'We want socialism. But whether it comes under the name of Social Democracy, or Labour Party, or Municipalisation, or Collectivism is to me a matter of supreme indifference.' For all their differences in temperament and outlook, on this, at least, Hardie and Mac-Donald were agreed: that the committee needed both robust and powerful friends and that these could only be found among the unions which represented the LRC's core membership. Although commanding a majority on the executive, however, the unions remained as jealous of their power as their independence, one delegate at the TUC of 1901 warning: 'We shall no longer allow the [LRC] tail to wag the dog. We shall wag our own tails.'

He exaggerated. The unions remained the power-brokers, but, slowly yet inexorably, they were changing their political stance. At the LRC conference in Newcastle in 1903 there was a four-to-one vote in favour of a resolution tabled by Pete Curran of the Gas-workers that:

> Members of the Executive Committee and officials of affiliated organisations should strictly abstain from identifying themselves with or promoting the interests of any sections of the Liberal or Conservative parties, inasmuch as if we are going to secure the social and economic requirements of the industrial classes Labour representatives in and out of Parliament will have to shape their own policy and act upon it regardless of other sections of the political world.

As a declaration of political independence there could be no mistaking the intent. The nascent party was committed to Labour, or Labourism as Hardie preferred it to be called, though the exact terms of its programme had yet to be determined. All that was certain was that this was a clean break with the fudge-and-mudge of the past, and this by an overwhelming majority. Albeit piecemeal, the party was developing its persona, long nurtured by Hardie and now empowered by the growing militancy of the unions. Four years had passed since the Liberal *Daily News* had accused employers and, by association, the Tory government of judicial 'union-bashing', it having twice rejected measures to reduce working hours. And worse was to come. In the following eighteen months the courts had not only rescinded the rights to peaceful picketing but ruled that employers could sue unions for damages resulting from strike action.

Ammon Beasley was a man who enjoyed litigation for its own sake. General Manager of the Taff Vale Railway Company, he had little patience and even less sympathy when his work-force staged an eleven-day walk-out in support of a colleague who had been sacked in August 1900. As far as Beasley was concerned, *The Times* had been right when it declared that 'the unreasonable and pernicious rule [of trade unions] must be suppressed', and he felt he was the man for the job. Ignoring the advice of the company's lawyers, Beasley determined to bring an action for damages not against the strikers but their union. For a year the case engaged the courts, the first hearing finding for the plaintiffs, only for the judgement to be reversed on appeal and reversed, once again, by the Law Lords in July 1901. The blow was a crippling one. Henceforth any stoppage at work, however lawful, could be made the subject of an action brought against a trade union.

For six years the judiciary had been squeezing the unions, but it was the Taff Vale decision that finally convinced them of the vulnerability of their situation and of the need to establish an independent party to represent their interests in the Commons. Indeed, as Clement Attlee was to reflect many years later, the emergence of the Labour Party 'was not [the result of] the inspiration of a great leader . . . but rather a judgement of the House of Lords which deprived the Trade Unions of legal status which they had enjoyed for many years'. It was this that steeled the faint hearts to vote for the Curran resolution of 1903, and it was this that provided the LRC with the means to create a third force in British politics.

Within the year membership of the LRC almost doubled, to 861,150 individual members, and the number of affiliated unions rose from sixty-five to 127. Much had changed since that February day of 1900, but when the *Daily Telegraph* wrote that the election of Will Crooks, the LRC candidate, as the new Member for Woolwich presaged the rebirth of Chartism, not even it could have imagined how prescient it was to be proved.

At the General Election of 1906, the committee fielded fifty candidates, of whom twenty-nine were returned, for Arthur Balfour to reflect in the aftermath of the Tories' crushing defeat: 'We have here to do with something much more important than the swing of the political pendulum . . . We are face to face (no doubt in milder form) with the Socialist difficulties that loom large on the Continent. Unless I am greatly mistaken, the election of 1906 inaugurates a new era.'

4

The Great Unrest

'I pondered how men fight and lose the battle . . . and other men have to fight for what they meant under another name.' – William Morris, A *Dream of John Ball*, 1886

The Liberals came to power in January 1906, and the ailing Prime Minister, Campbell-Bannerman, was replaced by Herbert Henry Asquith in 1908. The 'coarse-grained and unimaginative' lawyer of Beatrice Webb's description had come far since he had entered the House of Commons in 1886, and for the next eight years he was to lead one of the most talented and radical administrations of the twentieth century. So radical was it that it was to generate new and corrosive tensions within the labour movement. Committed to adapting the individualism of the nineteenth century to the socio-economic needs of the twentieth, it seemed as if Asquith's New Liberals were bent on stealing the Labour programme, with the tacit support of the Labour group in the Commons and to the growing distrust of their rank-and-file supporters.

Immediately, however, the rift that was to polarize the party and precipitate a major national crisis was disguised by the party's success. Arthur Henderson, later to be described by David Lloyd George as 'the greatest political organizer in Britain but not normally a man given to flights of rhetoric, was to capture the spirit of the moment: 'The wage-earners have at last declared in favour of definite, united independent political action, and we this morning can rejoice in an electoral triumph which can safely be pronounced phenomenal.'

All that remained to be answered, as the final report of the LRC noted, was: 'What does the Labour Party want? What will it do?' The new name adopted by the committee sounded all very well in principle, but precisely what did it represent? Precisely what programme – of all the options on offer – would it pursue? These were questions that the twenty-nine Labour Members were hesitant to address, recognizing not only that they had so few answers but that what answers they had might expose the differences between them – differences that were quickly revealed when they came to elect the first chairman of the Parliamentary Labour Party. Keir Hardie, who had devoted two decades to uniting the movement, was the natural candidate for the post, but he was altogether too fond of declaring that 'Socialism is much more an affair of the heart than the intellect' for his comrades' commonsensical tastes. Such sentiment might sound all very well on the hustings, but the new Labour Members in the Commons (half of whom were trade unionists) were pragmatists rather than visionaries. What they wanted of their leader was a practical man who reflected their own down-to earth convictions, a quality that David Shackleton, longtime Secretary of the Darwen Weavers' Association, had in full measure.

The election, when it came, was a close-run thing, only MacDonald's vote on second ballot securing Hardie's appointment. Momentarily, sentiment ruled, but the election was a portent of things to come. Where Hardie represented grass-roots socialist activism, Shackleton represented the trade union interest – and the unions were interested primarily in themselves. Always a delicate balance, it was too soon to expose the divisions at the heart of the movement, personal as much as ideological. While MacDonald was later to write: 'I voted for Hardie as chairman with much reluctance, as I could not persuade myself that he could fill the place', the Fabians were both more caustic and more prescient, writing within six months of the General Election:

> The Labour Party in the House of Commons is as yet not disliked because it is not feared. Until it has made itself both disliked and feared it will be far short of having fulfilled the objects of its very existence . . . inasmuch as nothing short of an economic revolution

can vitally or permanently improve the wage-earner's condition, it
is at an economic revolution that the Labour Party must aim . . .
A Labour policy which hurts no one will benefit no one.

The caveat, essential to the Fabians, was that such a revolution could only be achieved gradually, although the anonymous
author was realist enough to recognize that it would take more
than twenty-nine MPs to build the New Jerusalem. None the less
Tract 127, *Socialism and the Labour Party*, revealed how quickly the
hopes vested in the Labour group in Parliament had been disappointed, the more so because it was the Fabians, a society committed to carrying moderation to extremes, which had mounted
such an attack.

No signature was attached to *Socialism and the Labour Party*,
but H. G. Wells may well have been its author. Five years had
passed since the Webbs had first permeated his thinking, and
while Beatrice was, as ever, patronizing about his plebeian background ('His mother was the housekeeper to a great establishment . . . his father the professional cricketer attached to the
place'), she was quick to recognize that his 'great knowledge of
the lower middle class, their habits and thoughts' would be of
inestimable value to the Fabians as an 'instrument for popular-
izing ideas'. Already established as the author of such best-sellers
as *The Island of Dr. Moreau* and *The Invisible Man*, Wells was to
reinforce his reputation with the more radical Fabians with the
publication in 1905 of *A Modern Utopia*.

It was the shape of things to come. A student of Plato, Wells
invented a new Republic in which a superior caste of benevolent
despots, the Samurai, would manage an ideal world. If that was for
the future, however, the critics of the Webbs' authoritarian ways
read a much more immediate message in *A Modern Utopia*.
Whether or not Wells's remark to Beatrice that 'The chapter on
the Samurai will pander to all your worst instincts' was in earnest
or in jest, the Webbs underestimated both his disruptive capacity
and his determination to rewrite the Fabian agenda. They were

soon to learn the full extent of their mistake.

Within a month of the General Election, and presaging Tract 127, Wells launched a vitriolic attack on the society. It was 'small, shabbily poor . . . collectively inactive'; it was 'remarkably unbusinesslike, inadaptable, and uninventive in its way', while as for the policy of permeation:

> The mouse decided to adopt indirect and inconspicuous methods, not to complicate its proceedings by too many associates, to win over and attract the cat by friendly advances rather than frighten her by a sudden attack. It is believed that in the end the mouse did succeed in permeating the cat, but the cat is still living – and the mouse can't be found.

Now humorously, now contemptuously, Wells dismembered the entire Fabian project:

> Measure with your eye this little meeting, this small hall . . . then go out into the Strand. Note the size of the buildings and business palaces, note the glare of the advertisements, note the abundance of traffic and the multitude of people . . . This is the world you are attempting to change. How does this little dribble of activities look then?

In pursuit if not of socialism then of collectivism the society had succumbed to conservatism, while of all its petty defects the worst was the membership's fondness for private jokes and its endless capacity to 'giggle'. The butt of Wells's remark was his fellow egocentric, Shaw, the giggle being his 'particular victim':

> It pursues him with unrelenting delight, simply because he is not like everybody else, as he rises, before he opens his mouth to speak it begins . . .you will not suppose than in attacking laughter I am assailing Bernard Shaw. But I do assail the strained attempts to play up to Shaw . . . to fall in with an assumed pretence that this

grave high business of Socialism, to which it would be a small offering for us to give all our lives, is an idiotic middle-class joke.

The echo was of William Morris, and Wells's critique was to
rack the society for the next two years. Although centred largely
on the clash between those titanic egoists Wells and Shaw, it
exposed, in microcosm, the differences that rent the party itself.
Where Wells would have aligned the society with Hardie and the
more radical wing of the movement, going so far as to suggest that
the Fabians should be renamed the British Socialist Party, Shaw
and the old guard rejected all take of radicalization, confident in
the efficacy of gradualism. As the controversy progressed it
became progressively more acerbic, and in 1908 Wells resigned,
his palace revolution having failed, although not before Shaw had
taken his revenge.

The last debate in the long-running controversy took place
at a meeting of the society in the summer of 1908, and Shaw
dominated the proceedings. After dismissing Wells's demands
for reform, he turned on Wells himself. During a visit to the
USA Wells had written a book – 'and a very good book too'
added Shaw – 'but while I was drafting our reply I produced a
play.' He paused, and there was silence. Seemingly Shaw had
lost his train of thought, and the silence lengthened. Then, as
the audience grew restless, he added: 'I paused there to enable
Mr Wells to say "And a very good play too."' Wells, and with
him his case, were damned not by the giggle but the gale of
laugher that followed.

Whoever wrote Tract 127 was right in all but one respect. The
Labour group in the House was not feared; it was too small for
that, not least, because the Liberals had won one of the most
resounding victories in electoral history, to command an overall
majority of eighty-four seats. And while Labour sat on the Opposition benches it had little to oppose in the opening sessions of the
new Parliament. Indeed at times it appeared as if the Campbell-

Bannerman administration was gearing its programme to appeal if not to liberal sympathies then to the political tastes of the trade unionists who formed the core of the infant party.

Small wonder that the word socialism was rarely heard in debates or that the phalanx of trade unionists in the party felt that patience was all that was required to achieve their New Jerusalem. Indeed they subscribed wholeheartedly to Ramsay MacDonald's opinion that 'The old order changeth' – until the Liberals published their Trades Disputes Bill. Five years had passed since Ammon Beasley had triumphed in the courts, five years during which the unions had grown increasingly restive at the legal stronghold imposed on their activity as a result of the Taff Vale judgement. While still in opposition the Liberals had implied that they would reverse the decision, and in his maiden speech as chairman of the party Hardie urged the new government to honour its previous commitment: 'If an officer offends the law, punish the officer, but do not punish the whole of the members for his indiscretion or want of judgement.'

On this question, at least, the entire Labour Party was united, as it was soon to unite with a powerful group of Liberal MPs who had committed themselves at the hustings to reversing the Taff Vale decision only to find that, once in power, their own front bench was attempting to stall on the issue. Based on the report of a Royal Commission established by the previous Tory administration, the Trades Disputes Bill went some way to allowing peaceful picketing and to establishing that an act done in combination was not necessarily illegal. Crucially, however, it left the courts to decide which act should be regarded as wrongful, while the financial immunity of trade unions remained in doubt. For all the government's seeming impregnability, a growing revolt among its own back-benchers forced Campbell-Bannerman to abandon the Bill in the course of a debate in the Commons and to announce that he intended to adopt a Labour Party measure that would provide complete legal immunity for trade union funds.

Considering the size of the Labour group, it was a major

achievement. The party, if not yet feared, was already a force to be reckoned with. The experience of power was a heady one, but having realized its goal Labour once again went into retreat, causing Hardie to write in May 1907: 'I am struck by the fact that the part in Parliament is somehow dropping out of notice. When one is on the spot, one does not notice it just the same. The cartoonists seem to be forgetting us, and somehow we don't seem to bulk so large in the eye of the public.'

Hardie's disenchantment was cankerous, and towards the end of the year he was actively considering retiring from the chairmanship of the party:

> My strongest reason for desiring to get out of the Chair is that I may be free to speak out occasionally . . . The [party's] tendency evidently is to work in close and cordial harmony with the Government and if this policy is persisted in we shall lose our identity and be wiped out along with the Liberals, and we should richly deserve our fate. By another session those of us in the party who are Socialists and who believe in fighting will have to get together on our own account and if we cannot drag the party with us we will 'gang oor ain gait'.

Not that Hardie was alone in his disillusion. It was reciprocated by MacDonald and Philip Snowden's disillusionment with Hardie himself. It was very well for him to protest that 'Nature never intended me to occupy an official position'; what they found inexcusable was Hardie's cavalier attitude to the day-to-day business of the House, Snowden complaining that his chairmanship was a 'hopeless failure' and MacDonald contemplating that his 'old resentment' against Hardie resulted in 'the elements of discord . . . gathering in a most menacing way'. The resentment was as much in MacDonald's mind as connected with Hardie's performance.

As Secretary of the ILP for six years MacDonald had lived in the shadow of a man with whom he shared much in common yet whose character was very different from his own. Each of them was as proud as he was vain, but where Hardie remained the visionary MacDonald adopted pragmatism; where Hardie, the rhetorician, was the radical individualist, MacDonald, the adroit politician, was the past master of party games; and while Hardie suspected MacDonald of his taste for 'luncheons and confabbing with Cabinet ministers', MacDonald regarded Hardie as an exhibitionist: 'From the beginning Hardie's greatest weakness [for showmanship and stage management] has lain there and long ago I had to make up my mind that I must accept him with his defects or not at all . . . I take his vanity as a necessary product of his finer self.'

At best, an uneasy relationship, at worst, a fissile one, it was soon to be reflected in the elements of discord within the movement that were gathering in 'a most menacing way'. The return of the Liberal government coincided with the first signs of a downturn in the economy, although the Labour group in the Commons appeared careless of such developments. Having once been admitted to 'the finest Club in Europe', it seemed to a growing body of their supporters that they had become little better than supernumeraries in the theatre of Westminster, showing little regard for and even less understanding of what was happening out of doors.

They were soon to learn. In June 1907, less than eighteen months after Labour's parliamentary début, Victor Grayson entered his name on the electoral lists for a by-election in the Colne Valley division of Yorkshire, for long a Liberal stronghold. At twenty-five he was already an inspiring public speaker who had been nominated by the local branch of the ILP, to the indignation of the ILP establishment, which refused to sponsor his candidacy. A militant, whose contempt for those 'crank socialists who believe that collectivism means living on cabbage and carrots and drinking cold water' did nothing to endear him to the nonconformists of the party hierarchy, Grayson's charisma allied to his uncompromising radicalism appealed powerfully to the voters.

The Labour group in the Commons were not so charitable, however, MacDonald writing shortly after Grayson took his seat: 'He puts up the backs of our own men very badly.'

Grayson proved merely a foretaste of the troubles to come, triggered by the growing suspicion among the party's rank and file that its MPs were betraying not only their election pledges but the trust of the electors themselves – a suspicion that was to be fuelled with the publication of *Is the Parliamentary Labour Party a Failure?* in the summer of 1908. The author, Ben Tillett, was no stranger to Labour politics. In 1889 he had been among the leaders of the London dock strike, and as a founder of the Dockers' Union he had been its Secretary for two decades – qualifications that gave his criticism of the party leadership a pungent authority. When he wrote of men such as Arthur Henderson, David Shackleton and Philip Snowden as 'liars at five and ten guineas a time' he knew something of what he was talking about, while his description of them as 'softly feline in their purring to Ministers and their patronage' revealed the full extent of his disenchantment. It was all very well for them to plead that expedience made it necessary for them to trade with the Liberals in the interests of their electors, but there was more to socialism than expedience, he felt.

As careless of *realpolitik* as he was conscious of grass-roots opinion, Tillett was to intensify a debate that was to rack the labour movement in the years immediately ahead and, if momentarily the accession of the fourteen MPs representing mining constituencies was to bring some relief to the party leaders, the ILP conference in 1908 was to expose a growing rift between the moderate and militant wings of the movement. Superficially there appeared to be little to distinguish between two of the major resolutions tabled. As so often, however, the appearance disguised the reality, much of the history of the party turning on the terminological subtleties of conference resolutions.

The SDF, which had campaigned alone and disastrously during the 1906 elections, none the less remained affiliated to the

ILP, and it was an SDF member, William Atkinson, who tabled an amendment to the Labour Party constitution, proposing that the party's ultimate aim should be the 'obtaining for the workers the full results of their labour by the overthrow of the present competitive system of capitalism and the institution of a system of public ownership and control of all means of life'.

The radical wing, among them Victor Grayson, applauded, prompting one MP to accuse the amendment's backers of employing entryist tactics to manipulate conference business and another to subject the amendment itself to savage criticism for attempting to impose a doctrinaire formula on what was, in practice, a heterogeneous alliance of the left. When put to the test, the amendment was voted down by a nine-to-one majority, yet less than two days later the conference was to vote for a resolution that was to become the touchstone of Labour probity for the next ninety-seven years:

> That in the opinion of this Conference the time has arrived when the Labour Party should have as a definite object the socialisation of the means of production, distribution and exchange, to be controlled by a democratic State in the interest of the entire community.

Of such semantic niceties are political differences made.

Although lacking the authority of an amendment to Labour's constitution, the resolution provided a practical goal for the party, although that was for the future. Meanwhile there was more pressing business to hand. In the first decade of the twentieth century the purchasing power of the pound fell by 18 per cent and wages in major industries rose by only 0.31 per cent, while the number of unemployed in the trade union movement alone (comprising less than a third of the total work-force) doubled between 1906 and 1909.

During the boom years of the late nineteenth century it had appeared that the gap between the Two Nations was narrowing, however slowly and inadequately. With the onset of the depression of the pre-war years such hopes were exposed for what they were: illusory. In 1905 the Liberal MP Chiozza Money calculated that an eighth of the population shared half the national income and that the remaining 38 million people shared the balance. As economic conditions deteriorated, so the margin increased, to precipitate a national crisis in the mid-term and, more immediately, to create a crisis in the labour movement itself – a crisis compounded by the Osborne judgement.

Like Ammon Beasley before him, W. V. Osborne enjoyed nothing more than a little litigation, and he had powerful financial backers to indulge his litigious tastes. A member of both the Liberal Party and the Railway Servants' Union, he strongly objected to his union dues being used for the upkeep of the Labour Party. Maintaining that the practice was *ultra vires*, Osborne brought an action against the Railway Servants in the summer of 1908, and on the High Court rejecting his petition he took it to appeal, where the decision was reversed. In depriving Labour of its major source of funding, the judgement struck at the foundations of the party. Only three years had passed since the Taff Vale decision had been reversed, yet again it seemed that the law was being employed to undermine the existence not only of the unions but of the entire labour movement – and this at a time when the praetorian guard of the movement, as Hardie regarded the ILP, was at its most vulnerable.

Since the publication of Tillett's pamphlet, the party establishment had been under mounting pressure from left-wing 'impossibilists', MacDonald's catch-all phrase to describe virtually any individual or faction in advance of his own position. Already contemptuous of the feeble performance of the Labour group in the Commons, and more especially when Hardie was replaced as chairman of the parliamentary party by the former Liberal and come-lately Fabian Arthur Henderson, the impossibilists' suspicions of Labour's taste for Liberal policies were to be reinforced in April 1908 when Asquith became Prime Minister and appointed

Lloyd George as his Chancellor. Where, previously, the Liberals had paid lip-service to radicalism, it now appeared that they were bent on root-and-branch reform to secure their own power base at the expense of the Labour vote.

It was a gambit at which the party was adept. Since the Whig grandees of the 1688 had sent James II on his travels they and their Liberal successors had played a five-finger exercise on power, now piano, now forte, but always tuned to the perpetuation of their dynasty. To their critics it had long seemed that there was something in Dr Johnson's charge that the first Whig may have been the Devil, his progeny having appropriated all the best tunes. More than seventy years had passed since Gray had championed reform to secure the vote of the industrial bourgeoisie. And now the party was shifting its ground once again to secure its own ascendancy.

For all the Liberals' commanding majority in the Commons Asquith and his colleagues were quick to read the mood of the country and alert to Lloyd George's warning that if they were to ignore social reform while in government 'then would a real cry arise in this land for a new party, and many of us here in this room would join in that cry'. There was no need to remind his audience that the party already existed, or the advantages to be gained by appropriating its policies. On grounds of pragmatism, if not of principle, a radical programme of social reform would not only help the government to outflank Labour in the country but also test the nerve of the Labour vote in the Commons by exploiting the emergent rift in the party. Henderson and his group had no more taste for the likes of Grayson and his politics than Asquith or his colleagues, and if the situation demanded making sacrifices to fortune then why not make a sacrifice of the Labour faction?

Within weeks of taking office, the Asquith administration had introduced a series of measures that gave substance to their new-found radical commitment: a Trade Boards Act designed to establish minimum wages in certain trades and eliminate the evil of 'sweating'; a Coal Mines Act to secure an eight-hour day for miners; and, most significantly, a non-contributory Old Age Pensions scheme that represented a new and formidable use of the power of taxation to redistribute income. Measure by measure, the Liberal programme attacked Henderson's and the moderates' position, causing Bruce Glasier, Editor of the *Labour Leader* and a Council member of the ILP, to write in November 1908: 'He [Henderson] is reckoned . . . as playing the Liberal game. Were he to resign, the rupture would end there, I have no doubt that the feeling in our movement would be one or relief.'

Glasier was wrong. The rupture was not healed, and the relief never came. Rather than resign Henderson soldiered on as chairman of the parliamentary party for the next two years, to complain at the ILP conference of 1909 at having been listed among: 'the betrayers of the class that willingly supported them . . . the press flunkies of Mr Asquith'. His bitterness mirrored the mood of the conference. Even before the delegates met, MacDonald was reflecting: 'The movement is more shaken at the moment than it has been for a long time, and the trouble is that it is an internal rent not an external blow that is the source of our weakness.' No mention was made of Grayson, but since entering the Commons his militant rhetoric and cavalier lifestyle had come to haunt the party establishment. And as their aversion for his extravagances burgeoned, so his popularity among the rank and file increased. In November 1908 a meeting was called in an attempt to re-establish socialist unity, but Grayson refused to attend, preferring instead to mount a venomous attack on Hardie and, by implication, all that the old guard represented.

This was the internal rent that the Liberals played on and MacDonald feared. At the ILP conference in Edinburgh his fears were quickly realized when an amendment tabled by Grayson was carried against the old guard. In protest Hardie, MacDonald, Snowden and Glasier announced their intention of resigning from the executive of the ILP, and in spite of the fevered efforts of delegates to make them withdraw their resignation they refused. Their gesture was one of principle rather than pique, concerned as much with asserting the party's commitment to gradualism as to making an example of Grayson and all that he represented: the recrudescence of socialist militancy. Nine years had passed since Labour had achieved a degree of unity, even if its goals had yet to be defined. In 1909 it was as much a question of what goals Labour should be pursuing as how they could best be achieved that was to undermine the fragile unity of the party, to divide the movement against itself.

And while the law ruled (in 1909 the Law Lords confirmed the Appeal Court's decision in the Osborne case) and the Labour Party wrangled, the Liberals intensified their assault on what Winston Churchill termed 'the radical conscience' and, indirectly, on Labour's position. After speaking for four hours Lloyd George ended the Budget speech of 1909 with a forthright challenge to the Opposition:

> This is a War Budget. It is to raise money to wage implacable war against poverty and squalidness. I cannot help hoping and believing that before this generation has passed away we shall have advanced a great step to that good time when poverty, and the wretchedness and human degradation which always follow in its camp, will be as remote to the people of this country as the wolves which once infested its forests.

The Chancellor resumed his seat at eight o'clock, leaving Labour Members to wonder at the gall of a man who had so blandly appropriated their radical credentials and Tories trying to absorb the full implications of what they had heard.

While the financial purpose of the People's Budget was to cover a government deficit of £126 million, there could be no disguising its political target, the one interest the Tories held sacred above all else: land. Among a number of measures Lloyd George proposed a 20 per cent tax on unearned increments in the capital value of land, an increase in estate and death duties and a super-tax on all incomes above £5,000. But while Lloyd George's audacity determined the Tories' response, it compounded Labour's dilemma. There could be no question of the party opposing the package, yet in doing so there was the risk that it would reinforce the suspicion that the party was no better than a left-wing appendage of a progressive alliance. And as Tory hostility to the budget intensified, the Duke of Beaufort suggesting that he 'would like to see Winston Churchill and Lloyd George in the middle of twenty couples of dog hounds', so the Liberal response became ever more radical.

Always contemptuous of the Tories' assertion that the Upper House was 'the watchdog of the constitution' – 'You mean it is Mr Balfour's poodle. It fetches and carries for him. It barks for him. It bites anybody he sets it on to' – Lloyd George set about attacking the established order of things with a relish that mocked Labour's political timidity. At a meeting in London's East End in July, in a speech of which the King later complained that it 'set class against class', he made a bonfire of the vanities of the great and good, contrasting the extravagance of their lifestyles ('a fully equipped Duke costs as much to keep up as two Dreadnoughts') with the cant of their principles:

> I was telling you, I went down a mine the other day . . . In the very next colliery to the one I descended, just a few years ago, three hundred people lost their lives. And yet when the Prime Minister and I knock at the door of these great landlords and say to them: 'Here, you know that these poor fellow have been digging up your royalties at the risk of their lives. Some of them are old . . . they are broken, they can earn no more. Won't you give something to keep them out of the workhouse?' they scowl at us, and we say 'Only a ha'penny, just a copper.' They say: 'You thieves!' And they turn their dogs on us, and you can hear their bark every morning.

This was the language of the militant rather than the moderate left, language that roused Sir Edward Carson to write to *The*

Times that Lloyd George had 'taken off the mask and openly preached a war of the classes'. To the Labour group in the Commons, who had spent a lifetime expunging the phrase from their political lexicon, such talk was taboo, and while MacDonald was quick to endorse the Budget ('an epoch-making measure') he was equally quick to assure the House that that was because 'Socialism is not in it.' The Lords disagreed, but even then it is probable that they would have hesitated about rejecting a Money Bill if they had not been provoked by the lash of Lloyd George's oratory. The House of Commons' exclusive control of finance was a central tenet of Britain's unwritten constitution, but after a six-day debate in late November the Upper House threw out the Budget, causing Lloyd George to declare that: 'the Lords may decree a revolution which the people will direct' and *The Times* to deliberate on the prospects of a constitutional crisis.

The issue was plain, and in January 1910 the Liberals went to the country with the slogan of 'Peers versus People'. The outcome was not what they expected. At the close, the government had lost 145 seats, and while it still commanded a wafer-thin majority the future of its legislative programme depended on the votes of the minority parties. If the Liberals had fared disastrously, proportionately Labour had fared little better, losing eleven seats formerly held by Labour and miners' members, to reduce the party's representation to forty MPs. The irony of the situation was not lost on Hardie. For all Labour's setbacks Labour and Irish Nationalist MPs now held the balance of power at Westminster and, while the party could no longer indulge in the luxury of opposition for fear of bringing in the Tories, it no longer needed to tug its forelock to its Liberal partners. Theoretically at least it could begin to flex its own political muscle, as demanded by an increasingly militant faction among the rank and file.

Among those who had lost their seat at the 1910 elections was Victor Grayson, but an altogether more formidable figure was to emerge or, rather, re-emerge to provide a focus for left-wing dissent: Tom Mann. Having served as a member of the Royal Commission on Labour, and briefly as Secretary of the ILP, he had quit England in 1901 to work as a political activist first in New Zealand and then Australia, where he had hammered out the skeleton of his political philosophy, maintaining that 'the present system of sectional trade unionism is incapable of combating effectively the capitalist system under which the world is now suffering'.

On his return to Britain he reiterated his convictions, to be welcomed by Hyndman of the renamed Social Democratic Party ('we have no more intelligent, active, vigorous and a capable exponent of Socialism than Tom Mann'), and the Editor of the SDP journal *Justice*, Harry Quelch, who declared that substantial as Mann's work had been in Australia, it was 'as nothing to the work he could do here . . on the scene of self-satisfaction which we had now reached Tom Mann came as a disturbing element – and we wanted someone to wake us up'. Quelch exaggerated. What MacDonald's 'impossibilists' lacked was not spirit but a coherent programme to canalize their militancy. However expedient Labour's concordat with the Liberals, and however admirable the party's gradualist strategy, there was little sustenance to be found in the inevitability of gradualism, the more so as economic conditions continued to deteriorate.

By 1910 unemployment was at its highest level since 1886 and still rising, while the purchasing power of the pound had fallen by almost a quarter since 1895 and was still falling. As early as 1908, a year during which working days lost in industrial disputes quadrupled, Ben Tillett noted that 'Britain is in an increasingly restless mood, but the movement lacks direction.' The syndicalists and, most notably, Tillett's long-standing friend Tom Mann were to provide it. Since the turn of the century the Socialist Labour Party in Scotland, an SDF splinter group, had been peddling the theories of the American academic Daniel De Leon who, contemptuous of parliamentary action, advocated that trade unions should declare economic war on capitalism. In France George Sorel had reached much the same conclusion. An engineer turned political activist, and a powerful champion of Drey-

fus, Sorel maintained that the general strike was the agent of revolutionary socialism.

In the USA De Leon's doctrine was to provide the founding
text for the International Workers of the World (IWW), established in Chicago in 1905. In France Sorel's major work, *Reflexions
sur la violence*, was to become the handbook of the Confédération
Générale du Travail, the revolutionary wing of French trade union
(*syndicat*) movement. In Britain Tom Mann was to become the
agent for both. After a brief visit to Paris in June 1910, where he
met the leaders of the CGT, he returned to London to publish the
first issue of *The Industrial Syndicalist* in July. Its tone was as direct
as its message was uncompromising:

> Chief among our [socialist] faults is our remarkable gullibility.
> We have been singularly willing to take the word for the deed –
> They [Labour MPs] are revolutionary neither in their attitude
> towards existing society nor in respect of present-day institu-
> tions. Indeed, it is no exaggeration to say that many of them have
> constituted themselves as apologists for existing society – The
> engines of war to fight the workers' battles to overthrow the Cap-
> italist class must be of the workers' own making – But what will
> have to be the essential condition for the success of such a move-
> ment? *That it will be avowedly and clearly Revolutionary in aim and
> method.*

Its agency? A general federation of trade unions. Its means?
The strike weapon. Its object? 'To change the system of society
from capitalist to socialist.' Sixty years had passed since the
Chartists had last massed, but in Tom Mann it was again possible
to catch an echo of Thomas Benbow's ironically titled revolutionary pamphlet *Grand National Holiday and Congress of the Production Classes,* of James Morrison's call for 'a long strike, a strong
strike, and a strike all together' to bring about 'a different order of
things'. As in 1910 it was the physical-force Chartists' disillusion
with the 'sponging house' of Westminster that had triggered their

call for extra-parliamentary action; and as in 1836 it was Mann and the syndicalists who were to mobilize the discontent abroad at what they regarded as the Labour Party's betrayal of the people's trust.

Not that the party's leaders had ever pretended that Labour's New Jerusalem could be built overnight. Cautious men, who had much to be cautious about, they knew very well that to imply as much would have been to disappoint their supporters. Yet, for all their protestations, the very fact of Labour's presence in the Commons had fed expectations among the rank and file of the movement that could never, realistically, be fulfilled. Always chimerical, their hopes were stillborn. Labour's handful of MPs, the majority of whom were of moderate persuasion, were hardly the material of which revolution were made, and their supporters were quick to learn that the leadership's promises of revolutions tomorrow were a poor substitute for revolutions today. Deferred gratification was not enough to satisfy the growing distress of workers who, disenchanted with reality, turned in growing numbers to extra-parliamentary action.

In the early days of what was to become known as the Great Unrest the author and journalist Fred Henderson wrote:

> At the very moment when the governing classes were congratulating themselves on having comfortably absorbed the Parliamentary Labour Party, there breaks out with a dramatic completeness this Labour Unrest everywhere. As for the Parliamentary Labour Party, its members had adapted to the club life of Westminster as to the manner born . . . The whole thing, after the scare of 1906 at the emergence of Labour's political class consciousness, had settled down, so far as Westminster was concerned, into a beautiful quiescence.

The quiescence was illusory. As the Liberals sanitized the Labour vote, to fortify suspicions of the leadership's integrity, militancy burgeoned: 'And then, suddenly, this fierce eruption of discontent everywhere, shattering the complacency and the dream of peace! – the explosive violence and unmistakable emphasis of a living fact as against the paper statutes of legislators' (*The Labour Unrest*, 1912).

Henderson was both right and wrong. When it came, the eruption was explosive, but the Great Unrest was a crisis that had been waiting to happen. Since 1906 the Labour Party had been in an impossibilist position, trapped between the appeal of New Liberalism and the demands of extra-parliamentary activists, a condition compounded by the inertia of the trade unions. The Taff Vale decision had been reversed, but the Osborne judgement remained, to hamstring the unions and to paralyse their ageing and conservative leaders.

This was the political vacuum that syndicalism was to fill. Where Grayson and Tillett had reflected the disenchantment with Labour's performance, Mann was to mobilize it by providing a focus for the widespread if fragmented discontent of the rank and file – not least in the South Wales mining valleys. In 1914 Stanley Jevons, author of *The English Coal Trade*, reflected that:

> In temperament the Welshman is distinct from the Englishman. There had been throughout the nineteenth century, and still is among the older miners, an extraordinarily religious fervour . . . During the past fifteen years, however, there has been a distinct falling off in attendance at chapels; and the younger generation is growing up mainly imbued with socialistic and political aspirations. To many of them the 'War against Capital' has become almost a religion.

A guerrilla war of strike and lock-out had racked the Welsh industry for a quarter of a century before the 10,000 pitmen of the Cambrian Combine struck in support of a wage claim in November 1910. By mid-month, with 23,000 men out and the strike movement still gathering momentum, Churchill ordered troops to be deployed in the valleys, Keir Hardie warning that 'their presence . . . may in the end lead to disorder which would altogether be obviated if the troops were not there'. His fears were soon realized. On the evening of 21 November troops cleared the streets of Tonypandy and a protester was killed. Six days later Tom Mann addressed the inaugural meeting of the Industrial Syndicalist Education League in Manchester. The events were coincidental, but in the minds of the 198 delegates, representing some 60,000 trade unionists, the one gave credence to the other, to reinforce Mann's declaration that 'We have no hostility at all to unions . . . but the capitalist organisations have travelled much faster than the workers. They have syndicated their forces. We are called upon to do the same on the basis of class, and not to act sectionally.'

While the miners had their martyrs, the leaders of Britain's 1,168 unions had no inclination to make martyrs of themselves. Preferring to manage the existing confusion of interests that were the source of their own often derisory portions of power, they were unanimously hostile to Mann's claim that if they were to syndicate their forces no more than fourteen industrial unions would be needed. Indeed this was virtually all that they agreed upon, concerned, as they were, more with inter-union rivalry (in the building industry alone there were nineteen unions, all contesting for their share of members) than with achieving any semblance of unity to challenge the union of capital.

The situation made a nonsense of their claims to represent the best interest of their members, as growing numbers of them realized, and by the close of 1910, encouraged by the Amalgamation Committees established by the syndicalists, the motley of dockers' and transport workers' unions combined to form the Transport Workers' Federation. Within the year the federation's success was to provide an example of what could be achieved by collaboration. Early in 1911 strikes by Lancashire weavers and the Society of London Compositors had been picked off, piecemeal, by management, but in June a localized stoppage by dockers in support of striking seamen quickly flared into a national strike. One after another Britain's major ports were strikebound. By August 100,000 workers were out in London, while in Liverpool, where two gunboats were stationed in the Mersey with their guns trained on the City, the local railmen came out in sympathy with the dockers to trigger an extension of the stoppage. Within the week 200,000 railmen were on strike, prompting the Home Secretary, Winston Churchill, to declare that Britain was under the control of the military authorities, 'practically every regiment . . . having now been mobilised'.

In their *History of Trade Unionism* the Webbs were to describe what Keir Hardie was to call the 'Russification' of Britain: 'an overpowering display was made with the troops, which were sent to Manchester and other places, without requisition by the civil authorities . . . In fact, a policy of repression had been decided on, and bloodshed was near at hand.'

A full-scale confrontation was avoided only when the government's nerve broke and it intervened to persuade the port authorities to meet the unions and settle their demands. Seemingly the case for syndicalism had been vindicated, although one prominent shipowner was later to declare that 'the Dockers had new leaders, men unknown before'. The Labour Party leadership knew better. While in public Philip Snowden accepted that 'The Syndicalist movement by directing attention to . . . points which Socialism had rather ignored', in private MacDonald was locked in discussions with the government in the belief that the Liberal radicals under Lloyd George were 'converging upon Socialist positions'.

What MacDonald meant by socialist remained imprecise, but the negotiations were to compromise his position. As bitterly critical of the deployment of force to intimidate the strikers ('One way to maintain law and order is not to allow a policeman to break a man's head') as he was of the media coverage of the strike, especially those papers that were 'spewing out a filthy slush of hypocrisy', his private dealings contrasted graphically with his statements of public concern. As the stoppage intensified, it appeared that MacDonald was intensifying his efforts to reach an agreement with the government, and Arthur Henderson was to claim later that as chairman of the Parliamentary Labour Party he had gone so far as to propose entering 'a coalition with Lloyd George and Balfour' (leader of the Tory Party).

True or not, Henderson's assertion revealed the rift at the heart of the labour movement. And if 1911 was to expose the differences that rent the movement 1912 was to prove even more damaging, if not to to the syndicalists then to MacDonald and the Parliamentary Labour Party. Since the collapse of the Cambrian Combine strike, an unofficial Reform Committee of the South Wales Miners' Federation had been drafting what subsequently proved to be the most notable pamphlet ever published by Britain's pitmen, *The Miner's Next Step*. Inspired in part by their own experiences, in part by the lessons of syndicalism, the authors asked why their union was so well respected by the coal owners, to provide their own reply:

> Because they had the men – the real power – in the hollow of their hands. They, the [trade union] leaders, become 'gentlemen', they become MPs and have considerable social prestige because of their power . . . Now every inroad the rank and file make on this privilege lessens the power and prestige of the leaders. Can we wonder then that our leaders are averse to change? Can we wonder that they try and prevent progress?

Until such Uncle Toms were removed, real progress towards creating an organization that would take over the mining industry and manage it 'in the interests of the workers' would never be achieved. And even then it would be impossible to realize such a goal in isolation: 'We cannot get rid of employers and slave driving in the mining industry until all other industries have organised for and progressed towards the same objective. Their rate of progress conditions ours, all we can do is to set an example and the pace.'

The pamphlet was published in November 1911, and two months later the Miners' Federation of Great Britain tabled a pay claim – five shillings a shift for men, two shillings for boys – which the management rejected out of hand. Possibly the conjunction of events was coincidental, possibly the one had no bearing on the other, but, whatever the case, the federation's leadership called for strike action, and on St David's Day 1912, 'about a million miners' ceased work according to the Board of Trade. The effect of the biggest strike that Britain had yet seen was soon to become evident. Starved of coal, Lloyd George's 'paramount Lord of Industry', British industry was in crisis within the fortnight, and as conditions continued to deteriorate the government acted, Asquith tabling a Wages Mining Bill in the Commons on 19 March. Its content was politically charged, proposing to establish a minimum wage for the industry, and the Commons' response was as explosive, the Opposition accusing Lloyd George of being a closet syndicalist and reminding MacDonald of his remark that 'On the day of his first triumph, when he declares his strike, the Syndicalist signs his own death warrant.'

The government's majority held firm, however, and on 26 March the Bill returned to the Commons for its third reading. The House was crowded. This was grand theatre. In less than a month, the miners had humbled both the country and the government, as Asquith was soon to make clear: 'I speak under the stress of very strong feeling. We have exhausted all our powers of persuasion and argument and negotiation. But we claim we have done our best in the public interest, with fairness and impartiality.'

Asquith's voice faded, then died. The House sat silent, transfixed. The Prime Minister was weeping.

Throughout the passage of the Bill MacDonald had defended the ends that the miners were demanding, their call for a minimum wage having 'taken its place among the axioms of moral men and women', while deploring the means they had adopted, condemning their leaders as 'syndicalist Anarchists of the ordinary type, who find in Socialism the greatest obstacle to their absurd economic and political ideas'. Careless of Lenin's verdict that 'If the railway strike of 1911 displayed the new spirit of British workers, the miners' strike positively represents a new epoch', MacDonald seemed to have learned nothing from the experience of the previous year. Sidney Buxton, President of the Board of Trade, dismissed with contempt 'the almost complete collapse' of the Labour Party in the Commons:

> They were not consulted with regard to, and had no share in the Seamen's or Transport Worker's movement last summer. During the railway strike they attempted to act as a go-between for the men and the government, but they had very little influence over the actions of the men, or on the result. During the Miners' Strike . . . the Labour Party exercised no influence at all.

The Liberals' contempt for their putative allies was mirrored in the scorn with which the rank and file of the labour movement viewed the party leadership. Like the union old guard it seemed that they, too, had joined the 'gentlemen' of Westminster. Mac-Donald's savage assault on a stoppage by London dockers in May tended to confirm their suspicions: 'If we are to go about our business in a harum scarum sort of way, breaking contracts and plunging the whole country into a state of unsettlement . . . we cannot retain that liberty of action which we have secured up to now.'

The dock strike was broken, but not before a new agent had entered the lists in defence of its cause: the *Daily Herald*. Launched, briefly, as a printers' strike sheet in 1911, it was relaunched in April the following year to make its political stance over the dockers' strike clear: 'We have considered the matter. We have considered every phase of it and we say, Prepare your organisation and strike. STRIKE AND STRIKE HARD.'

The primary targets of the *Herald*'s attacks were MacDonald, Snowden and the ILP for their 'sinister relationship' with the Liberals. G. K. Chesterton was among those who were to provide the paper with its cutting edge:

> Mr MacDonald had no position, high or low, in any of the three dimensions of the universe. It would not have made the slightest difference for good or evil, to the future of anything or anybody, if the tiger had eaten him. There would have been a Liberal MP for Leicester instead, who would have made the same speeches, given exactly the same votes; and, if he were the usual, successful soap-boiler, would have eclipsed Mr MacDonald in everything except good looks.

Like MacDonald's, Chesterton's words capture much of the bitterness that was racking the movement. As the dispute intensified, so attitudes hardened and the rancour became engrained. Jealous as much of their egos as of their principles, moderates and militants made a sacrifice of compromise in the name of ideological rectitude. Little more than a decade had passed since it had seemed that they had shared a common purpose, if the details for realizing their goal had still to be agreed. By the close of 1912 the accord had been exposed for what it was. The victim of its own animus, it appeared that the party was bent on its own destruction.

For Liberal radicals such as Lloyd George the schism improved the prospect of reaching an agreement with MacDonald and 'the closet Liberals' within the Labour Party and, in the process, of extending their own left flank. For MacDonald and his following in the House such a deal would not only conform with his own gradualist sympathies but also provide the means for sterilizing 'the syndicalism virus' within the labour movement. For MacDonald's 'impossibilists' such an accord represented only one thing: the betrayal of socialism. And throughout 1913 it was the militants who dictated the political terms, while MacDonald fought a rearguard action to maintain the unity of the party he led.

Shortly after his election as chairman of the parliamentary party, he had confided: 'I see nothing but storms and heartaches ahead.' The heartaches were deferred until 1931. The storm had already broken, and as the strike movement gathered force its success mocked what the *Daily Herald* regarded as MacDonald's 'politics of deference'. As first the miners and then the transport workers achieved their strike objectives it appeared to be nonsensical for MacDonald to protest that there was no realistic alternative to gradualism. For men in a hurry it seemed that there was. Careless of the fact that as Labour was a minority party in the House, as it was in the country (where it had obtained only 7.6 per cent of the vote at the 1910 election), the need was for political diplomacy rather than gesture politics, the rank-and-file activists had little patience and even less time for his defence of *realpolitik*.

Thirty-eight million man days had been lost through strikes during 1912, and the momentum was maintained the following year, for the government's industrial troubleshooter, George Askwith, to reflect in November: 'Within a comparatively short space of time there may be movements coming to a head in this country of which recent events have been a small foreshadowing.' He knew what he was talking about, having played a key role as peacemaker in the disputes that had convulsed the industry the previous year. What had triggered Askwith's alarm, however, was not the burgeoning support for direct action, rather the growing number of unions that were actively considering amalgamating to reinforce their strike and negotiating potential.

The Transport Workers' Federation had shown something of what could be achieved during the strike of 1912, and later that year three of the major rail unions – the Amalgamated Society of Railway Servants (with 132,000 members), the General Railway Workers' Union (20,000 members), and the United Signalmen and Pointsmen (4,000 members) – entered talks that led to the creation of the National Union of Railwaymen. Their initiative was to serve as the model for the formation of the Amalgamated

Union of Building Trade Workers and the Amalgamated Engineering Union, and, while still jealous of its federal composition, Britain's most powerful union, the Miners' Federation, was moving steadily towards integration.

Slowly, yet inexorably, the jigsaw of union power was taking shape. Where, once, Beatrice Webb had despaired of the flabbiness of the TUC leadership, a new generation of leaders as contemptuous of Westminster as they were committed to direct action had energized the movement, union membership rising by more than 30 per cent to 3.9 million members in the four years to 1914. This was 'the strong right arm of the Labour Movement' that Tom Mann commended and MacDonald condemned, to the growing alarm of the ILP. While the rank and file were 'eager to come to grips with capitalism', it seemed that the best MacDonald could do was to plead expedience to justify his continuing flirtation with Asquith's administration, for the *Labour Leader* to catechize the party's conscience:

> Are we to forget the Government's attempts to intimidate the railwaymen? Are we to forget the Government's callous betrayal of the London dockworkers? Are we to forget the Government's rejection of a minimum of 21s a week for railway workers? Are we to forget the Government's denial of a living wage and an eight-hour day?

Yet this was the government with which MacDonald connived in the belief that the Labour Party was 'in the true line of progressive apostolic succession from the Liberals'. As far as his critics were concerned, his pietistic tones did nothing to disguise his apostasy. Quietism was no longer a political option and the more vehemently men such as Snowden called up God in support of their cause ('The Sun of Righteousness is rising with its healing wings. The Christ that is to be appears'), the more it reinforced the radicals' suspicions of their political intentions. Seemingly it was the old, old story that they had heard not once but so many times before, but this time things were different, this time it appeared that power was where it should be – in the hands of the people.

For all the gloss that Labour apologists have subsequently placed on events, the movement was bitterly divided against itself, its constituents having diminishing confidence either in the integrity of the party leadership or in the policies they pursued. As direct action gained credence it exacerbated the tensions within the Labour establishment, Keir Hardie adopting an increasingly hostile attitude to MacDonald's position. Long suspicious as much of MacDonald's taste for fashionable society as of his unwillingness to show any fight over issues that might embarrass his Liberal associates, Hardie was to develop into an implacable critic of his protégé. As for MacDonald, he had come to regard Hardie as the elder statesman of socialism who had lived for too long off his reputation as the founding father of the party. Masterful figures and proud, their jealousies mirrored each other, as their political differences reflected the schism at the heart of the labour movement.

As early as the 1910 elections, Hardie had signalled his distrust of any extension of the Lib–Lab concordat, while welcoming evidence of the growing working-class militancy he witnessed at first hand in South Wales. The two issues were to point and counter-point his contest with MacDonald during the Great Unrest. While Hardie shared MacDonald's opinion of syndicalism ('anarchism in its industrial form'), it did nothing to diminish his regard for the value of strikes as a weapon of the working class or to modify his criticisms of MacDonald and his confederates. In the summer of 1912, when the party executive decided not to field a candidate at a Leicester by-election, allowing the Liberals to have an uncontested run at the poll, Hardie decried 'the slobbering talk with which the Liberal press was filled . . . about the friendly understanding between the Liberals and the Labour Party'. His suspicions of a Lib–Lab détente were to be reinforced in the spring of 1913 when Lloyd George (Hardie's 'pettifogging

attorney') sounded out MacDonald on the possibility of an electoral compact. The proposal was stillborn, none the less Mac-
Donald's specious denial that such a deal had ever been mooted
merely fortified Hardie's mistrust of his intentions.

As a catalyst the leadership's difference over the role of the
direct action movement intensified the conflict within the party,
MacDonald asserting that working men were being 'goaded into
revolt' by syndicalist agitators. In October 1913 MacDonald's
confidant , Philip Snowden, was to expand on the theme, declaring that 'the General Strike is General Nonsense'. An ascetic, of
whom Churchill was to say that he regarded 'militant Socialism as
a disease . . . like rickets or mange', Snowden accepted that, when
partially employed, strikes had their uses but maintained that
concerted extra-parliamentary action had no place in the Labour
programme. The alternative was to empower the Labour Party
and, in the process, augment its influence in the Commons.
Hardie was scathing. He maintained that, while strikes should
never be employed indiscriminately and should always be peace-
able, they were an essential weapon in the armoury of the labour,
for 'It is the experience gained by the strike which ultimately fil-
ters into the consciousness of the working class and makes political action a triumphant reality.' The echo was of Tom Mann ('The
purpose of Syndicalism is to educate the organised workers to
recognise their own power'), and if it was not Mann himself then
it was his syndicalist principles that were to dominate the industrial agenda in the early months of 1914.

Askwith's forebodings were to be realized more quickly than
even he had foreseen. On a small scale Britain was subjected to
an epidemic of strikes early in the year, and in March the transport workers and railwaymen agreed to support a miners' initiative and to form a Triple Alliance. Although the fine print of the
compact had still to be agreed, the overarching principle reflected
its syndicalist origins: that in future all three unions would coordinate the submission of their demands to management and none
would agree to a settlement unless the others agreed too. With a

combined membership of more than 1,200,000 workers in key industries, the Alliance was the most potent weapon yet forged by the union movement, a strike weapon which, if deployed, could reduce Britain to impotence within a matter of hours.

Samuel Butler once declared that the most perfect irony is unconscious. He would have been entertained by the coincidence that on 3 March 1914, at a time when the Triple Alliance was in the making, Lloyd George was again testing MacDonald's political will by broaching the idea of a Lib–Lab concordat. The proposal came to nothing, having been anathematized by Keir Hardie, and, while the conjunction of events was pure happenstance, the events of those March days none the less exposed the breach at the heart of the labour movement and the party that claimed to represent it.

Since 1900 the alliance of the left had always been an uneasy one, a marriage of convenience between partners to whom collaboration came hard and compromise even harder. The talk may have been of comradeship, but the word itself mocked the reality, for if moderates such as MacDonald were to damn Mann and the Industrial Syndicalists as 'impossibilists', holding that the future lay with 'evolutionary socialism', then, for their part, militants such as Tom Mann were to damn MacDonald and his circle as 'traitors to their class', holding that direct action was the only way in which the working class could succeed in securing 'the world for the world's workers'.

In the early summer months of 1914 it momentarily seemed as if Mann's prescription might have been realized. By mid-summer Askwith's department had recorded more than 900 stoppages, and in July the Scottish coal owners announced that they could no longer afford to pay the seven shillings a day minimum wage and were cutting it by a shilling. The scene was set for a major confrontation, the more so if the Triple Alliance should be mobilized in support of the miners, when at 12.20 a.m. on 5 August a telegram was dispatched from the War Office in Whitehall: 'War. Germany. Act.' The industrial crisis was averted, and it was to be

another six years before Ernest Bevin was to write the postscript
to the Great Unrest:

> It was a period which, if the war had not broken out, would, I
> believe, had seen one of the greatest industrial revolts the world
> has ever seen.

5

The War That Will End War

'The Labour Party, that sad failure of socialism.' – G. D. H. Cole, *The World of Labour*, 1913

The outbreak of war brought no peace to the Labour Party. The issues involved were too contentious for that. Since 1910, when the Second International had declared that 'If war threatens to break out it is the duty of working men in the countries concerned . . . to use every effort to prevent war by all the means which seem to them most appropriate', it had been an article of socialist faith that the proletariat would not take up arms against one another in defence of capitalist interests. The high summer months of 1914 were to expose the ideal for what it was, for Horatio Bottomley's chauvinist weekly, *John Bull,* to encapsulate the public mood at the news of the assassination at Sarajevo: 'To Hell With Servia'. Insular as always, the majority agreed. The Continentals could be left to fight their own wars, as they had done often enough in the past.

For five weeks, as the war machine gathered momentum, Britain counted down the days to the August Bank Holiday weekend, now fearful that the *Daily Mail*'s jeremiad that war was inevitable would prove to be correct, now convinced that the Bishop of Lincoln was right when he wrote to the *Daily News* on 1 August: 'For England to join in this hideous war would be treason to civilization and disaster to our people. God save us from the war fever.' It was a sentiment that was to be re-echoed the following day by the 'vastest crowd' that Trafalgar Square had seen for many years according to the *Manchester Guardian.* Called by the Labour Party to denounce the 'madness of warmongering', the demonstration – one among the many throughout the country – was empowered by a manifesto hastily drafted by Keir Hardie and Arthur Henderson:

Men and women of Britain, you have now an unexampled opportunity of your power, rendering a magnificent service to humanity
and to the world. Proclaim that for you the days of plunder and
butchery have gone by. Send messages of peace and fraternity to
your fellows who have less liberty than you.

Down with class rule! Down with the rule of brute force!. Down
with war! Up with the peaceful rule of the people.

The huge crowd applauded, to acclaim a resolution that: 'the
Government of Britain should rigidly decline to engage in war',
but their resolve was short-lived, as were the pacific hopes of
Hardie and Henderson and much of Labour leadership.

On the afternoon of Monday 3 August the Foreign Secretary,
Sir Edward Grey, informed the Commons that if Germany should
violate Belgian neutrality the government would regard it as an
act of war. Momentarily it appeared that the House was united in
agreement, then Ramsay MacDonald rose to speak:

The Rt Hon. gentleman has delivered a speech the echoes of
which will go down in history . . . But I think he is wrong. I think
the government for which he speaks is wrong. I think that the verdict of history will be that they are wrong.

So far as we [the Parliamentary Labour Party] are concerned,
whatever may happen, whatever may be said about us, we will take
the action of saying that this country ought to have remained neutral, because in the deepest part of our hearts we believe that was
right and that that alone was consistent with the honour of our
country and the traditions of the party that are now in office.

Whatever the conclusion of history, MacDonald himself was
to be proved conclusively wrong when he declared that Grey's
speech would 'not persuade a large section of the country' of the
case for war. Little more than twenty-four hours after it seemed

that Britain had rallied for peace; the crowds once again massed in Westminster and Whitehall, this time baying for war and to be done with what H. G. Wells had taken to describing as: 'this trampling foolery in the heart of Europe'.

But where the majority were united, the Labour Party was riven. Within forty-eight hours of the declaration of war MacDonald voted against granting the government credits to finance the conflict, a stance supported by only four other Labour MPs, and on 7 August he resigned his leadership of the parliamentary party. As the war fever intensified, the divisions within the labour movement burgeoned, only the ILP adopting an uncompromising stand against the fatal rapture of war:

> Out of the darkness and the depth we hail our working class of every land . . . In forcing this appalling crime upon the nations it is the rulers, the diplomats, the militarists who have sealed their doom. In tears of blood and bitterness the greater democracy will be born . . . Long live Freedom and Fraternity. Long live International Socialism.

The death of such ideals were to be measured by the extent of the tragedy that followed. Engaged in the name of a cause that few understood, Europe's working class dismissed the warnings of the leaders of European socialism, to find a new comradeship in death. For Shaw, far-sighted in his belief that militarism would lead to the collapse of the system that the militarists sought to defend and that henceforth there would only be two real flags in the world, 'the red flag of Democratic Socialism and the black flag of Capitalism', the war revealed that 'Nations are like bees. They cannot kill except at the cost of their own lives'. For Keir Hardie the conflict mocked all that he held dear. Only three days after he had warned the Commons that united working-class action would put a check on the government's hawkish intentions, he was to be howled down by jingoists at a peace meeting in his own constituency. The blow was a devastating one. As a man of peace he had been rejected by his own people, a hurt that was to inspire the bitter reflection 'I now understand the sufferings of Christ at Gethsemane.'

As the death toll rose, and the casualty lists lengthened, Hardie and MacDonald and the small anti-war faction were to become increasingly isolated. By the autumn of 1914 the unions had declared an Industrial Truce under which most of the strikes then in progress were settled, and in May 1915 Labour joined Asquith's coalition government. Arthur Henderson, who had succeeded Ramsay MacDonald as leader of the parliamentary party, entered the War Cabinet as President of the Board of Education. The appointment owed more to its symbolism than to its substance, signalling the majority of the parliamentary party's abandonment of the policy of independence upon which the party had been founded and its commitment to what the ILP condemned as the government's 'pitiless tribute to Moloch'. While the charge was to gain in credence in the years to come, the ILP won little support for its contention that the war was 'a monstrous product of the antagonisms which tear apart the capitalist society' and even less sympathy for those who advanced such views, Wells condemning Hardie and MacDonald's opinions as 'the spiteful, lying chatter of the shabbiest scum of Socialism'.

Twenty years after the publication of *The War That Will End War* Wells was to deplore his own jingoism ('My own behaviour in 1914–1915 is an excellent example of that inability to realise that a sovereign state is essentially and incurably a war-making state'), but his words reflected the mood of the time. By 1915 the majority of people applauded his indictment of 'conscientious objectors and war resisters' and, while Lloyd George was to reflect later that 'Had Labour been hostile, the war could not have been carried on effectively', he had little cause for concern. Both the Labour Party and the unions had been conscripted for the war effort, leaving only the warring fragments of Hyndman's SDF (the Socialist Labour Party, the British Socialist Party and the Socialist Party of Great Britain) and the ILP to campaign against the war, and this with increasing difficulty. In March 1916 Ramsay MacDonald, expedient in many things but steadfast in his opposition to the war, delivered one of the most courageous speeches of his career at Briton Ferry in South Wales:

> The ILP is bending under the force of a blinding storm today, and our ultimate confusion is the hope of our enemies. But they will not succeed. We shall go on, and when the fair weather comes again, we shall confront the world unashamed, and shall say to posterity: 'We await your verdict.' And the verdict will be: 'Blessed is the peacemaker, for he is called the child of God.'

It was a message that few wished to hear and fewer were to heed. Even where militancy did re-emerge it generally resulted from economic rather than anti-war motives. Within months of the outbreak of war a shortfall in the labour market had already become evident, with the result that the ubiquitous George Askwith formulated what was to become known as the 'Shells and Fuses Agreement' under which union leaders accepted the substitution of skilled for unskilled labour, in part by men but more generally by women. At shop-floor level the so-called 'dilution of labour' generated intense hostility, especially among the craft unions, which was to be compounded in March 1915 by the passage of the Treasury Agreement under which the unions agreed to abandon the strike weapon for the duration of the war and to accept government arbitration on all disputes. With profits soaring and costs rising (food prices rose by a third in the first year of the war), while wages were controlled, it seemed that patriotism was a one-way trade. A normally circumspect Whitehall mandarin wrote to the Minister of Munitions, Lloyd George:

> I am quite satisfied that the labour difficulty has been largely caused by the men being of the opinion that, while they were being called upon to be patriotic and refrain from using the strong economic position they occupy, employers, merchants and traders

were being allowed the fullest freedom to exploit to fullest the
nation's needs.

The difficulty to which he referred was a rash of uncoordi-
nated and sporadic strikes by railwaymen, the miners of South
Wales miners and the engineers in the Clydebank shipyards. Condemned by the national officials concerned, the Clyde workers
took matters into their own hands, deputing their own shop stewards to negotiate for them and eventually establishing the Clyde
Central Withdrawal of Labour Committee under the guidance of
the Socialist Labour Party and the ILP. On a visit to Clydeside in
December 1915 Lloyd George and Arthur Henderson were given
a rough reception, and the following month the unofficial strike
leaders were arrested and imprisoned under the Defence of the
Realm Act. The model they had established, however, was to be
imitated elsewhere, leading to the creation of the National Workers Committee Movement, designed to provide a link between
the unofficial shop steward movement throughout the country.

As the war entered its second year, and losses continued to
mount, the pressure on Britain's labour resources mounted, to
intensify the political pressures on Henderson and the Parliamentary Labour Party. On joining the coalition Henderson had been
assured that there would be no conscription for the armed forces.
By the autumn of 1915, however, there were already signs that the
government intended to renege on its pledge. More than 3 million
men were already under arms, but the appetite of war was insatiable. In October the government introduced a scheme under
which all men of military age were called upon to 'attest' for service, and by Christmas a Military Service Bill was laid before Parliament, designed to introduce compulsory military service for
single men. Labour's response was uncompromising. At a special
Congress of the entire labour movement the measure was rejected
by a two-to-one majority, and the Labour Party determined to pull
out of the coalition.

Henderson's letter of resignation to Asquith was revealing.

Careful not to be seen allying himself with the anti-war faction in the party, he concentrated on the growing threat to civil liberties: 'No-one who has studied the recent history of Labour will doubt that it is the fear of encroachment on civil and industrial freedom – on a man's right to choose his own trade and his own master and to make his own terms of service – that makes the opposition to military compulsion a question of principle.'

The fears that Henderson identified were widespread, but on Asquith's assurance that there would be no conscription of married men he and the parliamentary party agreed to remain in the coalition. Four months later Asquith's pledge was revealed for what it was: meaningless. In May 1916, with Haig gearing up for the Somme offensive, the Military Service Act was extended to cover married men, a measure approved by both the unions and the Labour Party, with the proviso that it should be accompanied by 'the conscription of wealth'.

The caveat was as impotent as it was vain, a face-saving formula to disguise the signatories' embarrassment at their own retreat from a position they had adopted less than six months earlier. But while the party had reneged on its own commitments, even the leadership was beginning to have doubts as much about the government's conduct as its conduct of the war. For more than a year Lloyd George had been undermining Asquith's position, leading one of his closest friends, George Riddell, owner of the *News of the World*, to wonder at his dealings with the hard men of the Tory Party. And in December the coup succeeded. Asquith was ousted from office, to be replaced by Lloyd George. To secure credibility for his new-found coalition, however, Lloyd George needed Labour support and on 6 December he invited a deputation from the party to cross-examine him on his political intentions. The composition of the deputation reflected the rift within the party – on the one hand, Henderson and Clynes and J. H. Thomas; on the other, MacDonald and Snowden.

The meeting was a stormy one, and the final decision on what was later to be described as 'the most serious position the party has had to face in the whole of its existence' was bitterly divisive – the more so because Lloyd George's undertaking that he was prepared to give reasonable consideration to a negotiated peace settlement contrasted starkly with his hawkish views. Only three months had passed since he had dismissed President Wilson's offer to act as a mediator between the combatants, assuring a United Press International correspondent that the Allies would fight to the finish: to 'the knock-out blow'. Apparently the man could not keep track of his own fabrications, yet, as far as the majority of the deputation was concerned, too many compromises had been made to circumstance for them to turn back, and the party executive agreed to enter the new coalition. While Henderson was to justify the decision on the grounds that it would continue to provide the Labour with a voice in government, Ramsay MacDonald was to write bitterly:

> The crisis has developed and Brutus has killed Caesar. Of course Labour is in. It will not leave its position in a hurry. It is professing simple patriotism again & Mr Henderson after saying that Asquith was indispensable last week told us at a specially summoned meeting of the Labour Party today that he thought he should be allowed to stay in the new government . . . He reminded me of the story of the virgin nuns who kept Satan behind them until someone suggested spiritual service & thereafter kissing and holiness were combined.

Significantly, another of Lloyd George's confidants, C. P. Scott of the *Manchester Guardian*, was to juxtapose Henderson's appointment to the inner War Cabinet as a Minister without Portfolio with reports from Petrograd that pro-German reactionaries were 'doing their utmost to stir up a revolution in order to make this an excuse for breaking the compact of London and making a separate peace'. Events were to prove him wrong. It was the breakdown of power in Russia in March 1917, and the subsequent establishment of a Liberal government, that marked the first phase of Russian Revolution – and reinforced Henderson's case when he came to present Lloyd George with Labour's plans for post-war reconstruction. Drafted by Sidney Webb, the proposals included plans for the nationalization of the railways and the mines and a programme for the prevention of unemployment and the provision of a living wage.

Plausible as ever, Lloyd George upstaged Henderson's deputation at their own demands: 'I'm not afraid of the audacity of these proposals. I believe that the settlement after the war will succeed in proportion to its audacity . . . If I could have presumed to be the adviser to the working classes, I would say to them: Audacity is the thing for you.'

Henderson required no prompting about the need for audacity. Inspired in part by the shop stewards' movement that had mobilized an army of grievances (more than 4 million days had been lost through strikes in 1916), in part by the radicalization of the labour movement following the revolution in Russia, a new and restless spirit was abroad. In May 1917 a strike by a quarter of a million engineers at the continuing 'dilution' of labour and the proposed extension of conscription threatened to paralyse industry, while on 1 June 100 delegates attended a hastily convened meeting in Leeds to hear MacDonald and Snowden declare that the Russian Revolution had once again given workers the chance to take the political initiative. In a rare alliance of force, moderates and militants joined in a resolution calling for the establishment of Workmen's and Soldiers' Councils that would support Russia 'in her demand for the repudiation of all war aims and the establishment of a peace without annexations or indemnities'.

After three years of war the hope was reborn that the workers of world might, indeed, unite to impose a peace on the war-weary combatants. Illusory as it was, it was an illusion that the Labour Party did not share with the rank and file. Committed to the government's fight-to-the-finish policy and fearful that Russia would unilaterally sue for peace, the leadership proscribed the Leeds conference, but not before Henderson had cabled Petrograd to

117

declare the party's support for the new Russian regime: 'Organised Labour in Britain is watching with the keenest sympathy the efforts of the Russian people to deliver themselves from the power of reactionary elements which are impeding their advance to victory.' A brief visit to Russia in June 1917 reinforced Henderson's conviction of the need to sustain the Russian alliance and affirmed his belief that Russia's attendance at an international socialist conference called to define the war aims would be the best way of ensuring that she remained 'on active service'.

Lloyd George disagreed. Having lost faith in Russia's will to fight he wanted nothing whatsoever to do with a conference that would provide Russian socialists with a platform to promote their pacific views. As for his Minister without Portfolio, it seemed to Lloyd George that Henderson had caught 'the revolutionary malaria', and on 1 August he was invited to explain his aberrant views to his Cabinet colleagues. The meeting was timed for four o'clock. An hour later Henderson was still waiting 'on the door-mat' as his colleagues discussed his case in the Cabinet room. When finally admitted, he challenged them to demand his resignation. Aware of what it could cost the government in terms of working-class support they refused. Henderson resigned eleven days later, having secured a three-to-one endorsement for the Stockholm initiative at a special Labour Party conference held in Central Hall, Westminster.

The debate as to whether a British delegation should travel to Stockholm was long and venomous, Henderson coming under sustained attack for his supposed new-found pacific sympathies ('If you go there you will only be going to discuss terms of peace'), for supposedly giving comfort to the enemy ('To go to Stockholm was to go to meet men who had not repudiated masters whose hands were red with the blood of Nurse Cavell') and for his supposed betrayal of Britain's fighting men ('I believe that the only way of ending this war is the way in which our brave boys at the front are trying to end it'). Ironically, it was a scathing aside by a Labour MP that Henderson was joining MacDonald's 'new majority' that marked a turning point not only in the debate but in the mood of the party itself, MacDonald supporting Henderson's call 'to use the political weapon to supplement our military activities . . . to secure such a victory as will ensure for the world a lasting, honourable and democratic peace'.

The Stockholm conference never met, the hopes vested in it being overtaken by the October Revolution and the Soviet government's opening of unilateral peace negotiations with Germany. Meanwhile the *rapprochement* between Henderson and MacDonald marked the first tentative signs of a realignment as much in the policies as in the balance of power within the Labour Party. Although the Caxton Hall conference, and Henderson's subsequent resignation, did not lead to Labour's withdrawal from the coalition, a new alliance was in the making between two of the agents of the party's post-war fortunes. Always an uneasy relationship, it was born more of *realpolitik* than amity, more especially when it emerged that Lloyd George was considering forming a new party, and it was possible that some of their Labour colleagues would join him.

Whether a serious proposition or a mischievous ploy, the very idea that Lloyd George was thinking such a thing helped to focus the party leadership's mind on the future. Since the New Liberals had cast themselves as the architects of social revolution, they had been encroaching on what Labour regarded as their natural constituency, concerned to secure their presence in the political centre ground. For it was there, in the space between the extremes, that power in the British political system ultimately lay. Suspicious of ideologues of whatever persuasion, the humdrum, even pragmatic tastes of the British electorate have long served as the stabilizer of British politics – a point that Henderson and MacDonald were quick to remember, and Lloyd George would never forget. Political veterans, they could read the runes well enough, and while Lloyd George had taken to talking about 'the war to end wars', MacDonald and Henderson set about formulating what Labour would make of the peace.

The Labour movement was coming to terms with itself, but the question remained: on what or, rather, on whose terms? The catch-all formula devised by Hardie to provide the party-in-embryo with the appearance of unity in 1900 ('That this Conference is in favour of establishing a distinct Labour Group in Parliament') no longer served. In the years between, the aim had been realized, but a precise definition of what purpose the party had been established to serve remained to be determined. Topsy-like, the party had just grown, but without any sense of ideological cohesion.

Bertrand Russell wrote in 1918: 'Socialism, like everything else that is vital, is rather a tendency than a strictly definable body of doctrine. A definition of Socialism is sure to include some views which many would regard as not Socialism, or to exclude others which claim to be included' (*Roads to Freedom*).

Little more than a year later, on a visit to Leningrad, Russell was to reflect: 'I am troubled at every moment by fundamental questions, the terrible, insoluble questions that wise men never ask.' Ironically, it was exactly because they did dare to ask questions about the nature of Soviet power that the Labour leadership rejected the communist path to socialism and condemned communism to play a secondary role in British left-wing politics. It could well have been different.

The Russian Revolution provided the British Socialist Party – numbering no more than 10,000 members – with a charisma disproportionate to its size. During the closing stages of the war, and in the early days of the peace, it had momentarily appeared that Britain was in a revolutionary mood, but that was before an ILP delegation visited Moscow to catechize the Soviet leadership as to its intentions and what would be entailed if Labour were to join the Communist International. If the pat answer to the delegates' questions was ill-informed – 'in no country can the dictatorship of the proletariat be applied better or more directly than in Great Britain' – what followed was to damn the entire project. Communism, the delegation was instructed, was the only true form of socialism, and those who compromised the purity of its dogma were mere 'lackeys' of the bourgeoisie.

Disabused, the delegation returned home. Effectively, the arrogance of the Soviet leadership had undermined what it sought to achieve: the establishment of a viable communist presence in the UK. But if the Labour Party was to reject outright the extra-parliamentary strategy recommended by the Soviets – that the working class should prepare 'not for an easy parliamentary victory but for victory by a heavy civil war' – there was no shortage of alternative paths to the New Jerusalem on offer, each the product as much of Britain's wartime experiences as of the Great Unrest that preceded it.

The experience came as an unpleasant surprise to Britain's intellectual elite. In challenging the existing order, and the comfortable assumptions of the elite, it seemed as if the British workman had taken leave of his senses. Perhaps the typical working man of their imaginings was not such a phlegmatic fellow after all. Perhaps his very taciturnity disguised a dark and revolutionary nature. A renegade notion, it was to disturb the cloistered calm of the ideologues of the left, although not of R. H. Tawney. Unlike many left-wing intellectuals he had experienced at first hand the conditions about which he wrote, first in London's East End and later in the Lancashire cotton belt. If his time at Oxford convinced him that it was the duty of socialists to base their principles on ethical precepts, he argued it was exactly this that they had failed to provide during the Great Unrest:

> At present the agitation of the workers is like the struggles of a man who feels he hears a message of tremendous significance, but who cannot find words in which to express it. He gesticulates, he struggles with himself, he is borne by the spirit. But the fire within him finds no expression in speech, and consumes himself instead of quickening others.

121

The words. The spirit. The fire. The language was that of the Nonconformist charismatics, but the descent was not from Wesley's quietism ('Where then shall mankind find this transforming power? – in the Cross of Christ') but from the principles of Charles Kingsley and the Christian Socialist brotherhood of the mid-nineteenth century, entrenched in the belief that if Christianity failed to address the social and economic problems of its times then it failed in its mission. Yet it seemed to Tawney that the likes of the Webbs, with their obsession with facts and statistics, were reducing socialism to a series of minute readjustments of the socio-economic structure, as if 'the economic classes and institutions had stepped out of a kind of political Noah's Ark, sharply defined, highly coloured, with an unalterable destiny graven on each wooden feature'.

Such a desiccated approach to the human condition held little appeal to Tawney. Statistics were all very well as far as they went, but they did not go far enough. What they lacked was an ethical dimension, a pivotal idea that would provide coherence for all the rest: 'There is no creative force outside the ideas which control men in their ordinary actions.' Contemptuous as much of the gradualist approach of the Fabians, with their belief that major social change could be achieved without conflict, as he was of the Marxist interpretation of history on the grounds that it was as materialistic as the capitalist system it opposed, Tawney placed his faith in the mediating power of equality, in combination with his own Christian faith: 'In order to believe in human equality, it is necessary to believe in God.'

A fusion of the spiritual and the temporal, it empowered Tawney's ideology and fortified his conviction that equality was the only way to achieve a just and stable society, yet left open the practical question of how his ideal could be achieved; of how it might be possible to redress the inequality of the human condition. Among others, his contemporary G. D. H. Cole believed that he could provide at least some of the answers.

At the Fabian Summer School of 1914, held on the last weekend of the peace, Cole had mounted a scathing attack on the society's old guard and its programme of gradualism. Unlike previous critics, Cole was as constructive in his criticism of the Labour agenda as he was scornful of the Labour Party's leadership of the working class, declaring that should it ever to come to power it would 'be sadly at a loss to know what to do'.

At the age of twenty-five, as precocious as he was talented (he had been elected a Fellow of Magdalen College, Oxford, in 1912), Cole had no doubts about his own prescriptions for socialism, convinced that the Great Unrest was evidence of 'the awakening of the fighting spirit in the ranks of organised labour'. The vision was that of William Morris, of the call for the fellowship of labour – a vision the Labour Party had appropriated, only to degrade. Yet the fighting spirit remained, offering Cole the prospect that 'Instead of the reformist Labour Party, there is hope that some day we shall have a revolutionary party imbued not with the spirit of blind revolt but with a real consciousness of what the State must be made.'

Cole was not alone in his disenchantment with reformist Labour, and it was not only militants who were critical of the party's parliamentary performance and its lack of a coherent agenda. In 1907, A. R. Orage, a brilliant journalist, had established New Age, a polemical journal that was to provide a forum for a critique of Labour policy and to act as the midwife to Guild Socialism. In the pre-war years the movement gained a small but significant constituency, more especially following the foundation of the National Building Guild, which attracted the backing of many unions. It was Cole, however, who was to refine the guild's thinking and provide it with intellectual rigour.

Even the name Guild Socialism smacked of William Morris, whose works had converted Cole to socialism, and it was in an attempt to give direction to 'the revolutionary consciousness' of the working class that Cole developed a theory of industrial conflict which, in challenging the received wisdom of the Labour establishment, drew heavily on the Marxist canon and shared much with the tenets of syndicalism. As confident in his belief that economic power precedes political power as he was in the existence of 'a real class war', Cole rejected the top-down political approach to reform ('the political super-structure which reflects the economic basis of society . . . will change with it'), to deploy the trade unions in the van of social revolution, maintaining that 'Economic action, and still more, economic organisation, are the need of Labour today.'

As for the action, Cole eschewed the general strike weapon of the syndicalists; as for the organization, he rejected both the syndicalist's call for worker control of industry and the socialist's conception of the control of the means of production, distribution and exchange by the state:

> The ordinary Socialist still expects the State merely to step into the employers' shoes, and run industry, much as the private capitalist has run it, for its own profit . . . The worker will still be a 'cog in the machine', the State will merely take the master's place as skilled machine-minder.

Only the unions could break the impasse and, in the process of empowering the workers ('From fighting bodies, organised against capitalism, they must develop into controlling bodies, capable of carrying on production'), provide them with a countervailing force to the state, in which state and guilds would form a partnership of equals:

> The conditions on which the producers consent to serve and the community to accept their service must be determined by negotiation between the Guild and the State. The Guild must reserve the right to withdraw its labour; and the State must rely, to check unjust demands, on its equal voice in the decision of points of difference and on the organised opinion of the community as a whole.

Utopian as it was, Cole's vision was ominously flawed, the casual reference to the 'organised opinion' of the community disguising its authoritarian implications. It was not this, however, that the Fabians and, more especially, the Webbs objected to, rather Cole's faith in ordinary people's capacity for intelligent decision-taking. Paternalistic as always, the Webbs held fast to Sidney's axiom of the need for 'A discreetly regulated freedom', to be managed by mandarins such as themselves, who conformed to the three Bs of Beatrice's definition: 'benevolent, bourgeois, and bureaucratic'. As authoritarian in their way as Cole, the Webbs, too, were compelled to rethink many of their ideas as a result of the Great Unrest.

In 1912 the Webbs were travelling through India, but Clifford Sharp, who was later to become editor of the *New Statesman*, kept them posted with news of the industrial disputes that were racking the UK:

> Labour will surely never forget that it has had the strongest government of modern times practically on its knees suing for peace. And this must give a tremendous impetus for industrial versus political methods . . . Things will never be the same again, this affair [the miners' strike] marks the beginning of a new phase in the class war.

What it might involve, and who was to lead it, was to point and counterpoint Sharp's subsequent letters: 'Socialist thought (as well as outside opinion) is in a condition of flux – Everybody is at it waiting for a lead, and as things stand Socialism is not offering one. If it does not strike fairly soon I think it will not have another chance.'

It is not difficult to imagine the Webbs' frustration at not being on hand to provide the lead that socialism demanded, yet on their return even they we compelled to admit that they had no immediate answers to the questions raised by 'the new spirit and temper being manifested by the industrial classes'. It was something they found hard to understand. For two decades they had mistaken statistics for reality, a kind of bloodless simulacrum of the human condition, only to discover that reality defied their computations. Political necromancers, it seemed as if they had helped raise spirits they could not lay. Beatrice wrote: 'The Socialist Party has aroused great expectations as to the construction of a New Social Order. Unless we can meet these expectations by carefully drafted and tested specifications, we shall be adjudged by the rising generation of thinkers and workers intellectually bankrupt.'

This was one thing the Webbs were unwilling to admit. The bureaucratic mind-set remained, but it was now to be complemented by a more radical prescription. Although critical of syndicalism as impractical, they were as quick to recognize its role in focusing people's attention on what Tom Mann excoriated as 'the tyranny of capitalism' as they were to accept that the Great Unrest had raised acute questions about devising alternatives to the existing system of private ownership and management of the means of production.

Ironically, in view of their aversion to Marxism, they found part of the answer in the role of the state which, seemingly, had already become 'a busy house-keeper, whose object is to serve citizens' and whose future function would be benign rather than coercive: 'a sort of extended Co-operative Society, performing for the great public of consumers the services they require, and supplying those, not necessarily compulsorily, or even universally, but often only by individual request'.

But if the state was to safeguard the consumers' interests, what of the producers? Where should economic power lie? Less than ten years had passed since Wells had mocked the Fabian project as 'some little odd jobbing about water and gas', but now the Webbs were beginning to think the unthinkable: the wholesale nationalization of industry. In June 1914 Beatrice was to write to Shaw: 'Sidney and I will do our best to work out the distribution of power among persons and among classes. You must work out the distribution of wealth.' It was a project that was to be deferred. Two months later war broke out, for Tawney to serve with the Manchester Regiment and to be severely wounded on the Somme; for Cole to enter the Fabian Research Department; and for Sidney Webb to join the War Emergency Workers' National Committee, the only independent voice of the united labour movement after August 1914.

The special conference of the motley of interests that composed the Labour Party in February 1918 was a set piece of political stage management. Labour managers, called upon to debate and approve a new constitution for the party, were quick to recognize the dangers implicit in such an undertaking. Where once, comparatively recently, the party had been in search of a policy, by the last year of the war there were a number of ideologies on offer: Christian Socialism, with its visceral appeal to the Nonconformist conscience; Guild Socialism, with its promise of balancing out the interests of the unions and the state; the ILP, with its commitments to nationalization; and the congeries of Marxist factions (the Socialist Party of Great Britain, the Socialist Labour Party, the British Socialist Party) all in bullish mood following the events of October 1917.

In the free market of ideologies, only moderation was at a discount, and it was the vehemence of the debate that threatened what the conference organizers were seeking to achieve – a leading rather than a secondary role for the Labour Party in British politics. As Arthur Henderson and Sidney Webb realized, it was a high-risk game they were playing in drafting a new constitution for the party, for if, in debating its contents, the conference were to degenerate into a political knock-about it would jeopardize the purpose of the exercise and make a laughing stock of Labour. Yet the risk had to be taken if Labour was to command political credibility.

Almost two decades had passed since the original constitution had been approved, in part because of a lack of concrete policies.

The omission had been deliberate – and not only to secure the appearance of unity for the infant party. Political commitments are dangerous things, as subject to changes in circumstances as to shifts in the public mood, but by the autumn of 1917 political ambiguity would no longer serve a party bent on power. In order to challenge the New Liberal conscience, and its widespread appeal to the electorate, it was imperative that Labour stake out its position, the problem again being to devise a formula that would provide the party with a programme of substance while retaining an image of unity.

It was a task for which Arthur Henderson and, more especially, Sidney Webb were well qualified. While Cole and Tawney may have derided Webb as one of those writers 'who pile up statistics and facts, but never get to the heart of the problem', the arcane skills he had learned in a quarter-century of preparing submissions to government inquiries and reports for the Fabian Society were to stand Labour in good stead when it came to revising the party's constitution and, of equal importance, to drafting the programme detailing its policy: *Labour and the New Social Order*. The new constitution, which not only marked a real break with the Lloyd George coalition but also the end of what little remained of the Lib–Lab concordat, was approved unopposed at the February conference which itself was a testament to Henderson's and Webb's skills.

The constitution's proposal to recruit individual members at local level – aimed at transforming the party from a loosely based federation, able only to act through its affiliated unions and socialist societies, into a nationally based party, capable of replacing the Liberals as the alternative party of government – encroached directly on the ILP's bailiwick as the principal organization of socialism in the constituencies. And it was the ILP which, in providing the cutting edge of the movement's radicalism, was regarded as a bogy by many of party's trade union paymasters. It was problem that demanded all of Henderson's and Webb's political legerdemain, prompting Richard Crossman to write forty-five years later:

> The Labour Party required militants, politically conscious socialists
> to do the work of organising the constituencies. But since these
> militants tended to be 'extremists', a constitution was needed
> which maintained their enthusiasm by apparently creating a full
> party democracy which excluded them from effective power.

Henderson's and Webb's solution was as elegant as it was art-
ful: that while nominally sovereign power in the party would rest
with the delegates to the Annual Conference, in practice such
sovereignty would be circumscribed by the deployment of the
union block vote. It was a formula that allowed Henderson to
steer through all nineteen clauses of his plan for the structural
reorganization of the party virtually unscathed.

And if Henderson now had the blueprint he required to create
an effective party machine, Clause IV of the revised constitution
was to provide the motor that was to power it:

> To secure for the producers by hand or by brain the full fruits of
> their industry, and the most equitable distribution thereof that may
> be possible, upon the basis of the common ownership of the means
> of production and the best obtainable system of popular adminis-
> tration and control of each industry and service.

This was the keystone for all the rest, the party's definition of
socialism – although the word itself was studiously avoided. After
two decades Labour had determined its purpose but remained
unwilling to pronounce its name. The word was altogether too
contentious for that – a cockshy between left and right. Even the
so-called 'Reconstruction Manifesto', *Labour and the New Social
Order*, which fleshed out the new constitution and which was
debated at the first party conference held under its aegis in June
1918, remained leery of the word, preferring rather to declare that
the party aimed at:

the gradual building up of a new social order based not on internecine conflict, inequality of riches and domination over subject classes, subject races or a subject sex, but on deliberately planned co-operation in production and distribution, the sympathetic approach to a healthy equality, the widest possible participation in power both economic and political and the general consciousness of consent which characterises a true democracy.

A testament to Fabian gradualism and to the subtlety of Sidney Webb, the Manifesto none the less was a seminal work, its twenty-seven proposals including the abolition of the Poor Law and the development of a Municipal Health Service; the emancipation of women and complete adult suffrage; state subvention of unemployment benefits and the nationalization of 'the whole function of insurance'; regional devolution and reform of the Lords; the nationalization of the railways and the mines; and the control of capitalist industry. While the details were critical, it was Clause IV of the constitution that was to serve as the benchmark of Labour probity for the next seventy years. Even in 1918, however, there were questions raised as to whether the clause went too far or whether it went far enough – an ominous foretaste of disputes to come.

6

We Fight Alone: The General Strike

We hold that evolutionary Socialism is not enough. Time presses
in the turmoil of the war's aftermath.' – Oswald Mosley, *Revolution
in Reason*, 1925

The Great War ended on 11 November 1918, and Field Marshall
Sir Henry Wilson declared: 'Our real danger now is not the Boche
but Bolshevism.' It was not the fear of revolution but the
euphoria at the ending of the war that swept the coalition government to power in December, however. Lloyd George, as quick
to exploit the triumphalist mood as he was to campaign on a platform of 'making Germany pay until the pips squeak' called a snap
election within forty-eight hours of the cessation of hostilities.
The outcome was to justify his decision, the coalition winning an
overall majority of 249 seats. Significantly, virtually all the ILP
anti-war campaigners lost their seats, among them Ramsay Mac-
Donald, Philip Snowden and George Lansbury, while, of Labour's
new parliamentary intake of fifty-nine MPs, forty-nine were trade
unionists of moderate persuasion and chauvinist tendencies.

It was not so much the size of the government's majority that
troubled MacDonald, however, rather the way in which it had
been obtained. The coalition's blatant appeal to vengefulness,
reflected in slogans demanding death for the Kaiser, led him to
write that the campaign had been ''an assassination rather than a
battle' – not least of tolerance and reason. Their loss, he feared,
could only lead to reaction, more especially when Labour Members spent so much of their time deprecating the militancy of their
own constituents who, inspired by the Soviet example, were
demanding a more radical approach to the peace settlement than
that offered in the party's *Reconstruction* document. Even Philip
Snowden, normally as economic with his sentiments as he was

later to prove conservative with the economy, appeared to have caught the mood: 'Capitalists must either get off the back of Labour with good grace, or get flung off with perhaps rather more than the necessary degree of violence.' Hyperbole possibly, but within weeks of the election it seemed that MacDonald's fears might well be borne out: 'After the war the world goes mad. And our own people go mad. We have our dreams of a better world . . . but after war these dreams become frenzied. The furious violence of hate takes possession of them.'

He was describing conditions in Europe, but his concern was for Britain where, at the war's end, 353,000 ex-soldiers were unemployed – and the number was rising daily. Britain may have helped win the war, but by January 1919 it seemed she was already in danger of losing the peace. On 6 January 1919, 12,000 troops mutinied in Folkestone and Dover, and some 60,000 at other camps, while at Osterley Park, Middlesex, men of the Service Corps seized a squadron of lorries, drove into London and demonstrated outside 10 Downing Street. For the next forty-eight hours Whitehall resembled an armed camp and when, at the end of the month, 20,000 troops in Calais refused to obey their officers' order, the War Office issued a questionnaire to all commanding officers asking whether their men would stay loyal in the event of a revolution.

But it was not only the armed forces that were restless. For all of Lloyd George's high talk of building a land fit for heroes to live in, the reality was very different. During 1919 wholesale prices rose by 72 per cent, against a 20 per cent increase in the average wage, while everywhere the queues at the Labour Exchanges lengthened, unemployment rising to 12.2 per cent in the post-war year. And as Lloyd George and his Cabinet colleagues, among them ultra-conservatives such as Lord Curzon and F. E. Smith, invoked images of the fall of the Bastille when a crowd attacked Luton Town Hall, Lord Sydenham was writing to *The Times* about 'certain dark forces which, with alien intention, are being directed to bring about a red revolution in this country'.

Sydenham's charge was ill-founded. The majority of the

Labour movement rejected the revolutionary solution to their problems. While the courage of the Soviets in their contest with the counter-revolutionary White Armies commanded their admiration (and one of the few positive steps taken by the Labour Party was to foil the coalition's attempt to intervene in Russia in support of the counter-revolutionaries), they had little taste for the doctrinaire policies being peddled by Moscow, demanding complete subservience to the party line.

Only the newly formed Communist Party, made up largely of the dissolved British Socialist Party, subscribed to 'the Soviet idea as against Parliamentary democracy, i.e. a structure making provision for the participation in social administration only of those who render useful service to the community' in pursuit of the dictatorship of the proletariat. Numbering no more than 10,000 members, the Communist Party applied for affiliation to the Labour Party in August 1920 only to receive the first of many rejections. Although justified on the grounds that the new party's first allegiance was to Moscow, the decision exposed the ideological space between the gradualist and Marxist positions and, in the process, helped consolidate the rift at the heart of the movement that was to have such damaging longer-term consequences.

Not that the future was of immediate concern to a growing army of the disillusioned in 1919. For them there was more pressing business to hand, and if the Labour Party was unable, or unwilling, to provide them with the leadership to articulate their grievances they would find it elsewhere. In the last week of January a general strike involving more than 100,000 workers paralysed Glasgow, once the heartland of the shop steward movement. On the last day of the month a march was planned to George Square in the city centre, for Scotland Yard's Director of Intelligence to ponder the irony that many of the strikers had only recently been demobbed and that if rioting should take place 'for the first time in history, the rioters will be better trained than the troops'. Some 40,000 demonstrators took part in the march, to met by a baton charge of mounted police as they entered the square, prompting one reporter to describe the scene as 'a miniature battleground' and another to call up memories of the Great Unrest.

Five years had passed since George Askwith had warned of the revolutionary potential of British workers; the war had defused the unrest. Seemingly, however, the situation had not been resolved, simply deferred. Through the spring and into the summer of 1919 a series of piecemeal strikes racked industry, to be followed in the autumn by a strike of railmen, which Lloyd George was to denounce as part of an 'anarchist conspiracy' but which was settled within a week, in part owing to a deal struck between Lloyd George and the General Secretary of the National Union of Railwaymen, Jimmy Thomas. A political changeling who was a model for later champagne socialists, Thomas's rhetoric disguised his conservative disposition. Elected an MP in 1910, he had been among the architects of the pre-war Triple Alliance, and it may have been his recognition of the dangers implicit in the re-emergence of the Alliance that provided him with leverage in his negotiations with Lloyd George.

But if the railmen were to settle for the status quo on the wages front without having to enlist the support of the Alliance, the miners knew no such reservations. In January 1919 the Miners' Federation lodged a new pay claim, together with a demand that the government should 'proceed at once with the nationalisation of all mines and minerals' – and called on the Alliance to buttress their claims. The idea was altogether too radical for the Cabinet, although it recognized that an outright rejection of the miners' demand could trigger an economic crisis. Lloyd George was a past master of prevarication, a quality that he was to deploy with all the guile of 'the goat-footed bard' of Keynes's description at a hastily convened meeting of the leaders of the Alliance:

> Gentlemen, you have fashioned in the Triple Alliance represented by you, a powerful instrument. I feel bound to tell you that in our opinion we are at your mercy. The Army is disaffected and cannot be relied upon. Trouble has already occurred at a number of camps.

We have just emerged from a great war, and people are eager for the reward of their sacrifices, and we are in no position to satisfy them. In the circumstances, if you carry out your threat and strike, you will defeat us. But if you do, have you weighed the consequences? The strike will be in defiance of the government of the country, and by its very success will create a constitutional crisis of the first importance. For if a force rises in the state which is stronger than the state itself, then it must be ready to take on the functions of the state, or withdraw and accept the authority of the state.

As Bob Smillie, President of the Miners' Federation, recalled: 'From that moment on we were beaten, and we knew we were.' For all the cataclysmic visions of the right, *The Times* declaring that the miners' leaders 'lurked in the shadows of political anarchy', the leadership of the Alliance had no ambition to turn the world upside down, although on one count Smillie was wrong in his reading of the outcome of the meeting. Lloyd George may have won the battle, but the war had only just begun.

For the next two years, the government and the miners circled each other like swiving cats, each testing the nerve of the other. In March 1919 the government established a commission which found in the miners' favour, not least in their demand for the nationalization of the industry, for Lloyd George to reject the proposal which, until shortly before, he had espoused. In July 1920 the miners renewed their wage claim, for it to be contemptuously dismissed by the Coal Commissioner acting on behalf of the government, at which the miners staged a twelve-day strike that forced Lloyd George's hand. In January 1921 the government set 15 March as the date for the decontrol of the industry, at which point the reinstated owners announced that new employment terms would have to be negotiated, not least regarding wages.

For the Miners' Federation there was no mistaking the owners' meaning: either their members accepted a wage cut or they would be locked out. After six years, during which the industry had been under state control, the owners were back to their old game, a game at which two could play. On 31 March the federation mobilized the Triple Alliance and twenty-four hours later a million miners were locked out for having rejected the owners' wage ultimatum. The impasse was complete and when, eight days later, the leaders of the railmen and transport workers issued their strike orders, to take effect on 12 April, it seemed that the countdown to a general stoppage had begun. The appearance was deceptive. The Alliance was by no means as united as it appeared. While the transport workers remained solid, the railmen were beginning to waver, and on 12 April the strike call was postponed for seventy-two hours, in large part owing to the misgivings of Jimmy Thomas.

Like the Emperor Frederick I, Thomas liked nothing more than an army, provided that it never engaged the enemy. And by 15 April that is what he feared most. That afternoon he joined other rail and transport leaders at a reception at Number 10, where Lloyd George 'was supported by several government Ministers and high government officials'.

The Times was to report the following day that Thomas was the only sign of an accommodating spirit in the whole proceedings: 'He repudiated all desire for a revolution, and declared that if the strike was an industrial means to secure a political end, he would have nothing to do with it . . . He deplored the war-like preparations, and said he was anxious, at the eleventh hour, to avoid the conflict.'

This was precisely what he helped to achieve. At 4 p.m. on 16 April Thomas announced that the strike of railmen and transport workers had been cancelled, leaving the miners 'to carry on the fight alone'. It may have been that Thomas was justified in his fears and that he had helped to avert a constitutional crisis, if not a revolution, although *the Daily Herald* had no doubts about the damage that he and his members had inflicted on the unions: 'Yesterday was the heaviest defeat that has befallen the labour movement within living memory. It is no use trying to minimise it. It is no use pretending it is other than it is. We on this paper have said throughout that if the organised workers would stand together they would win. They have not stood together, and they have lost.'

The echo was of Ernest Bevin's caution – 'I have said it over and over "When the test comes if you do not make it [the Triple Alliance] a real organisation it will be found to be a paper alliance"'– and if the divisions among the unions led to the débâcle of Black Friday, then *The Times* was to read more into the outcome than a temporary setback for the Alliance:

> The story of how and why this momentous decision [of the railmen and transport workers to desert the miners] was reached is obscure, and we shall not attempt to penetrate the obscurity . . . Perhaps the true story will come out presently, but it does not concern us now. It is enough that the struggle between the Left and Right wings of the Labour movement, which has been one of the hidden influences in the shifting sequence of events, came to a decisive issue yesterday, and the Right wing won.

And the right was to win again at the Labour Party conference later in the year when the Miners' Federation backed the Communist Party's renewed application for affiliation, for it to be rejected for a second time. Following Black Friday, militancy was at a discount among the unions, the majority of which preferred to place their faith in political action and the Parliamentary Labour Party – more than two-thirds of whose Members represented mining constituencies. Even Ramsay MacDonald had difficulty in explaining how they squared their political consciences, to damn the group's performance in the Commons as incompetent, and to ask despairingly: 'Where is the Opposition?' Although no longer an MP, it was an answer that MacDonald was attempting to provide according to his own Fabian terms of reference.

In her diary Beatrice Webb was to call MacDonald 'the mystery man', but for all his gnomic utterances there was diminishing mystery about his political intentions. In 1907 he had written 'Socialism retains everything of value in Liberalism', and it was these values he endorsed when joining the Union of Democratic

Control shortly after the outbreak of the First World War. Founded by a group of eminent Liberal MPs and intellectuals, and committed to open diplomacy and a negotiated peace settlement, MacDonald's membership of the union signalled not only his rejection of labour militancy but provided a lead to his game plan for the future: to sustain the Progressive Alliance but under Labour control. His policy, pragmatic rather than visionary and still to be fully fleshed out, was to be tested to near destruction in the political turbulence of the post-war years.

In 1919 MacDonald agreed to take charge of the post-war reorganization of the ILP, to become engaged in a savage contest with the left over its dalliance with Sovietism, direct action and workers' control. Initially MacDonald had some sympathies for the difficulties that Lenin faced, but these soon gave way to a deep distrust of the Soviet leadership and outright hostility to the policies it pursued. The majority of the ILP was more radical. In 1920 George Lansbury, the pacifist editor of the *Daily Herald* and among the best loved figures in the history of the movement, returned from a visit to Moscow with the assurance that Lenin had no wish to see other socialist parties following the Russian model. Anxious to hear only what it wanted, the ILP subscribed to Lansbury's interpretation, careless of the fact that it contradicted virtually all previous pronouncements coming out of Moscow. MacDonald was scathing, writing in *Forward* that it now appeared that revolution was not revolution, that dictatorship was not dictatorship and that 'in the Russian turmoil the English language as well as the bourgeoisie has been upset'.

The delegates to the ILP annual conference in 1920 were as unmoved by MacDonald's outburst as they were careless of the implications of what he was to write in the conference's aftermath: 'Perhaps the most essential thing said at Scarborough was by Colonel Wedgwood when he urged that the Labour Party should become the Opposition in fact (as well as in name). This involves a mental change, as well as great Parliamentary activity.'

If MacDonald teased his readers with his call for 'mental

change' , there could be no mistaking the significance of his complimentary reference to Colonel Wedgwood. A descendant of Josiah, Wedgwood had sat on the Liberal benches for thirteen years before joining Labour in 1919 – one of a small but growing band of Liberal grandees, many of them former Asquith acolytes, who crossed the political divide to join Labour in the post-war years. The defections marked a tectonic shift in British politics: the end of the great Liberal dynasty. Indeed where as recently as 1914 Labour had played little more than a walk-on part in the theatre of Westminster, and this to a Liberal script, it was now the Labour Party to which men such as Wedgwood looked for effective opposition and, by implication, the capacity to form a government.

Contemptuous of Lloyd George, who had once represented the progressivism they espoused, they despaired for the future of the Liberal conscience once it fell into his hands. The bitterness was widespread and deep-rooted, leading a former editor of the Liberal periodical *The Nation*, H. W. Massingham, to write: 'The capitalist reaction of 1921 and 1922 makes a shabby chapter in the story of British statesmanship. And it can never be forgotten that its instrument, if not its author, was a Liberal Prime Minister', and the Liberal economist Sir Leo Chiozza Money to declare: 'When Mr Lloyd George elected to sell out our national war property to the capitalists . . . he took a stand which enabled many of us to decide which way to go. It is just as well that the issue should be made pellucidly clear. Labour stands for the national ownership of the nation.'

MacDonald had read the runes well. Seemingly the inconceivable had occurred. He may not have anticipated the full measure of the shift that was to take place in political allegiances, or the extent of the damage that it would inflict on the Liberal Party, but he was quick to recognize the invaluable support that it provided in his contest with the militants in the party. Conversely, the more that he could do to marginalize the left, the more attractive Labour progressivism would appear to Liberal apostates. But if this was his hidden agenda, he continued to disguise it well, complaining at one moment that the radicalism of the ILP was threatening the entire Labour project, at the next of the need 'to keep the ILP going vigorously to see that its Socialist Idealism will not be swamped in the political opportunism of the Labour Party'.

MacDonald made a talisman of the words Idealism and Socialism – yet in permutating their meaning according to circumstances he compounded the mystery as to his own intentions, the irony being that if Beatrice Webb could not fathom his meaning then no one could. The past mistress of permeation and gradualism, they were qualities that MacDonald had first debated in her 'hard little house' in Westminster a quarter of a century earlier and which he was now to deploy with consummate skill in his wrangle for the Liberal conscience, the renewed failure of direct action in the post-war years serving not only to reinforce his progressive convictions but also his appreciation of the role that the Liberal defectors could play in containing the impossibilists in his own party.

MacDonald's position was reinforced by the knowledge that the coalition government might not run its full term. Nothing concentrates Labour's mind like the prospect of a General Election even if, in 1922, the party leadership had little notion of what it wished to achieve. Early in the year the ILP published *Now for Socialism* in an attempt to force the party to commit itself to a much more precise programme of legislation than that outlined in *Labour and the New Social Order*, but the party establishment wanted nothing of the ILP's headstrong ways. Relying more on the old formula that it was time for a change than on providing an effective prescription about either the nature of such change or how it might be achieved, Labour's 411 candidates went to the polls in November 1922 to surprise even themselves by winning 142 seats.

For the Tory leader Bonar Law the election was a triumph, the Conservatives taking 345 seats; for Lloyd George and the riven Liberal Party it was a disaster, the two factions within the party winning only 116 seats; and for Labour a mixed blessing, the momentary euphoria being replaced by self-doubts about the party's capacity to form His Majesty's Opposition. MacDonald shared them. For two years, he had been critical of ineffectiveness of the Labour group in the House, and his return to Commons for Aberavon did nothing to allay his concern, not least following his election as chairman of the Parliamentary Labour Party. The contest was a close-run thing, Jimmy Clynes, who had previously held the post, calling in old favours and MacDonald drawing heavily on the support of the Scottish members of the ILP, the majority from Clydeside. Whatever the reasons for their choice, whether out of ignorance or a mistaken belief in MacDonald's radical credentials, the irony is inescapable: that as representatives of the most militant section of the party they proceeded to vote for the one man committed to exorcizing all they represented.

MacDonald was not slow to make his intentions plain. Having once established himself in power, there was to be no more dissembling, for as he was to write in the *Leader* nine days after the election:

> The failure of the party in the last Parliament was that it was never
> an Opposition and was never led as an Opposition. It never
> impressed itself upon the country as an alternative Government
> with an alternative national policy . . . There are only two advan-
> tages on the Front Bench. The first is that you can put your feet on
> the table, and the second that you have a box of nice convenient
> height whereon to lay your notes . . . The importance of its pos-
> session, however, lies in the fact that it is a symbol of authority.

The message was clear. MacDonald was determined to impose his own authority on the parliamentary party and to mould it into an effective Opposition – the problem being to determine the nature of an alternative national policy. It was all very well for the *Leader* to editorialize about MacDonald's ability to provide 'a powerful expression to the will and ideals of the whole Party', but if it is the job of the Opposition to oppose, then such opposition has to be based on a rational alternative – and even where such alternatives did exist they were open to dispute within the party itself.

The ten Glasgow MPs who had been returned to Westminster

had not been elected to play parliamentary games, to enter into deals and trade off their principles. A quarter of a million people had packed the streets surrounding St Enoch's Station, Glasgow, to see them off to London. The mood had been evangelical, and between choruses of 'Jerusalem' and the 'Red Flag' Jimmy Maxton, imprisoned in 1916 as a pacifist agitator and a leader of the 1919 strike, warned the government that it could expect nothing from them but implacable opposition. While MacDonald subscribed to the sentiment, he had no time for the strategy of harassment that Clydesiders adopted on arriving in Westminster: 'My difficulty is to interpret myself to three or four good fellows who have no sense of Parliamentary methods & who expect Front Benchers to live in a perpetual state of fighting exaltation.' But if the Clydesiders quickly grew restless under the whip of parliamentary procedures, they were equally quick to question MacDonald's 'drawing room fashion' of leadership, for David Kirkwood, once a leader of the shop stewards' movement, to complain later:

> While MacDonald was worrying about the glorious traditions of the Mother of Parliaments there were other mothers worrying more . . . I don't think that it is good business to be taming our movement. It is a movement of fighters, of working men in revolt . . . We insist on our right to fight and to shock the fine ladies and gentlemen, and to have as little regard for their old institutions as they had for our mothers. These institutions exist to keep my class in subjection.

And fight and shock they did, and not only the fine ladies and gentlemen. Careless of parliamentary niceties, they harassed the government and the Opposition with even-handed contempt, Jimmy Maxton going so far as to accuse his own front bench of being a party to murder in approving cuts in the health budgets of local authorities. The charge caused uproar in the chamber, which redoubled when Maxton accused one protester of being 'the worst murderer of all'. Ignoring an order from the Speaker to withdraw the remark, Maxton continued to defend his position until, exhausted, he resumed his seat, to be followed by three of his Clydeside colleagues, each of whom repeated his charge. Mac-Donald was white-faced with anger, but Maxton's protest made little difference. At the division, the Labour front bench abstained, and the measure went through virtually unopposed.

There was more to the left's differences with MacDonald than his style of leadership, however. Sceptical of Parliament as 'territory occupied by the class enemy', they suspected that the Labour front bench was trading its principles in pursuit of power. The charge was not new. The sell-out theory of socialism had been around since Morris had entered the lists against Shaw and Hardie had expressed fears that the Labour and Liberal parties were becoming indistinguishable. The Labour Party, always a compromise and frequently an acrimonious one, may have succeeded in papering over the cracks in its ideological foundations, yet it continued to be undermined by the problem of defining its own identity and, consequently, of devising a formula by which its goals could best be achieved.

If in 1923 MacDonald appeared to be making a virtue of carrying political moderation to extremes, an encomium in *The Times* to the statesmanlike qualities of his leadership only served to reinforce the fears of Tom Johnson and his Clydeside colleagues that 'Unless we go ahead creating Socialist opinion and not merely an opinion that we are tame and harmless substitutes for the Liberal Party, we shall only get office and not power.'

In less than a year Johnson's fears were to be borne out. In November 1923, after little more than a year in office, Stanley Baldwin, who had replaced Bonar Law as the Tory leader, called a snap election. Although the Conservatives won 258 seats, they lost their overall majority, Labour taking 191 seats (an increase of forty-nine on the previous year's performance) and the reunited Liberal Party taking 159 seats. Unable to form a government, but none the less holding the balance of power, the choice for Liberals was either to keep the Tories in or to join with Labour and keep them out. For more than a month the inter-party haggling continued before the first Labour government was formed, with tacit Liberal support. Less than a quarter-century had passed since the delegates at the Memorial Hall had voted in favour of 'establishing a distinct Labour group in Parliament', and on 22 January 1924 it seemed that the political world had been turned upside down – although on visiting Buckingham Palace to present his new government MacDonald reassured George V that he would do his best to discourage Labour MPs from singing the 'Red Flag' in the Commons.

As for the new Ministry itself, Jimmy Clynes, newly appointed Lord Privy Seal, captured something of the mood of the moment on visiting the Palace: 'As we stood waiting for his Majesty . . . I could not help marvelling at the strange turn of Fortune's wheel, which had brought MacDonald the starveling clerk, Thomas the engine driver, Henderson the foundry labourer and Clynes the mill hand to this pinnacle beside the man whose forebears had been kings for so many splendid generations. We were making history!'

The euphoria was short-lived. The Liberals had not reached their decision on the principle of Buggins' turn, rather on the shrewd calculation as to where the party could exert maximum influence. As Asquith had made clear, if Labour were to come in 'it could hardly be tried under safer conditions', for whoever took office 'it is we, if we really understand our business, who will really control the situation'. Indeed so much was implicit in MacDonald's agreement to form a minority government: that the Liberals would give Labour independent support provided that the party did not attempt to launch socialistic legislation. Privately, MacDonald might rail at being 'a sort of kept party' of the Liberals, while within weeks of taking office he was under growing pressure from his own left wing, confiding to C. P. Scott, the editor of the *Manchester Guardian*, that 'They threaten, if they see any signs of political subservience, to vote against me.'

And for all Asquith's early confidence about playing the puppet master, the Liberals were soon to become disillusioned with the role, for Lloyd George to denounce the whole arrangement as adulterous in April 1924:

> They [Labour Members] give themselves the airs of Eastern Poten-
> tates and say 'Liberalism? We have no further use for it. Off with
> its head!' Liberals are to be the oxen to drag Labour over the rough
> roads of Parliament for two or three years, and at the end of the
> journey, when there is no further use for them, they are to be
> slaughtered. That is the Labour idea of co-operation.

MacDonald was equally resentful: 'The Liberals get meaner and meaner, & we respect the Conservatives more and more.' Bitterness is there, and possibly something more – betrayal perhaps? A political realist, MacDonald had long recognized the potential for a centre-left political grouping. It was for this as much as for any personal preferences that he had adopted progressivism as the touchstone of his political agenda. It was for this that he had alienated much of the left wing of his own party in the post-war contest for power. It was for this that he had been damned by his critics as a traitor to his class. Opinionated as he was, MacDonald did not lack courage, yet within weeks of taking office the hopes that he had vested in the inevitability of moderation had been decimated by the power play of Westminster.

In his first speech in the Commons as Prime Minister, MacDonald appealed to the House not for tranquillity 'but for security and confidence based upon goodwill', and Labour's legislative programme was as modest as his ambition which, while it may have satisfied the Liberals, incensed his own left wing. Even before MacDonald had formed his government, Tom Johnson had warned: 'There's going to be no Lib/Lab alliance . . . If the Labour Party were to betray the working class by allying itself with a Capitalist Party, the Labour Party is finished.' Always a lethal word in the Labour vocabulary, the composition of MacDonald's Cabinet appeared to confirm Johnson's charge of betrayal. Only two radicals, F. W. Jowett and John Wheatley, were given posts, a number equalled by Liberal defectors, while an ex-Tory lawyer, Lord Parmoor, was appointed Lord President of the Council, and a Peer who made no pretence of being a socialist and who was not even a party member was appointed First Lord of the Admiralty. Where previously there had been doubts, there was now open distrust, a mood reinforced as it became increasingly evident that the new Chancellor, Philip Snowden, intended to devote as much time to pursuing the left as he was to handling economic affairs.

At best an unstable, at worst a fissile combination, MacDonald found himself leading a push-me-pull-you administration in the style of the Duke of Plaza Toro, for when the left cried 'Forward', the Liberals cried 'Back', and when the Liberals cried 'Back', the left cried 'Traitor.' Emasculated politically, it was only a matter of time, or circumstance, before the government fell. In May Labour shocked its supporters when they learned it was prepared to use the Emergency Powers Act against striking dockers and London tramwaymen. The left had suspected much but had never imagined that a Labour government would consider employing such punitive measures against its own supporters. And worse was soon to come.

In July the ministry triggered a new crisis by moving against the *Workers' Weekly*, a communist news-sheet, for publishing an open letter calling on the army 'to let it be known that neither in the class war, nor in a military war, will you turn your guns on fellow workers'. This was part of a campaign by the Communist Party to discredit Labour as a tool of reaction, and two Conservative MPs were quick to exploit the article. On 28 July they raised the issue in the House, for the Attorney General, Sir Patrick Hastings, to declare that in his opinion the article came under the Incitement to Mutiny Act of 1795 and, as such, he intended to take proceedings against the journal and its editor, John Campbell.

A week later, when Hastings reported that the offices of the paper had been raided and the editor arrested, there was turmoil in the Chamber. Seemingly the whole Labour back bench was on its feet when the MP for Lanark, Tom Dickson, challenged the

Attorney General to say whether, if any Member of the House was to express opinions similar to those that had appeared in the offending weekly, they, too, would be subject to prosecution. 'If so,' Dickson concluded, indicating the Treasury bench 'they will probably lose half their party.'

Directed not so much at Hastings as at Ramsay MacDonald, the Campbell case was to provide the lighting rod for the left's pent-up anger, the more so when Hastings accepted that his original advice to the Cabinet was flawed and therefore that he intended to drop the proposed prosecution. Although he was quick to deny that the volte-face had been the result of political pressure, few believed him, and following the summer recess the Conservatives tabled a censure motion on the government to which the Liberals tabled an amendment calling for the establishment of a select committee to examine the facts of the case.

Even before the debate MacDonald sensed that the government had run its course – 'The papers are full of the coming election . . . Friends remarked that I was happy and lively and wished to know why: "Because it is the end."' The experience of office had proved as painful as it was likely to be short-lived but now, at least, he had the opportunity to clear his name of the charges levelled against him. In the censure debate of 8 October, however, MacDonald appeared like a man with a death wish, prompting Asquith to remark that he had preached the government's funeral oration before the patient was dead. At the division the Liberal amendment, with Conservative support, was carried by 166 votes, and at 11.30 that evening the Cabinet met to approve MacDonald's decision to see the King and ask for a dissolution.

After little more than eight months, the high hopes of January had been dashed. Always the hostage to Liberal caprice, and constantly aware of the disruptive potential of its own back-benchers, what little chance the first Labour government had of survival, let alone of pursuing a socialist programme, was damned from the day that it took office, to be twice damned by the left at its fall for having failed socialism. And if the left were quick to complain of the administration's faint-heartedness, the *Daily Mail* was equally quick in its effort to taint Labour with subversion in the election that followed.

Consistent only in its hostility to anything to the left of its own brand of paranoia, the paper obtained a copy of the so-called Zinoviev letter in the run-up to the election. Where the letter had originated, and whether it was genuine or forged, remains an open question, not that such ethical considerations troubled consciences at Conservative Party headquarters or the *Daily Mail*. Purporting to be from the President of the Comintern, Zinoviev, for the eyes only of the leaders of the British Communist Party, the letter instructed the party to prepare for an insurrection in Britain and, in passing, anathematized MacDonald for his anti-Soviet views. Three days before the election the *Mail* carried the letter under the banner headline: 'Civil War Plot by Socialists'. On seeing the story Jimmy Thomas remarked: 'We're bunkered.' He was right. On election day Labour lost forty seats and the Conservatives under Baldwin were returned to power with an overall majority of 223. The irony is inescapable, that the Labour Party under MacDonald should have been bunkered by the Red Bogy.

The election over, the in-fighting began, although there was near unanimity as to who was responsible for Labour's electoral defeat. As careless of the fact that Ramsay MacDonald had led a minority government as they were of their own part in the débâcle, both the right and left wings of the party turned on him with all the savagery of frustrated men, Philip Snowden confiding to Mannie Shinwell that Labour's opportunities had been 'wantonly thrown away by the most incompetent leadership which ever brought a government to disaster', and John Wheatley condemning MacDonald's 'timid, statesmanlike attitude' to echo Jimmy Maxton's relief that the government had fallen as: 'every day they were in led us further from Socialism'.

Much had changed in the two years since MacDonald had become leader of the parliamentary party, but all the old ideological differences, all the old personal rivalries remained. Indeed, the brief taste of power had sharpened the expectations of what might have been. Throughout its history Labour has been bedev-illed by the qualifying clause – if only this policy had been adopted, if only that course had been pursued, if only there had been other than Ramsay MacDonald – and in the aftermath of the 1924 election the party lost no time in reverting to its auto-destructive ways. But if MacDonald was to serve as a scapegoat, it was the policies he pursued as much as the shades of his char-acter that were to be subjected to intensifying scrutiny. With the exception of a Housing Act, which gave local authorities addi-tional funds to build homes for controlled rents, Labour's nine months in power appeared to its critics to have achieved little beyond discrediting the party.

Twenty-four hours after the election MacDonald and his record were put to the test when the parliamentary party met to elect its officers, most notably that of leader. MacDonald was eventually reappointed but not before a predatory debate of which he was later to write:

> The Left wing were out for my blood & had not the sense to restrain itself. Some members do no work but much talking & wish to turn the floor of the House into a sort of national street corner soap box . . . The difficulties of the party are more within than without, and though I write 'the Left wing', the inspiration really comes from those who were disappointed that I did not put them in the Ministry.

MacDonald's counter-attack was on two fronts: at the mili-tants of the ILP who subscribed to Wheatley's view that 'There can be no freedom for the toiling multitude under capitalism. Knowing that, we should fight to end it, not to mend it'; and at the trade unions, still smarting from not having received what they regarded as their rightful share of Cabinet posts in the Labour administration. Although re-established as leader for want of a better candidate, MacDonald's political credibility was at low ebb, and the left wanted nothing more of his casuistry. Led by George Lansbury, Jimmy Maxton and John Wheatley, the radical wing of the ILP formed an inner caucus committed to purging it of gradualism, while at the Labour Party conference of 1925 Ernest Bevin moved that 'in view of the experiences of the recent Labour government, it is inadvisable that the Labour Party should again accept office whilst having a minority of Members in the House of Commons'.

As with the ILP, the message was clear. The experience of government had shown there could be no compromising with capitalism. In the debate that followed MacDonald rejected the motion, for Bevin to launch a scathing attack on his 'dictatorial attitude' which, he declared, would have been enough 'to make Keir Hardie turn in his grave'. Although voted down, the motion revealed a new and more militant mood among certain of the larger unions that was to be reinforced by growing evidence that the Conservative government intended to launch a major offensive against labour. Its first target was the miners. Faced with falling demand, the coal owners had resorted to their time-worn tactic of demanding a cut in wages and an extension of working hours from their work-force. Once again the miners were to act as the stalking horse for government, the Prime Minister, Stanley Baldwin, extending the offensive in July 1925 when he warned all workers that they, too, would have to accept wage cuts. The response was immediate, the rail and transport workers' unions pledging themselves to support the miners' call for a complete stoppage of all movement of coal on 31 July, to be followed if necessary by a sympathetic strike.

On 30 July Baldwin's nerve broke, and on the offer of peace terms the strike was called off. Temporarily the Prime Minister's rhetoric had overreached his government's capacity to contain a major industrial dispute. The setback was only temporary, however. Having promised a nine months' subsidy to coal owners, mainly to support wages, and having established a commission to report on the case, the government set about making plans for a confrontation which it certainly anticipated if not engineered. As for the Labour Party, G. D. H. Cole was to later to summarize its response to the emerging crisis as 'a mixture of inopportune pacifism and over-confidence', compounded in Ramsay MacDonald's case by an outright rejection of direct action.

Speaking at a meeting of the ILP, he maintained that the government's surrender to the miners 'had handed over the appearance of victory to the very forces that sane, well-considered, thoroughly well examined Socialism feels to be probably its greatest enemy. The Tory government, in . . . the methods it adopted to bring this temporary settlement into being, has sided with the wildest Bolshevik, if not in words, certainly in fact and in substance.'

MacDonald was soon able to take comfort from a shift to the right in the General Council of the TUC and more especially in the composition of its Special Industrial Committee, the agency set up to coordinate union action 'to defend any principle of an industrial character which might be deemed vital by the allied organisations'. Indeed only one thing may have made him question the appointment of his aide, Jimmy Thomas, to the committee, a confidential report that 'J.H.T quite expects to be the next P.M.' As socially ambitious as he was politically untrustworthy, Thomas had long made a practice of blowing the trumpets to advance to cover his own retreat from socialism. First elected an MP in 1910, he had none the less retained his post as General Secretary of the National Union of Railwaymen, where he had developed an uncompromising formula for dealing with union militants: 'When the buggers give you trouble, give 'em a mass meeting. That gets it out of their system.'

Different tactics were demanded in the miners' case, however, and while the government accelerated its preparations for the showdown to come the Special Industrial Committee spent three months deciding whether or not it should meet. Small wonder that one Junior Minister in Baldwin's first administration considered that 'If the socialists are left to themselves, they will do our job for us.' As indeed they did. Jealous of its respectable and statesmanlike image, the Shadow Cabinet under MacDonald wanted no part of industrial militancy, while the resolve of the TUC declined progressively as the April deadline neared.

As Labour distanced itself from the promised dispute, and the General Council of the TUC wrangled as to which course to pursue if a dispute should occur, the Samuel Commission finalized its report, to conclude that there could be no alternative to a temporary wage cut, although as and when appropriate the government should take steps to ameliorate the lot of the miners. Having hand-picked the commission, it was not surprising that this was precisely what Baldwin wished to hear – for the owners, immediate gratification; for the miners, deferred expectations. Even after the publication of the commission's findings in March, however, the Industrial Committee continued to play its dilatory games, so that with only seventy-two hours remaining until the subsidy ended on 30 April no organization to carry out a General Strike had been countenanced, let alone been put in place.

On the 29th a meeting of trade union executives was held at the same Memorial Hall in London where the Labour Party had been founded a quarter of a century before and where, in the following forty-eight hours the unions were to recover their collective nerve. On Friday the 30th the subsidy ended, and with the government refusing to intervene any further the mine owners demanded their wage cuts. That evening lock-out notices were posted on collieries throughout Britain. On May Day 1926 the General Council of the TUC asked for a mandate to call a General Strike, and when the final figures were announced – For 3,653,529, Against 49,911 – Ramsay MacDonald and Jimmy Thomas joined in singing the 'Red Flag'. The euphoria disguised the reality that the unions were totally unprepared for a national strike, and even at that late stage the General Council believed it could negotiate its way out of the impasse.

The next three days were to prove how disastrously it had misread the situation. The government wanted no more talk. For nine months the innocuously named but powerfully disciplined Organization for the Maintenance of Supplies (OMS) had been counting down the days to the receipt of the one-word telegram: Action. At midnight on 3 May, following the collapse of a final meeting between Baldwin and a union delegation, it was dispatched.

The General Strike lasted nine days, but it was lost before it began. Although the Ministry of Labour reported that 1.5 million workers in key industries (including transport, rail and public utilities such as gas and electricity) had 'stopped' on the first day in support of the locked-out miners, the OMS's contingency plans were already beginning to limit the strike's impact. Hurriedly trained volunteers recruited by the organization had begun to run skeleton bus and rail services, while troops and naval personnel moved into selected power stations and docks. Over the next forty-eight hours the government intensified its pressure, dispatching a convoy of a hundred trucks escorted by twenty armoured cars through London, for the police to report 'that the East End is absolutely quiet, the entire population being cowed by the display of force'. Where intimidation failed, the law served to supplement the government's hard-line policy. At the week's end there was a nationwide crackdown on demonstrations in favour of the strike, which resulted in more than 2,000 people appearing before magistrates on public order charges.

Britain, as the *New York Herald Tribune* reported, resembled nothing so much as an armed camp, yet still the strike remained solid. The feminist MP for East Ham, Susan Lawrence, exclaimed to Beatrice Webb: 'We are living in momentous times, on the eve of great things . . . A revolutionary re-action – a terrible time perhaps – many of us in prison.' Webb disagreed: 'There will not even be a revolutionary reaction. Thomas and Baldwin will see to that.' She was right. Five days into the stoppage Thomas was already colluding in the lie that support for the miners among the railwaymen was collapsing (in fact, only 2 per cent of the work-force of the four rail unions had returned to work by 8 May), to bolster a colleague's claim that 'Unless the General Strike is called off now there will be hundreds of trains running. The result will be a débâcle.'

Their nerve badly shaken, the lie was to be made the scapegoat for the General Council's subsequent breach of faith. By the evening of the 10th there was growing support for the view that if the miners did not settle for a hastily revised but little improved version of the commission's original report that had been drafted by Samuel on Baldwin's instructions, they would have to go it alone. Twenty-four hours later the miners' leaders, Arthur Cook and Herbert Smith, were presented with what amounted to a *fait accompli* by the council and, on being asked by them whether Samuel could deliver on his promise, Thomas replied: 'You may not trust my word, but won't you trust the word of a British gentleman who has been governor of Palestine?'

Whether they did or not made little difference. The council's mind was already made up, Thomas having dismissed any doubts that remained, asserting that the miners 'were not trade unionists in a proper sense', for they neither understood nor cared for the rest of the labour movement.

The following morning Ramsay MacDonald and Ernest Bevin made a final attempt to persuade the miners to abandon their position, to be asked for a final time what guarantees they had that the government would stand by its word and not be a party to the victimization of striking miners. They were questions that only the government could answer, and by midday a deputation from the General Council was at Number 10 where its leader, Arthur Pugh, became so muddled by his own verbiage that Baldwin had to interrupt, to ask brusquely: 'That is, the General Strike is to be called off forthwith?' The trade unionists agreed. The government had demanded unconditional surrender, and after nine days that is what they had achieved. The news was received with incredulity by the strikers, the actor Lewis Casson recalling bitterly: 'We simply couldn't believe it, and were convinced that the pass had been sold in London.' He, too, was right. The General Council had secured peace at the price of betraying their members and abandoning the miners, In the coalfields, the lock-out continued.

7

1931: This Is a Lonely Job

'The financial policy of the Labour Party is even more conservative than the bankers themselves.' – John Strachey, *Socialist Review*, July 1927

It was not only the strike that the government succeeded in breaking on 12 May 1926 but the political will of the trade union leadership and, with it, the will of much of the labour movement. The hopes of syndicalism had finally been crushed, for even if the rank and file of the movement had been capable of sustaining a concerted attack on capital their leaders had neither the desire nor the temperament to engage in such a contest. As Beatrice Webb was to note in her diary on 18 May 1926: 'The failure of the General Strike shows what sane people the British are' – a conviction that was to lead her to the conclusion that 'the proletarian distemper has run its course'. Seemingly the Fabians had been right all along. Seemingly gradualism was the only way.

Certainly MacDonald and his circle had no doubts on that score. For fifteen years he had argued that if the unions tried to coerce the state, the state would win. Nine days in May were to confirm his verdict, and while condemning the triumphalism of the government there was a note of quiet satisfaction in his remark shortly after the strike ended that 'the hot air merchants . . . will have to be kept in their place in the future'. There was no mistaking his target. Only three months had passed since he had confided:

The ILP is a terrible problem. The way in which it is at present being handled is making it a mere tool of the Communists . . . The result will be that the ILP will come into serious conflict, and the Labour Party will bring to bear on it the massed votes of

the Trade Union movement. The grip that the ILP has on the
larger movement will then be loosened, and there will be the end
of the chapter.

MacDonald underestimated the resilience of the radical wing
of the ILP. The General Strike may have convinced the TUC of
the futility of direct action, and reinforced MacDonald's standing
as leader of a party committed to gradualism, but the leadership
of the ILP remained as critical of MacDonald's personal credentials as they were sceptical of his political agenda. MacDonald's
growing fondness for the company of society hostesses such as
Lady Londonderry (the wife of a noted reactionary) did nothing
to recommend him as a tribune of the working class. And it
seemed that in making play with the word socialism he was progressively emasculating its meaning. His behaviour was to prompt
Maxton and his Clydesiders to mount a full-frontal assault on
MacDonald's leadership to determine who should command the
ideological heights of socialism.

Not that the ILP's challenge to gradualism was the product of
the 'frustrated anarchism' that its critics liked to claim. Following
the fall of the first Labour government, the ILP had published
Socialism in Our Time in an attempt to promote a radical constitutional formula for change and had subsequently produced a
series of position papers covering such issues as parliamentary
reform, land nationalization and, most notably, the living wage. In
advancing a carefully formulated and coherent strategy, *Socialism
in Our Time* and its supplementary reports armed the ILP with the
means to dispute party orthodoxy, the more so as the official
Labour line was to make as few commitments to the electorate as
possible, preferring to fall back on the general statement and aims
of *Labour and the New Social Order*.

Where the *New Social Order* traded in generalizations, however, *Socialism in Our Time* dealt in specifics, not least in demanding that any future Labour government should make the provision
of a minimum living income for every citizen the cornerstone of

its domestic policy. Subsequently described as 'a milestone in the history of the British left', the living wage proposal anticipated, albeit in embryo form, the welfare programme that was adopted by the Attlee government in 1945 – nineteen years after it had proved altogether too radical for the tastes of MacDonald and the Labour establishment.

Heralded as an alternative to the obscurantism of party policy, the ILP programme aimed to challenge 'the deadening idea that Socialism can only be established by slow gradualism over generations of time'. Thirty years had passed since William Morris had charged that time was the bondsman of capitalism. Now it was time that it served other masters, rather than being employed to defer expectations that had already been deferred for too long. Although eschewing direct action, even the charge implicit in the title, *Socialism in Our Time*, contradicted everything for which MacDonald had stood since that day in childhood when he came across 'the lightest burden I ever brought home', Orr's *Circle of the Sciences*, and discovered Darwin's theory of evolution:

> The real distinction between the evolutionist and the revolutionist is that the former believes that Socialist growth is to come from the vigorous activities of society forcing new forms of life, whilst the latter uses the unhealthy and dead parts . . . These policies may be good or bad in themselves, but they will have to be decided on their merits. They are not Socialism. (*Forward*, March 1926)

For all the supposedly impossibilist ambitions of the ILP radicals, however, their challenge – not least the call to effect 'a constructive but rapid transition' to socialism – demanded a positive response. It was all very well for critics to demonize the ILP programme as a concoction of 'flashy futilities', but even its advocates recognized that the *New Social Order* no longer served as a meaningful policy document. At a meeting of the National Exec-

utive Committee in the summer of 1927 Arthur Henderson proposed that the Executive should draft a programme of 'legislative
and administrative action' for an incoming Labour, a resolution
that was moved by MacDonald at the party conference later in
the year. A decade had passed since Snowden had reflected that
MacDonald's speeches were open to any interpretation that anyone cared to place on them, and at Blackpool in 1927 he excelled
himself:

> He was one of those who regarded unauthorised programmes with
> a good deal of suspicion . . . Authorised programmes might have a
> certain number of inconveniences, but unauthorised programmes
> had many more inconveniences. What they were asking the Exec-
> utive to do was to consider all the resolutions that had been con-
> sidered at the Conference from time to time . . . not for the
> purpose of stating what the Labour Government was wanting to do
> in its first year of office, but for the purpose of providing a plan
> which a Labour Government could work at.

Even MacDonald's capacity for obfuscation could not disguise
his intention. For all his reservations about committing the party
to the production of a policy document, however, he may have
taken comfort from the fact that in the process of supporting the
Executive's resolution the General Council of the TUC, in the
impressive figure of Ernest Bevin, had publicly distanced itself
from the radical wing of the ILP:

> I agree with a bold programme, but a good many delegates talk as
> if all the people in this country were class conscious socialists . . .
> When some of our friends draw up programmes, they are some-
> thing like manifestos. I would rather see a short programme of
> immediate objectives that Labour can really hope to accomplish
> and then we can go back and say 'At least we have done what we
> have said we would. We have delivered the goods.'

A critical element in the power game being played out in the always uneasy alliance that was the Labour Party, the TUC was to prove an invaluable ally to MacDonald in his contest with the ILP which, under Maxton's leadership, had come to regard itself as the keeper of the socialist conscience. It was a presumption that the TUC scorned. Consisting of fewer than 30,000 members the ILP was regarded by the TUC as a puny thing compared with the collective might of the unions. Yet still it pretended to dictate Labour policy. While the unions could adopt a hard-line policy towards the ILP, however, MacDonald had to be more circumspect, not least in the aftermath of May 1926. Contemptuous as he was of the ILP's claim that Labour was 'in a state of apathy, almost hopelessness' for having failed to address the crisis of socialism constructively, MacDonald could not dismiss the criticism of Maxton, Wheatley and the Clydesiders out of hand. They commanded too much clout in the Commons for that, two-thirds of all Labour MPs belonging to the ILP, twenty-seven of whom sat as Members for whose candidature the ILP was solely responsible.

Within weeks of the end of the General Strike, however, MacDonald had succeeded in alienating both the ILP and the unions, having published a damning review of the General Strike ('a weapon that cannot be wielded for industrial purposes') and, by implication, of the role of the General Council of the TUC in its mismanagement ('I hope that the result will be a thorough reconsideration of trade union tactics'). Momentarily, he appeared isolated, the ILP condemning him as a traitor to the working class, the unions protesting that he had misrepresented their role and Ernest Bevin going so far as to accuse him of stabbing the labour movement in the back which was why 'I cannot see my way clear to supporting the Labour Party so long as Mr J. R. MacDonald as its leader continues his present policy in relation to the industrial side.'

As the MP Mannie Shinwell was to write later: 'All political parties are acquainted with conspiracies, but the number I have known in the Labour Party would, I am certain, exceed those in all other parties.'

A past master of intrigue, Shinwell knew what he was talking about. A Clydesider, and formerly a close friend of Jimmy Maxton, he had witnessed the internecine feuding that racked Labour in the aftermath of the General Strike and, more especially, the power play of Ernest Bevin. Still in his early forties, Bevin was already a dominant figure in the inner councils of the TUC. A square-cut and massive presence, with an insatiable appetite for power, he was as jealous of his own reputation as he was of the good name of the Transport and General Workers' Union, of which he was General Secretary. But if Bevin distrusted Mac-Donald, he suspected the ILP even more, disdaining its radical programme and rubbishing its proposals for a minimum wage; 'You will discover that you cannot handle wages by attaching them to the tails of a particular slogan.' The harder the ILP pushed to the left, the more intractable Bevin became, first to reach an accord with MacDonald and then to endorse his resolution at Blackpool in 1927.

For MacDonald it was a major tactical victory, which may have done something to account for the note in his diary at the close of the conference, which appropriately enough fell on his sixty-first birthday: 'Blackpool has made it easy to be old. How fine our movement is.' In the light of the conference's outcome, he might well have added: Not least in its capacity to apply gradualism as much to its everyday practices as to its long-term principles. There was more to MacDonald's satisfaction than the fact that the party had again postponed taking any immediate decisions on future policy, however. By securing the backing of the unions he had gone some way towards marginalizing the challenge of the ILP and ensuring that when it emerged the party's new policy document would be to his taste – the more so as he was one of the committee appointed to produce its first draft. As for the other members, only one was an unknown political quantity, and he was a favourite of

MacDonald himself: Sir Oswald Mosley.

Thirty-one years of age, handsome, well connected and rich, Mosley was already a rogue politician, having quit the Conservatives, for whom he had sat as an MP since 1918, to join Labour in 1924 and win a by-election in Smethwick in 1926. Three months later he had secured a seat on the party's National Executive Committee, to the delight of his 'Dear Chief', Ramsey MacDonald. It was to prove a fateful liaison, although MacDonald appeared careless of the risks it entailed when Mosley drafted his own memorandum for consideration by the Executive's working party. A radical statement, only slightly more modest in its ambitions than the ILP's *Socialism in Our Time*, Mosley recommended a thoroughgoing revision of monetary policy, allied to a wide range of welfare initiatives, including improved pensions and child allowances. The precision of Mosley's programme was exactly what MacDonald wished to avoid. As far as he was concerned the party should offer no hostages to political fortune, and on this the rest of the committee was agreed. Mosley, the ILP and the Liberals might favour radical measures to revive the economy and curb the rising level of unemployment, but this was not Labour's way.

The first draft of *Labour and the Nation* was submitted to the party conference in 1928, MacDonald writing in the preface that 'the Labour Party unlike other parties is not concerned with patching the rents in a bad system, but with transforming Capitalism to Socialism' by way of 'the practical recognition of the familiar commonplace that "morality is in the nature of things" and that men are all, in very truth, members of one another'. MacDonald's oracular style was matched by the open-endedness of the programme itself.

Having demolished to their own satisfaction the Liberal programme, based upon Keynesian prescriptions and soon to be detailed in the Liberals' *Yellow Book* of 1928, the drafting committee advanced five general principles that Labour should pursue on its return to office:

(i) to secure for every member of the community the standards of life and employment necessary for a healthy and self-respecting existence;

(ii) to convert industry step by step . . . from a contest for private gain into a co-operative undertaking, carried on for the service of the community and amenable to its control;

(iii) to extend various forms of social provision – education, public health, pensions and so on;

(iv) to adjust taxation to provide for industrial expansion and ensure that any surpluses generated by society should be distributed for social ends;

(v) to establish peace, freedom and justice among nations by removing the causes of international disputes by political and economic cooperation through the League of Nations.

The left, under Maxton, were derisive. Nothing, it seemed, could be more non-committal that the right's commitment to socialism: 'A Labour Government cannot run Capitalism any more successfully than Baldwin or the others.' Maxton's criticism made no difference, and, having seen off the ILP's proposal for a living wage by a seventeen-to-one majority, the conference proceeded to adopt *Labour and the Nation* as the revised statement of the party's aims and objectives. It was with a good deal of self-satisfaction that MacDonald was to write at the end of the conference: 'He who conquers believes he can – and we have that belief.' Whether or not he was employing the royal 'we' remained unclear. What was clear was that the left had been neutralized, while the delegate's endorsement of a loyalty oath had reinforced the diktat of the Executive.

On this issue, at least, there was no ambiguity, the declaration laying down that:

affiliation to the Labour Party implies general loyalty to the decisions of the party conference and debars affiliated organisations and their branches from promoting or associating in the promotion of candidates for Public Office in opposition to the Labour Party.

Designed to exorcize all forms of dissent except those sanctioned by the party establishment, Maxton none the less welcomed the introduction of the oath on the understanding that the ILP was recognized as 'a Socialist Party within the Labour Party'. A sophism that even MacDonald must have admired, it was a formula which, temporarily at least, the party was happy to accept, for by the autumn of 1928 there was more pressing business to hand.

With a General Election in prospect, the need was to secure the appearance if not the substance of unity. After five years all the signs were that the electorate had lost faith in Baldwin's administration, in part for what was widely regarded as its mismanagement of an economy over which it had diminishing control. Long before the Wall Street crash of October 1929 there had been growing evidence of the fragility of the world economy. Whereas world trade had grown by at least 25 per cent in every decade between 1830 and 1914, it grew by only 8 per cent during the 1920s, with punishing consequences for the UK which was heavily dependent on its exporting capacity. Until 1914 the UK's exports had risen by an average of 3 per cent a year for thirty years, 30 per cent of all exports being produced by five core industries: coal, iron and steel, cotton, wool and machinery. In contrast, the volume of British exports during the 1920s was a fifth below what it had been in the pre-war years, with all that implied in employment terms. Although subject to variations, the underlying trend for unemployment rose consistently from the mid-1920s onwards, and it was the issue of unemployment that was to dominate the election of 1929 – and the Liberals who were to dominate the unemployment debate.

Lloyd George may have been 'this goat-footed bard, this half-human visitor from the . . . enchanted woods of Celtic antiquity' of Keynes's description, but he was one of the first politicians to grasp the revolutionary significance of Keynes's economic theories, most notably that during downswings in the economic cycle governments should intervene actively in the economy to stimulate demand and curb unemployment. In February 1929 the Liberals published their *Yellow Book*, a 500-page analysis of Britain's economic malaise to which Keynes was a major contributor. A month later the sixpenny pamphlet *We Can Conquer Unemployment* appeared under Lloyd George's name, for its pledge to explode in the political consciousness:

> If the nation entrusts the Liberal Party at the next General Election with the responsibilities of Government, we are ready with schemes of work of a kind which are not merely useful but essential to the well-being of the nation. The work put in hand will reduce the terrible figures of the workless in the course of a year to normal proportions and will, when completed, enrich the nation and equip it for competing successfully with its rivals in the business of the world.

And the means for achieving this economic miracle?

> At the moment, individual enterprise alone cannot restore the situation within a time for which we can wait. The state must therefore lend its aid and, by a deliberate policy of national development, help to set going at full speed the great machinery of industry.

The Tories were as contemptuous as Labour was captious. The carefully detailed and costed Liberal programme, which included proposals for a major road-building programme, for the upgrading of the telephone network and for the building of 200,000 houses a year, made nonsense of received economic wisdom, and on economic issues Labour was as conservative as the Conservatives. None the less, MacDonald was quick to realize that some sort of response was necessary in face of the Liberal challenge, and in the spring of 1929 Labour published a counterblast of its own – *How to Conquer Unemployment* – full of the sort of generalizations of which MacDonald was so fond: 'Roads will be built as a system, bridges broken and reconstructed, railways reconditioned, drainage carried on, afforestation advanced, coasts protected, houses built, emigration dealt with, colonial economic expansion planned.'

Neither for the first nor the last time, Labour stole the Liberals' clothes. In doing so, however, the party was careful to ensure that it made no specific commitments to its own undertakings, which led Shinwell to write caustically that the programme's only commitment was to establishing a committee to examine its own agenda if returned to office 'the curbing hand of MacDonald having erased the risks involved in outright change'.

But if MacDonald was responsible for the non-committal tone of *How to Conquer Unemployment*, Snowden was the author of its innate conservatism. Always weak in economic affairs, MacDonald had long made a practice of saying 'Leave it to Snowden', and Snowden was only too happy to oblige. A man who brought all the flair of the junior excise man that he had once been to the office of Chancellor, the essence of Snowden's character was captured by Churchill after the fall of the first Labour government: 'The Treasury mind and the Snowden mind embraced one another with the fervour of two long-separated kindred lizards.'

The years between had done nothing to shake Snowden's orthodox faith. As far as he was concerned, the New Jerusalem was to be built on the foundations of the doctrines peddled by the Treasury mandarins: that borrowing was contrary to every dictate of sound finance and that 'An expansion of the currency issue must respond to genuine demand arising out of real purchasing power and not be used to create demand.' Indeed there was a note of real pride in his declaration of February 1929 that there was 'a good deal more orthodoxy to Labour's financial policy than its critics appear to appreciate', a remark which may well have inspired the *Punch* cartoon featuring John Bull saying 'This impossible Bolshie' and the Bolshie saying 'This impossible bourgeois' and then both saying together: 'Well, my friend, what about business?'

Once labelled a Bolshie, it was business that Snowden was about during his time as Chancellor. Raised in the Nonconformist heartland of West Yorkshire, and convinced that socialism itself was a luxury, he brought his own early experiences to bear on his time at Number 11, the ascetic discipline of a young man who had come to terms early with his near poverty 'by the simple process of reducing his own wants to so rigorous a compass that upon thirty shilling a week . . . he was able to lead a life of proud independence'. Applied privately, the prescription had served well enough. Applied to the office of Chancellor of the Exchequer, it was to bring the second Labour government to disaster within two years of taking power.

At the election of May 1929 Labour was returned to office with 288 seats, although not with an overall majority. With the Conservatives having won 260 seats, the Liberals, with fifty-nine seats, held the balance of power. The right-wing bias of MacDonald and the party was reflected in the composition of his new Cabinet. Only one left-winger, the widely respected former editor of the *Daily Herald*, George Lansbury, was given a post. Even this amounted to a snub to the left, however, for as Snowden was to write of the office of Commissioner of Works, it was an appointment where Lansbury 'would not have much opportunity of squandering money, but would be able to do a good many small things which would improve the amenities of government buildings and public parks'.

But there may have been more to MacDonald's proscription of the left than either his own or the party's prejudices. In his autobiography Snowden suggested that in 1929 MacDonald was seriously flirting with the idea of doing a deal with the Tories to secure an extended term of office for Labour, rather than having to trade with the Liberals whose 'madcap finances' were too radical for the incoming administration. Indeed, the King's speech revealed how modest Labour's domestic programme was, preferring to defer legislation rather than addressing key issues, more especially of unemployment. The left were scathing, John Wheatley mounting a bitter attack on his front bench and its policy of government on the instalment plan:

> This is the day of the Government's power. Today the Government could do anything. Today the Government are not showing the courage that their supporters on these benches expect. If they displayed that courage . . . the parties opposite would not dare to wound them, however willing they might be to strike; but after twelve months of this halting, half-way legislation . . . and having been discredited in the country, there will be no Party in this House poor enough to do them honour.

It was not what the party wished to hear. As Jimmy Thomas remarked, Wheatley would have been better sticking to the facts than 'playing the soothsayer'. Temporarily at least, the future was put on hold, and at the annual conference in September 1929 the party was in a self-congratulatory mood, the Executive declaring that: 'The Labour Party has seized the imagination of the people. Despite our Parliamentary limitations, events are being shaped with a vigour and a spirit that are refreshing after the alternative inertia and reaction of the past four years.'

Little more than a month later Wall Street crashed. On Thursday 24 October 12,894,650 shares on the New York exchange changed hands at the onset of a collapse that was to shatter the dreams of those who had played the markets with psychotic abandon. Even before the crash, the withdrawal of US finance from Europe had been threatening to undermine its already fragile economy, but it was those seven days in October, described by

J. K. Galbraith as 'the slaughter of the innocents', that precipitated the crisis that was to ravage the world and, with it, the UK economy. When the Labour government took office in June 1929 9.5 per cent of the population, or 1,163,000 men and women, were registered as unemployed. Twelve months later they numbered 1,912,000, or 15.4 per cent of the working population, while by Christmas 1930 2,725,000 people, accounting for almost a fifth of the total work-force, were unemployed.

This was 'the economic blizzard' of MacDonald's description for which he and his Cabinet were totally unprepared. Save for a limited package of measures introduced by Thomas in July 1929 little had been done and even less time had been devoted by Labour to redeeming its election pledge of tackling unemployment. As Lord Privy Seal and Minister for Employment, Thomas was virtually bereft of constructive ideas, a charge that could not be laid against a leading member of his ministerial team, the Chancellor of the Duchy of Lancaster, Oswald Mosley.

For five years, Mosley had been pursuing an aggressive line on employment policy, and in January 1930 he produced a memorandum on the subject which bore a close resemblance to the ILP programme detailed in *Socialism Now*. MacDonald expressed cautious interest, but Thomas had as little time for the radical contents of the memorandum – which centred on the expansion of the purchasing power of the home market to increase demand and the 'insulation' of the economy by the control of imports – as he had for the charisma of its author.

It was neither Mosley's character nor his ideas that offended Thomas most, rather his breach of protocol for having sent Mac-Donald a copy of his memorandum before submitting it to Thomas. Subscribing to the view that in his position it was impossible to be anything but a snob, Thomas made Mosley's *faux pas* a resigning issue. MacDonald would have none of Thomas's posturing, however, and it was Mosley who was to resign, although not before Snowden had succeeded in negating any positive measures to stimulate the economy and check the rising tide of unemployment.

In the early days of the crisis triggered by the Wall Street crash, MacDonald had appointed an Economic Advisory Council, of which G. D. H. Cole was a member, and of which Cole was later to write:

> The Council . . . discussed the issue [of unemployment] time and time again; and some of us, including Keynes, tried to get MacDonald to understand the sheer necessity of adopting some definite policy for stopping the rot. Snowden was inflexible, and MacDonald could not make up his mind, with the consequence that Great Britain drifted steadily towards a disaster of whose imminence the main body of Labour MPs and of the labour movement was wholly unaware.

Seemingly the council was only agreed on one point: to have nothing to do with Mosley's programme: 'Right or wrong – and I feel sure that it was largely right – it stood no chance of acceptance as long as Snowden was at the Exchequer.'

Apparently, there was no way out of the deadlock. Paralysed by Snowden's resistance to Keynes's 'irrational theories' and his continuing devotion to the economic orthodoxy, it seemed that the crisis was self-perpetuating, a débâcle that was living off itself. The Tories were disparaging, and Labour defeatist, and when Baldwin declared in the Commons that 'the enthusiasm is running out of your Party all over the country, because you have lost faith with Socialism' several Labour MPs cheered and shouted: 'Come over here, Stanley.' In reply, Thomas admitted that he knew of no effective way of dealing with the crisis and jokingly confessed that he was breaking all records in the numbers of the unemployed. Neither MacDonald nor Snowden were seen to laugh.

Nor was MacDonald amused when, on 28 May 1930, Mosley

resigned from the government to deliver a blistering speech in the House, damning the inadequacy of Labour's economic policy and declaring contemptuously that at a time when unemployment was nearing the two million mark its public works programme was providing jobs for no more than 80,000 people a year. Three days later sixty Labour MPs signed a petition calling for Thomas's resignation, and in the first week of June MacDonald issued an invitation to Baldwin and Lloyd George to attend an all-party conference to discuss the issue of unemployment. With its own policy in ruins, the search for a new one began, but not before the first ominous cracks in the façade of Labour unity had appeared. In fact, it was MacDonald who personified the innate differences that had always racked the party and which the depression had thrown into sharp relief. In despairing mood, he wrote in August 1930: 'The whole economic scheme is breaking down for the very reasons foreshadowed by the Socialists.'

The reflection begged the question: What did MacDonald now represent? Once he, too, had been proud to adopt the title Socialist, but by the autumn of 1930 it may well have seemed to him that the political compass by which he had steered for so long had become disorientated; as W. B. Yeats put it: 'Mere anarchy is loosed upon the world.' The Labour Party had always been held together as much by political expedience as ideological conviction, and it may well have appeared to MacDonald that the party, which he had helped to construct over three decades, was once again in danger of imploding, for during the summer recess it became increasingly clear that Mosley was actively lobbying to become leader of Labour's left wing and, in due course, of the party itself.

Frustrated by the treatment his memorandum had received at the hands of the Labour establishment, and arrogant enough to believe in his own Messianic credentials, Mosley had no qualms about intriguing against his 'Dear Chief'.

It was not only Mosley's charisma but his circle of confidants that provided him with a power base; among them Oliver Bald-

1931: This Is a Lonely Job

win, the son of the Conservative leader; John Strachey, a formidable left-wing polemicist; the socialite Harold Nicolson, husband
of Vita Sackville-West; and the young and still little known Welsh
firebrand Aneurin Bevan. A politician in a hurry, Mosley quickly
came to realize that he had as little hope of leading the left as he
had of replacing MacDonald, and on 8 November 1930 Nicolson
noted in his diary: 'He [Mosley] is evidently thinking of leading
some new party of younger Nationalists', to add three weeks later:
'Tom Mosley tells me he will shortly launch his manifesto practically creating the National Party.'

Ironically, in the light of what was to come, the manifesto of
Mosley's new party, written by Mosley, Strachey and Bevan and
published in December 1930, shared much with the radical
agenda of the ILP in its claim to represent 'applied socialism'.
The party's nationalist thrust, however, was soon to belie its
socialist origins as Bevan was quick to recognize. In February
1931, when Mosley finally broke with Labour to form the New
Party, Bevan, to whom the Labour Party was the trustee of socialism, broke with Mosley to predict: 'You will end up a fascist
party.' To Mosley, impatient with the toil of democracy, this may
have been a solution he had always fancied. An essentially
authoritarian figure who, like his contemporaries Hitler and
Mussolini, believed that only he could resolve the crisis of capitalism, Mosley's egocentricity was soon to give way to the virus
of nationalism. And while he and the New Party drifted inexorably to the right, to confirm Bevan's prediction, the ILP maintained its pressure on the government to adopt a more radical
policy to contain the spread of unemployment, Jimmy Maxton
charging it with 'timidity and vacillation in refusing to apply
Socialist remedies'.

If the need for party unity in the pre-election period had
tempered the differences between the Labour establishment and
the ILP, a post-election comment in the *Daily Telegraph* that
Jimmy Thomas had 'all the instincts of a capitalist' synthesized
all that Maxton and the Clydesiders suspected of the new

administration: that MacDonald's government had sold out to the class enemy. The disillusionment was corrosive and created a crisis of conscience among the left-wingers of the ILP. How long could they continue to subscribe to policies of which they disapproved? How long was it possible to continue supporting a party in which they had lost faith? Where, ultimately, did their loyalty lie?

For Alfred Salter it was a matter as much of *realpolitik* as of principle: 'We are tied to the ILP by ties of conviction, interest and sentiment, and we don't want to see our movement come to an inglorious end or degenerate into a little rump of "rebels" or quasi-communists engaged in pin-pricking and harassing the Labour Party and its chief.'

All the angst of a man divided against himself was there – of conviction, interest, sentiment ranged against the interests of the party itself – but it was an indulgence that both the ILP and the Labour Party found intolerable. Neither were willing to forgo their role as the keepers of the socialist conscience. At its annual meeting in 1930 the ILP tightened its membership rules while expressing the hope that the Labour executive would refrain from taking any punitive measures that would prevent 'liberty of action on matters of deep conviction'. Such special pleading made little impression on the party leadership. Faced with a direct challenge to their authority, the Executive responded by amending the party's constitution to ensure that all Labour MPs conformed 'to the Programme, Principles and Policies of the party'. And, to reinforce the ruling, Labour's Chief Whip was soon to elevate loyalty above principle, maintaining that he would rather see the parliamentary party do the wrong thing unitedly than allow any criticism of the leadership's policies.

The nuances of the power play, however, could not disguise the fundamental differences on which they turned or avert the final clash between the left and the right of the party as to where its future lay.

Almost a century had passed since the Chartists had divided

against themselves and Bronterre O'Brien had raged at 'the faint hearts of our brotherhood'; almost fifty years since Morris had disputed with Shaw 'the real business of Socialists'; and now, once again, the ideological breach was opening at the heart of the movement. In February, 1930, Ramsay MacDonald left the ILP: 'In view of what is going on it was impossible for me to keep up my association. The ILP has lost its grip on socialism and its sense of the meaning "comrade". If the salt has lost its flavour, it is henceforth good for nothing.'

The bitterness was mutual, the sense of betrayal shared. For Maxton, MacDonald was the Judas of socialism. For MacDonald, Maxton was yet another of those impossibilists waging 'a guerrilla fight with Capitalism'. Half a lifetime had passed since he had joined the ILP to subscribe to Keir Hardie's visions that 'Socialism throbs with the life of days that are to be.' Then the mood had been evangelical, the pursuit of an ideal lacking definition. But, as Hardie had found, the harder he had tried to rationalize his vision, the more difficult it had become. And Hardie had never had to deal with the everyday management of government, of reconciling his ambitions to the realities of power. It was all very well to idealize, but to make a reality of ideals was a very different affair, and the harder events pressed in, the harder it became.

G. D. H. Cole was not alone in noting the difficulty that Mac-Donald was having in making up his mind during the intensifying economic crisis. Even Jimmy Thomas, never renowned for his sensitivity, noticed much the same thing, while by the autumn of 1930 MacDonald was writing: 'I am tired and wonder more and more if it is possible to go on.' The alternative, an increasingly seductive one, was to form a National Government on the lines being canvassed by Lloyd George, a scheme MacDonald himself had already considered: 'I have done everything possible to make such a thing possible. If there is a desire for it . . . I shall not stand in its way, and would be very glad to go into the background, if that would make it easy.'

The future was postponed, if briefly, but, as the situation deteriorated, there was growing evidence of splits within the Cabinet, leading to media-led rumours that MacDonald might resign ('This I fear would break the party, but it has broken itself'), or that Snowden would have to 'bend or go'. Yet for all his doubts about Snowden's loyalty MacDonald continued to trust Snowden's economic advice, and for all the pressures to adopt reflationary measures via the public sector Snowden remained wedded to the Treasury's orthodoxy, as he made clear in a Commons debate in February 1931:

> I say with all the seriousness I can command that the national position is so grave that drastic and disagreeable measures will have to be taken if Budget equilibrium is to be maintained . . . An expenditure which may be easy and tolerable in prosperous times becomes intolerable at a time of grave industrial depression . . . Schemes involving heavy expenditure, however desirable they may be, will have to wait until prosperity returns.

Snowden's message was straightforward: to balance his Budget public-sector spending would have to be sacrificed which, in practice, meant slashing benefit payments to the unemployed. His own back-benchers were incensed, one Member raging that his speech struck at 'the whole philosophy . . . upon which the Labour movement has been built', although Snowden did make one concession to his critics, accepting a Liberal proposal to establish a committee to examine all plans to reduce public expenditure to ensure that they were 'consistent with the efficiency of the services'.

Significantly Snowden retained the right to appoint the committee, and he was quick to pack it with his own nominees. A man obsessed, not least by hatred for the left wing of his own party, Snowden was determined to drive through his financial programme at any cost, even if it meant bringing the government down. And the May Committee was the means for achieving his ends. Indeed, as Snowden was later to admit, its purpose was to frighten the country and force the hand of Cabinet waverers into accept the draconian measures he was planning to introduce in order to ensure that his budget was 'balanced honestly'.

Even Snowden could not have foreseen where his intransigence would lead or how catastrophic his scheming would prove to be. On 31 July 1931 the May Committee forecast a £120 million budget deficit, to be compensated for by a 20 per cent cut in the standard rate of benefit, a £37 million reduction in a range of other programmes designed to assist the unemployed and swingeing wage cuts for teachers, the police and the armed forces. After the first shock had worn off, Labour's reaction was one of disbelief, the *Daily Herald* describing it as 'a nine days' wonder' and the *New Statesman* declaring that 'no government of any party' would dare to implement the report.

Both were proved wrong, the *Daily Herald* in less time than even its leader writer can have imagined. Inherently conservative, the financial markets had done more than simply subscribe to the rigidity of Snowden's thinking; they had helped to condition it, the irony being that it was the May report, a publication that reflected the City's own mind-set, that was to fuel the panic in the markets about the vulnerable state of the UK economy. Arguably, the crisis of 1931 was, in part, of the City's own making, for in making a bogy of public expenditure it was eventually to fall victim to its own inflated fears.

In the first week of August the Bank of England spent £21 million defending the parity of the pound, inspiring the British Bankers' Committee to warn MacDonald and Snowden of an escalating sterling crisis unless urgent steps were taken to balance the budget and improve Britain's trading balance. This was only a beginning. While Keynes argued that Britain should devalue by 25 per cent as a step to 'organising prosperity', Snowden held fast to the Treasury line that cuts in public expenditure were essential if market confidence in the economy was to be restored. By mid-

August, having already exhausted £50 million in credits, the Bank of England set about trying to raise a further £30 million loan – to be told that no further advances could be arranged until Britain balanced her budget in line with May's proposals.

MacDonald was between a rock and a hard place. Either he could meet the bankers' demands and abandon his election pledges or he could stand by the programme, albeit a minimalist one, on which he had been elected and the bankers would bring him down. If MacDonald vacillated, Snowden knew no such doubts. An economic Svengali, he manipulated both MacDonald and the Cabinet and steered through a package of economies until reaching the City's final and most onerous demand: that a reduced but still punitive cut in Unemployment Benefits should be complemented by the introduction of a means test for applicants. The Cabinet vacillated, but for the General Council of the TUC it was a demand too far.

On Thursday 20 August there were two meetings between a Cabinet team led by MacDonald and Snowden and the General Council of the TUC, one in the afternoon and one in the evening. On both occasions the trade unionists' response was the same: that the government was being jockeyed into abandoning its social policies by vested interests opposed to the existence of the Labour Party. As for Snowden's economic package: 'Not one of the Council's members . . . spoke in favour of the Government's proposals.'

For Labour it had been a disastrous day, for MacDonald the moment of truth. The party was tearing itself to pieces, for there could be no reconciling the differences between the unions and the Cabinet's position. On the evening of 20 August MacDonald was in a mood of 'furious despair', but the following morning he woke 'in fighting mood' to confide to his diary: 'If we now yield to the TUC we shall never be able to call our bodies or souls or intelligences our own.'

Having once decided, he did not care to ask to whom he might be yielding his intelligence if not his soul, reporting to the Cabinet that morning that as far as the City was concerned it was no longer simply a matter of balancing the budget but of balancing it by means of 'very substantial economies'. Seemingly, the more the Cabinet conceded, the more the markets demanded, and the more insistent their political agents on the Opposition benches became. Since the onset of the crisis MacDonald had been under growing pressure from the Tories and the Liberals to form a National Government, and on the evening of Friday 21 August Neville Chamberlain for the Tories and Sir Herbert Samuel for the Liberals again broached the idea, reassuring MacDonald that 'If I wish to form a govt. with their co-operation they would be happy to serve under me.'

The end, when it came, came quickly. On Saturday members of the Cabinet split on whether to make any further concessions to the City and authorized MacDonald to inform the King that they had placed their resignation in his hands. On tendering their resignation to George V, however, the King asked MacDonald to reconsider his decision, saying that 'he was the only man who could lead the country through the crisis'. And while the Opposition watched and waited in the ante-room of power, the bankers remained intractable. Either the government met their conditions or they would foreclose on the promised loan.

On Sunday 23 August the Cabinet accepted the bankers' ultimatum, but only on a split twelve-to-nine vote, coupled with a threat of mass resignation by the dissidents. With his Cabinet irrevocably divided, MacDonald had no alternative but to return to the Palace, where for a second time in twenty-four hours he tendered his government's resignation. This time, however, the King raised no objections, beyond expressing the hope that MacDonald would help 'in the formation of a National Government' which, he felt sure, would be supported by both the Conservatives and Liberals.

At 11.55 the following morning, a brief statement was issued by the Press Association: 'His Majesty the King invited the Prime Minister, Mr Stanley Baldwin, and Sir Herbert Samuel to Buckingham Palace this morning, and the formation of a National Government is under consideration.'

That night MacDonald noted in his diary: '4.10 . . . formally resigned and kissed hands on accepting to form a Govt. This is a lonely job.'

8

To Nationalize the Solar System

'Why cannot the leaders of the Labour Party face the fact that they
are not sectaries of an outworn creed, mumbling moss-grown,
demi-semi Fabian Marxism, but the heirs of eternal Liberalism?' –
J. M. Keynes, *New Statesman*, January 1939

Ultimately, the bankers had their way. A National Government
was formed, led by MacDonald, with Snowden at the Treasury,
and the stringent economic measures demanded by the financial
markets were imposed. In economic terms the crisis was over but
at punishing cost to the unemployed. As to who were the guilty
men, that remains a matter for debate. At the time, it seemed
more clear cut. The labour movement was riven by controversy,
although few had any sympathy for MacDonald. It was damning
enough that he had betrayed the electorate, but to have surren-
dered their interest to the City, as the *Daily Herald* asserted, was
a betrayal too far.

Only three colleagues of any substance joined MacDonald in
the political wilderness – Snowden, Thomas and Lord Sankey –
and on 28 August he was expelled from the party, and Herbert
Morrison turned his photograph to the wall at the offices of the
London Labour Party.

Apparently incapable of understanding the damage he had
inflicted on the party, or the bitterness that his betrayal had
caused, MacDonald was to write forty-eight hours after the fall of
the Labour government: 'My worst fear re desertion of Party
realised. We are like marooned sailors on a dreary island.' He was
to turn on his critics at the news that he might be asked to resign
his parliamentary seat: 'The desertion of colleagues & the flight of
the Lab Govt having grievous effect . . . If this is the best that
Labour can do, then it is not fit to govern except in the calmest
of weathers. Not only do I lose my seat, but I lose my confidence.'

As Snowden was to record, however, MacDonald was quick to console himself with the thought that as a reward for his betrayal 'every Duchess in London will be wanting to kiss him'. As for Snowden, the reception he received on introducing his emergency budget, which included a 10 per cent cut in Unemployment Benefit, was to justify his perfidy: 'Having unfolded a scheme of heavy sacrifices to balance his Budget, Mr Snowden sat down with the cheers of the United Unionists and Liberals ringing in his ears . . . It was an amazing scene. The House has known many changes, but surely none as dramatic as this one.'

Two months after forming the National Government Mac-Donald went to the country as leader of an anti-Labour alliance. Cosseted by the Tories and Liberals, he turned on the party he had once led to imply that to vote Labour would be to betray Britain's interests and to call for 'a doctor's mandate' that would place Britain's credit and reputation 'on a basis which will be unassailable for many long years to come'. It set the tone for all that was to follow, a campaign in which Labour was to be portrayed as 'the squandermaniac Party' and Snowden was to make a virtue of his apostasy: 'Every day from the first day of the election campaign to the eve of the poll I launched attacks on my late Labour colleagues.' G. D. H. Cole was later to suggest that the venom of Snowden's attacks was largely responsible for the enormity of Labour's subsequent defeat, the National Government (a coalition of Tories, Liberals of various persuasions and the so-called National Labour Party) winning 554 seats and Labour returning only fifty-two MPs.

There could be no disguising the extent of the débâcle. Even before the election, however, there were signs that MacDonald's and Snowden's defection had prompted Labour to examine its policies. For a decade and more it had played along with gradualism, yet seemingly this was the pass to which gradualism had led, to a humiliating and calamitous compromise with exactly the forces that the party had been created to oppose. The full disenchantment of the experience was captured by Jimmy Maxton at the party conference in October held in the shadow of the forth-coming election. For as long as he had sat in the House, and for all his doubts about its efficacy, Maxton had subscribed to Mac-Donald's agenda, but now:

> We are no longer frightened by the term Socialism. We must affirm
> it more than ever before in this coming election as an alternative
> to the crushing burdens of the vicious and foolish system of capi-
> talism which has produced poverty in the midst of plenty. In face
> of these facts I ask you unanimously to confirm your Socialist faith.

And it was a maiden speech by a newcomer to the conference that was to reassert this faith: 'We are not here to do hospital work to the Juggernaut of Capitalism. We are here to stop that Juggernaut from his progress through the world . . . The one thing that is *not inevitable now is gradualness.*'

The Webbs would have appreciated the irony, for the speaker was Beatrice's nephew Sir Stafford Cripps. At the age of forty-two he was already caricatured for his ascetic lifestyle (his service with the Red Cross during the First World War had destroyed his diges-tive system and compelled him to adopt an austere vegetarian diet). Churchill was later to mock Cripps's demeanour of pitch-pine-and-carbolic sanctity, remarking: 'There but for the grace of God goes God.' Dismissive of all talents but his own, Churchill's barb could not disguise the respect in which he held the polemi-cal skills of his opponent, the Wykehamist who had won a schol-arship to Oxford to study chemistry but who had abandoned the subject to read for the Bar, to become Britain's youngest King's Counsellor in 1927.

Elected an MP in January 1931, to be appointed Solicitor Gen-eral within weeks of his arrival in the Commons, Cripps had already been marked out as a coming man, and not only by Mac-Donald. The Countess of Warwick, widely known as the Red Countess, was a radical legend in her own lifetime. One of the most beautiful women in Britain, her marriage to the eldest son of the Earl of Warwick in 1881 had consolidated her social position. Then she met Robert Blatchford, editor of the SDF weekly *The Clarion* and author of the best-selling socialist handbook *Merrie England*: 'The next day I sent for ten pounds worth of book on Socialism. I got the name of an old Professor of Economics and under him I started my period of study without delay.'

More than thirty years later, in April 1931, the Countess was to hold the first of a series of house parties for a galaxy of intellectuals who were to bestride the left during the inter-war years, among them Harold Laski, G. D. H. Cole, R. H. Tawney, Clement Attlee, D. N. Pritt, J. N. Brailsford, Aneurin Bevan and Stafford Cripps. Devised to secure the adoption of 'a well-considered Socialist policy'. Cripps and Laski soon came to dominate the activities of the newly formed Society for Socialist Enquiry and Propaganda. Although never numbering more than 3,000 members, the society, quickly renamed the Socialist League in tribute to William Morris, was to replace the ILP as the forcing ground of socialism.

Since their 1930 conference, when delegates had declared that the ILP was 'an independent Socialist organisation . . . having a distinctive position within the Labour Party', a break between the two parties had become virtually inevitable. Almost forty years had passed since Keir Hardie had succeeded in cajoling and browbeating a motley of socialist factions to meet in Bradford and agree to the creation of an Independent Labour Party committed to 'the collective ownership and control of the means of production, distribution and exchange'.

Forty years on it seemed that the goal remained as distant as ever, the more so since the second Labour government had come into office. And as MacDonald's government moved inexorably to the right, the ILP responded by indicting the entire party programme and demanding an end to gradualism: 'We must concentrate upon securing and retaining such power that we will be able to carry through the decisive changes from Capitalism to Socialism without fear of effective interruption or obstruction . . . This policy inevitably means a break with the gradualism of the Labour Party.'

The issue was as clear cut as that, a challenge that the Labour leadership could not ignore. Racked by crisis, loyalty to the party was at a premium, yet it was loyalty to a programme to which Maxton and his dwindling band of radicals found it increasingly difficult to subscribe. The sense of *déjà vu* was compelling, of having compromised their principles not once but so many time since Keir Hardie had accepted that the Labour Party would always be a marriage of ideological convenience. And in 1932, after a decade of bitter wrangling over the custody of socialism, the partnership was annulled, for the ILP to quit the party it had largely been responsible for creating in 1893.

As far as the leadership of the Labour Party was concerned it was a parting that caused few regrets. Labour could no longer tolerate the existence of a party within a party, more especially when its policies clashed so often with its own. For while MacDonald had gone, those who replaced him shared his distrust of the left, even if, paradoxically, the new leader of the parliamentary party, George Lansbury, was to wonder at the extent of his previous innocence when he met MacDonald in 1932: 'I came away terribly distressed that a man with his mentality should have led us for so many years. He could never have believed in civil liberty or socialism. His whole mind is one web of tortuous conservatism. He has no solid root or belief anywhere except, perhaps, in a lingering kind of Protestant faith as expounded by John Knox.'

The attack is all the more remarkable having come from one of the most generous and gentle men ever to serve the Labour Party. At the age of seventy-two Lansbury had been appointed stopgap leader of a party machine that was increasingly dominated by three men, each of whom had little patience with what they regarded as the ideological pretensions of the ILP or its successor, the Socialist League: Hugh Dalton, Herbert Morrison and Ernest Bevin.

The son of a former tutor of George V, Dalton was educated at Eton and Cambridge and was appointed a lecturer at the London School of Economics at the end of the First World War, where his personal antipathy to J. M. Keynes did nothing to prevent his conversion to Keynesian views. An inveterate gossip, with an avid taste for intrigue, Dalton's aversion to anything to the left of his own opinions may well have been reinforced by his anti-Semitism, as personified by Harold Laski, whom he referred to as 'that undersized Semite' and whose radical opinions he damned as 'yideology'.

The contest between Dalton and the other two members of the triad that managed the Labour Party during its time of troubles could not have been more marked. As proud of his Cockney birthright as he was of his self-educated skills, Herbert Morrison was to win the first of his three elections as MP for Hackney in 1923, but it was his time as leader of the London County Council during the 1930s that not only shaped his political character but refined his administrative skills. And, as the years progressed, the latter tempered the former to make an administrator of the politician who regarded efficiency to be on a par with ideology.

This was where Bevin and Morrison agreed to differ, often bitterly. Although both men subscribed to the gospel of 'sensible socialism', as opposed to its 'impossibilist' variants, socialism for Bevin was more a matter of emancipating workers from the stigma of inferiority in a class-ridden society than of planning for the effective management of the New Jerusalem. In fact, it may well have been Bevin's innate sense of inferiority – of the former van driver who had made good to become the undisputed boss of one of Britain's most powerful unions – that accounted for his abiding hostility to the 'superior class attitude' of the party's left-wing intellectuals, although not for the streak of bullying anti-Semitism that he shared with Dalton.

Yet it was Bevin who was invited to become the first chairman of the Socialist League in the hope that he would be able to mobilize the unions behind the league's radical programme. It was a misjudgement on the part of both parties. For the league, Bevin was to become one of its most punishing critics. For Bevin, the experience was to fortify his conviction that 'intellectuals of the left were people who stabbed you in the back', for:

the difference between intellectuals and trade unions is this: You have no responsibility, and can fly off at a tangent as the wind takes you. We, however, must be consistent, and we have a great amount of responsibility. We cannot wake up in the morning and get a brain wave, when father says 'turn' and half a million people turn automatically. That does not work.

The fault line based, on the one hand, on the unions' distrust of the intelligentsia, on the other, of the intelligentsia's illusions about the working class, compounded the already strained relations between left and right at the Labour Party conference in 1932 – the same week in which the Socialist League was formally launched. The ILP may have gone, but its spirit lived on, Bevin reflecting: 'I do not believe that the Socialist League will vary very much from the old ILP attitude.' He was to be proved wrong in one respect – the league was committed to remaining within the Labour Party – but right in another – the animus that the league was to bring to the debate about the future of socialism following the débâcle of 1931.

While Morrison was fighting off the league's call for 'worker control', and Dalton was busy recruiting a new generation of young intellectuals (among them Hugh Gaitskell and Douglas Jay) to campaign against 'the melodramatics of the Socialist League', Laski and Cripps were challenging the entire basis of the party's gradualist agenda. Iconoclasts, as cavalier with political reputations as they were careless of the sensitivity of the unions, their full-frontal assault on the conservatism of the Labour establishment was to provoke an equally vituperative response from its apologists and prompt Dalton to write in his memoirs of a dream he had at the time: 'a dream in which he saw himself at a Labour Party conference moving a resolution to nationalise the Solar System. This was at first regarded as a brilliant idea, but towards the close of the debate a Socialist Leaguer got up at the back of the hall and moved an amendment to add the words "and the Milky Way".'

It was not so much a dream as a nightmare, for during the early

1930s the league was to haunt Labour's consciousness, more especially for the mounting ferocity of its attack on what Cripps and Laski had come to regard as a magic circle of power – legislature, crown and capital – that colluded to promote the illusion of a liberal democracy in order to perpetuate its own hegemony. Nothing was explicit, all was implied, a gentlemen's agreement to secure what Tawney called 'our religion of inequality' in the interests of the power elite. The analysis infuriated Dalton and the right wing of the party. Seemingly nothing was sacrosanct, not even the foundations of the party itself, for in providing a reasoned case for extra-parliamentary action it appeared that Laski and Cripps were undermining Labour's whole carefully constructed edifice of gradualism.

Even before the league's formal inauguration Cripps had been at the eye of a storm over whether or not he had declared that 'the day of evolutionary socialism was past, and the day of revolution, according to the manner of the Russian revolution, was now the political credo of the party'. Although Cripps was quick to deny the statement, smacking as it did of republicanism, it none the less gave notice that the league was in no mood to compromise with political correctness. It seemed to Dalton that in attacking the basis of the constitutional settlement, traditionally a political no-go area, Laski and Cripps were alienating precisely the constituency that the party was attempting to capture, a project of which Laski was to write dismissively: 'The right wing [Dalton, Morrison, etc.] are determined to make a party which will win Liberal votes at any cost . . . They will sacrifice everything and everybody to that.'

To Laski, Dalton was 'the Devil in the Labour Party', and it was Dalton's diabolism that he sought to exorcize. Once described as 'Everyone's favourite socialist', Laski's first contact with syndicalism while at Oxford, and a subsequent brief spell as a leader writer on the *Daily Herald*, were to help shape his radical outlook. Quite possibly the model for the hero of H. G. Wells's novel *Men Like Gods*, Laski spent four years lecturing at Harvard before joining the staff of the London School of Economics in 1920, to become Professor of Political Science at the University of London in 1926. Laski was more, much more than one of those 'desiccated intellectuals' that Bevin and the unions despised, however. A passionate man, he was deeply engaged by the crisis of the times and was not so much repelled as outraged by what he regarded as MacDonald's betrayal of 1931.

His contempt for MacDonald ('He is leading the gentlemen of England, and there is no price he would not pay for that') was matched by his conviction as to the unconstitutional role that George V had played in the downfall of the second Labour government: 'The new Cabinet was born of a Palace revolution . . . The Crown has rarely exerted so profound an influence in modern times.' It was to provide a rich source of speculation for the conspiracy theorists of the left, who were indifferent to the truth or otherwise of the charge, and became a launch pad for Cripps and Laski to mount a sustained attack on 'the illusion of democracy'. In 1933 Cripps wrote the league pamphlet *Can Socialism Come by Constitutional Methods?* to which Laski provided an extended reply in *Democracy in Crisis*.

The work was a political *tour de force*. Deploying all his forensic skills, Laski maintained that there could be no compromise between capitalism and socialism, no middle way 'between the motives of private profit and public service that it can continue half slave and half free'. Yet if an electoral victory for left-wing socialism were to threaten 'the possessing class', it was improbable that it would 'meekly abdicate' its power and privileges. On the contrary, there was every likelihood that it would mobilize 'all the essential weapons available' – the armed forces, the judiciary, the press, the educational system, the bureaucracy – to secure its authority:

> Under such conditions the suspension of the Constitution is inevitable. The government would then have to rule by the Defence of the Realm Act, which made it as certain as things can be in human affairs that its will would prevail. In these circum-

187

stances it appears that the resultant exacerbation of temper would produce the normal revolutionary situation, and men would rapidly group themselves for civil war.

Bleak as it was, it was a scenario to which much of the left wing of the party subscribed, including one as yet little-known MP, Clement Attlee. Memories of the catastrophic Gallipoli campaign, in which he had been severely wounded, may well have conditioned his reflection that the moment for any incoming Labour government to strike should be the moment it took power: 'The blow struck must be a fatal one and not merely designed to turn a sullen and obstructive opponent into an active and deadly enemy.' Cripps was to echo the message, to the fury of his opponents:

> When the Labour Party comes to power they must act rapidly and it will be necessary to deal with the House of Lords and the influence of the City of London. There is no doubt that we shall have to overcome opposition from Buckingham Palace and other places as well . . . There must not be time to allow the forces outside to gather and to exercise their influence upon the Legislature before the key points of capitalism have been transferred to the control of the State.

A letter to the *Daily Sketch* suggested that Cripps's choler was the product of his vegetarian diet. Others were not so generous. The establishment was incensed, as was the right wing of the Labour Party. Cripps and the league he represented were liabilities to the party, to be sterilized if not expunged, Dalton reflecting: 'This man is really becoming a dangerous political lunatic. It may become a duty to prevent him from holding any influential position in the party.'

Once again a breach had opened at the heart of the labour movement, to mock the comrades' protestations of amity. By 1933, however, the rift within the party was already being overshadowed by a more ominous development – the forward march of fascism – which, in its turn, was to precipitate new divisions within the party itself.

In August 1922 Benito Mussolini marched on Rome to declare: 'The century of democracy is over.' In January 1933 Adolf Hitler became Chancellor of Germany and proclaimed six months later: 'The National Socialist Workers' Party constitutes the only political party in Germany.' Even then there was already clear evidence of the Nazis' intentions, Victor Gollancz publishing an extraordinary exposé of the new regime's barbarity, *The Brown Book of the Hitler Terror*, 'Prepared by the World Committee for the Victims of German Fascism', in the autumn of 1933. As Lord Marley was to write in the preface: 'These manifestations of Fascism are appalling. But the memory of the public is short, and public opinion is unfortunately only too ready to reconcile itself to a *fait accompli*, as in the case of Italy.'

It was not so much public memory as political indecision that was to paralyse the Western democracies in the years immediately ahead. Only the Soviet government, faced with Hitler's stated intention of stamping out communism in all its forms ('The diabolical doctrine of Marxism must perish miserably on the battlefield of the National Socialist revolution'), reacted positively, calling for a united front in the face of the fascist menace. To European social democrats, increasingly aware of the fate of dissidents in the Soviet Union, the choice appeared to be between two totalitarian evils, while as far as the Labour Party was concerned Moscow's appeal, faithfully echoed by its mouthpiece, the Communist Party of Great Britain, smacked of entryism.

On the last day of his visit to Moscow in 1931 George Bernard Shaw may have lauded the regime ('Tomorrow I leave this land of hope and return to our Western countries of despair'), but the Labour leadership was not so naive. For almost a decade the party had resisted the Communist Party's attempt to infiltrate the party; now it appeared that it was adopting a back-door means for achieving its ends. While the ILP sided with the communists in calling for a united front, the Labour Party would have no part in their dealings, declaring: 'If the British working class hesitate now between majority and minority rule and toys with the idea of Dictatorship, Fascist or Communist, they will go down to servitude such as they have never suffered.'

Many on the left regarded the resolution as a specious defence of an indefensible position. Justified as Labour's fears of communism were, they none the less compromised the party's response to fascism. In lieu of a more resolute policy Labour intensified its campaign to proscribe any organization acting under communist influence, urging its affiliated societies to have no dealings with such bodies. And while Mosley, now leader of the British Union of Fascists, was staging the first of his demonstrations in London and the Germans were storming out of the Disarmament Conference in Geneva, the Labour Party was holding its annual conference in Hastings. Immediately it seemed that a degree of unanimity had been achieved in response to the threat of fascism. The appearance, however, was deceptive.

Two resolutions had been listed for debate, the first tabled by the National Executive Committee declaring that the party 'favoured the total disarmament of all nations throughout the world and the creation of an International Police Force' and proposing immediate cuts in arms expenditure; the second by the Socialist League pledging the party 'to take no part in war' and calling on it to consider employing the General Strike weapon if war should threaten.

Almost two decades had passed since Keir Hardie had issued much the same rallying call in Trafalgar Square on 2 August 1914, and it was Sir Charles Trevelyan, a one-time Labour minister, who caught the echo of those distant but still well-remembered days:

> At no time has there been such a black outlook in the world. The great instrument of keeping the peace, the League of Nations, some day will be the machinery for international safety, but it will be when

hearts are different and when governments are different. The resolution is one of action . . . The rulers must know that if war comes
they will fight with a divided nation. They can make their bourgeois
wars themselves, but they will make it without the workers.

The words were Trevelyan's, their inspiration those of Laski
and Cripps. Before the conference began Morrison had condemned Laski's habit of playing 'the loud pedal' when condemning the fascist dictatorships, 'the soft pedal' when condemning
their communist counterparts. It was Cripps's rationale, however,
that gave substance to the league's resolution: that war was the
inescapable product of capitalism and as fascism was the logical
outcome of capitalism, its emergence presaged war.

Significantly, the leader of the Parliamentary Labour Party,
George Lansbury, a lifelong pacifist, remained silent throughout
the debate, leaving Arthur Henderson, 'Uncle Arthur' as he was
known throughout the labour movement, to make a plea on behalf
of the Disarmament Conference he chaired in Geneva. For thirty
years a Labour MP, twenty-three of which he had been Secretary
of the party, Henderson was awarded the Nobel Peace Prize in
1934 when prospects for peace were already fading. Yet, slight as
the hopes were, Labour continued to vest them in the League of
Nations while toughening its stance against calls for a united front.

As the rift in the movement widened, so the debate grew
increasingly acerbic, to explode at the party conference of 1934.
During the summer the National Executive Committee had proscribed the Relief Committee for Victims of German and Austrian
Fascism as a communist front organization and proposed to expel
any party member who had connections with the committee, most
notably Harold Laski. Quick to protest that the move was designed
to protect 'the good name of the Labour Party', rather than from
'a desire for heresy hunting', Morrison indicted Laski as a political
innocent from whom other innocents deserved protection.

Beyond one low-flying jibe at Morrison ('the High Archbishop
of Orthodoxy in this movement'), Laski's reply was comparatively

restrained. Not so that of Aneurin Bevan, who had worked as a fund-raiser for the Relief Committee. Challenging the principle that 'in the future it is not membership of an organisation which is wrong but *association* with members of proscribed organisations', Bevan denounced the party executive for its 'inertia, lack of enterprise and insipidity' in allowing the communists to take the lead in combating Mosley's fascism, to conclude that in such circumstances it was not surprising that any Labour member who wanted a more active policy should associate with anyone who gave them a lead. Ernest Bevin was incensed. His namesake had been infected with the pretentious nonsense of those with whom he associated. In a furious tirade he denounced Bevan and the league for disloyalty to the movement and for trying to split the party. When Bevan appealed to the chair for protection, it redoubled Bevin's vehemence:

> Apparently my namesake can get on this platform and denounce the Executive, and he is so thin-skinned that he cannot take his own medicine. No, in this Conference, Aneurin Bevan, you are not going to get the flattery of the gossip columns that you get in London. You are going to get the facts . . . When people get on this platform and talk about liberty of association, remember the times we are living in. With the voice of dictatorship on every side, I hope that there is sufficient discipline in this Party . . . that everybody will stand four square against every attempt to divide us.

With the block votes of the unions secure, the National Executives' resolution was carried by an overwhelming majority. Ironically, Cripps was elected to the twenty-two-member executive shortly after the conference, the unions and the party establishment subscribing to the view that if it was impossible to contain dissent, it might be possible to absorb it. In practice, it proved otherwise. While the party continued to support the League of Nations' policy of collective security, Cripps combined his critique of 'the ring of capitalist power' with his attack on the league which reflected 'the inevitable conflicts of the capitalist system' to sap at the party line. In the summer of 1935, however, his case was seriously weakened with the publication of the so-called Peace Ballot.

The ballot was organized by the League of Nations Union, and more than 11 million of the 11.5 million respondents voted in favour of Britain remaining a member of the league, while nearly 10.5 million favoured 'an all-round reduction in armaments by international agreement'. Seemingly Labour's policy of 'preventing war by organizing peace' reflected the public's mood, but as far as the party was concerned what unity had been achieved was to be exposed at the Brighton conference later in the year. In North Africa Italian forces were already grouping on the borders of Abyssinia, and for two days the delegates indulged in a debate of unrestrained ferocity over what measures, if any, should be adopted to check the fascist menace.

Dalton opened for the Executive, asserting that the party was 'firmly united in its opposition to the policy of imperialist aggression' and calling on the government 'to use all necessary measures provided by the [league's] Covenant to prevent Italy's unjust and rapacious attack on the territory of a fellow member of the league', notably by the application of sanctions, Cripps's and the Socialist's League's distrust of the government, however, were matched only by their suspicion that the League of Nations was conniving to further the interests of the Western democracies. Before the conference opened, Cripps resigned from the National Executive, allowing him to mount a searing attack on the league's impartiality ('I cannot rid my mind of the sordid history of capitalist deception . . . events have satisfied me that the League of Nations has become nothing but a tool of satiated Imperialist powers') and to question the rationale of sanctions:

> When economic sanctions are applied a state of war automatically exists, and we must be prepared to defend these sanctions against military attack. Whether we call it military sanctions or war matters not. It is the same thing. That means the use by our gov-

ernment of the workers for military action against their fellow workers, in this case of Italy.

For all Cripps's forensic skills, this was not something the conference wished to hear, one delegate protesting: 'Let those who won't observe the decisions of the party get out'; another declaring that Cripps was 'the most colourful figure which the workers of this country have produced since Mosley', and Clement Attlee asserting that he did not believe that sanctions against Mussolini would lead to war.

But if Cripps incensed the conference, George Lansbury was to leave it confused. At seventy-six, a sick, tired man, he had led the parliamentary party for four years, and delegates fell silent as he climbed to the platform sensing that like some veteran from the theatre of politics this could well be his final appearance. The previous December he had written to Cripps: 'I am often very, very lonely, except for the persistent faith that that which we think of as God is all around us', and now he was to reiterate his faith in pacifism to rack the party he led:

> When I was sick and on my back, ideas came into my head, and one was that the only thing worthwhile for old men to do is at least to say the thing they believe and at least try to warn the young of the dangers of force and compulsion . . . It is said that people like me are irresponsible. I am no more irresponsible as leader than the greatest trade union leader in this country . . . If mine was the only voice in the conference, I would say in the name of the faith I hold, the belief I have that God intended us to live peaceably and quietly with one another – if some people do not allow us to do so, I am ready to stand as the early Christians did and say 'This is our faith, this is where we stand and if necessary, this is where we will die.'

Only seventeen years had passed since the end of the First World War, and the memories of that holocaust still bruised the delegates' minds. Sentiment had no place in Bevin's agenda, however, and he was on his feet even before the applause for Lansbury had died away.

> Let me remind the delegates that when George Lansbury says what
> he said today, it is rather too late to say it, and I hope that this
> Conference will not be influenced either by sentiment or personal
> attachment. I hope that you will carry no resolution of an emer-
> gency character telling a man like Lansbury what he ought to do.
> If he finds that he ought to take a certain course, then his con-
> science should direct him as to the course he should take . . . It is
> placing the Executive and the Movement in an absolutely wrong
> position to be hawking your conscience round from body to body
> to be told what you ought to do with it.

Accustomed as they were to the savagery of the brotherhood,
even the delegates were shocked by the venom of Bevin's attack.
All the personal rancour and ideological poison that bedevilled
socialism was there, and while Bevin was to write later, 'I go away
from conference after thirty five years of labouring with a sad heart.
I have lived through three splits in the movement and I do not
want any more', he offered no apology to Lansbury. The charge that
Bevin was the voice of the unions was never more true than at the
party conference of 1935. Lansbury's pacifism and the league's
rationale were brushed aside by 2,168,000 votes to 102,000, in large
part through the deployment of the union block vote.

At the close of the debate Lansbury resigned as chairman of
the parliamentary party, to be replaced by what the power-brokers
regarded as another stopgap leader: Clement Attlee. Self-effacing
to the point of transparency, Attlee was the product of a conven-
tional middle-class upbringing. Destined for the Bar, a visit to
London's East End in 1905 marked the beginnings of his transformation from a model of his class to a socialist with distinctly
radical sympathies. Apart from the war, when he rose to the rank
of Major, Attlee was to spend much of the next seventeen years in
Stepney, becoming Mayor of the borough in 1919 and MP for the
Limehouse constituency in 1922. This was the 'sheep in sheep's

clothing' of Churchill's description who was to succeed Mosley as Chancellor of the Duchy of Lancaster in MacDonald's ill-starred administration and the 'very small' man of Dalton's contempt who was to play a modest role in the tumultuous history of the Socialist League.

It may well have been this that recommended Attlee for the leader's post, that he appeared to threaten no one, least of all the ambitions of Dalton and Morrison. What reservations that they may have had were allayed by the knowledge that Attlee's tenure in office was likely to be short-lived, for in October 1935 the National Government went to the country on a platform of being true friends of the League of Nations, which was committed to making collective security work. While Labour tripled its previous representation, winning 154 seats, and the National Labour Party led by MacDonald was reduced to a rump of eight Members, the National Government, now led by Stanley Baldwin, was returned to power with 420 seats, 387 of which were Tory.

Within days of the House reassembling, the newly elected MPs met to chose a leader. Dalton managed Morrison's campaign, but Morrison's reputation for being a 'a bit too ambitious' – if not for his own good then for that of the party – militated against him, and on the second ballot Attlee was elected by a comfortable majority. Beatrice Webb was disparaging: 'the irreproachable and colourless Attlee elected chairman of the Parliamentary Labour Party . . . a somewhat diminutive and meaningless figure to represent the British labour movement in the House of Commons', and Dalton was to echo her sentiments: 'A wretched, disheartening result. And a little mouse shall lead them!' He would have done better to have reflected on the Elizabethan proverb that 'It had need to be a wily mouse, that should breed in a cat's ear.'

In 1937 Attlee was to write in *The Labour Party in Perspective*:

> During all these years [since he had first joined the party] there has never been a time when there were not questionings in the ranks and suggestions of breakaway movements . . . I have seen a

good many leaders of revolt arise, and very often I have seen them meet themselves coming back . . . There is today as much criticism of the Labour Party as ever, especially from those whose enthusiastic desires make official policy and action appear too slow. I am glad that this should be so. Self-criticism is a healthy thing so long as it does not lead to a paralysis of the will.

Even before he wrote, Attlee's toleration of dissent had been severely tested. In the early summer of 1936 Germany's occupation of the Rhineland in breach of the territorial provisions of the Treaty of Versailles was followed by the fall of the Abyssinian capital, Addis Ababa, to the Italians. Contemptuous of the League of Nations and the farrago of collective security, the fascist powers placed no limits on their ambitions. The Baldwin government, however, was pleased to accept Hitler's assurance that 'We have no territorial demands to make in Europe.' That mounting evidence of the Third Reich's martial intentions contradicted his words made little difference. It was a lie that the Western democracies wished to hear and one that was to compound the existing confusion within the Labour Party.

At national level, the party responded to the advance of fascism by reaffirming its support for the League of Nations and asserting that only a well-armed system of pooled security could hold the dictators in check. The parliamentary party agreed, while continuing to oppose any increase in arms expenditure on the grounds that 'no case has yet been made out for the vast commitments into which the Government were entering'. Only the constituency parties responded positively, calling for an anti-fascist crusade, a call that chimed in with the Socialist League's campaign for the formation of a United Front. To a party member such as Jack Clayton of Bury it was very much a case of 'You pays your money, and you takes your choice', a fractious lucky dip, while the news of the outbreak of the civil war in Spain only added to the confusion.

Although it was clear by August 1936 that both the Germans and the Italians were underwriting Franco's insurrection, the

British government was the prime mover in the establishment of a Non-Intervention Committee, which as Hugh Thomas, the historian of the Spanish Civil War, has written, 'was to graduate from equivocation to hypocrisy and humiliation and which was to last out the Civil War'. The full measure of Labour's disarray over exactly what policies should be adopted to contain this new eruption of fascism was thrown into sharp relief at the party conference in Edinburgh in October.

A highly ambiguous resolution tabled by the parliamentary party told the delegates everything, except what they wanted to know: whether or not the party would go on opposing the government's plans for rearmament. To Dalton the resolution meant one thing, to Morrison another. To Bevin, neither Dalton nor Morrison's interpretations were acceptable, while Cripps declared his total opposition to any measure that armed capitalist governments. In closing the debate Attlee added to the confusion by implying that only the parliamentary party could untangle the knot the parliamentary party had tied – and that would have to wait until Parliament reassembled.

Only the right-wing press took comfort from what Laski regarded as the ineptitude of the leadership at Edinburgh ('They provided no sense of direction, no clarity of purpose'), to place their own interpretation on the outcome of the debate, the *Daily Mail* (singled out by Morrison as the only paper accurately to cover the debate) reporting:

> Everyone has watched a flock of sheep driven through a five-barred gate – how they blunder and jostle, butt each other's ribs, shy from the entry at the last minute and then make a sudden clumsy bolt to get safely in. The process reminds us of what happened yesterday at the Socialist Conference at Edinburgh. After baulking and prancing and hoofing each other and giving vent to loud baas that sounded like 'collective security', the delegates – thanks to hot and trying work by Dr Dalton and other flockmasters – have been marshalled into the rearmament fold.

The *Labour Monthly* disagreed, vehemently, and not only on the key issue of rearmament:

> All the forces of capitalism are overjoyed at the result of the Edinburgh Conference. They see in the decisions . . . alike on Spain, on arms, on unity, a further step to the destruction of the Labour Party as an effective opposition force, and a check to the rising wave of working class unity.

The writer deceived himself. The unity he applauded was notional. As early as July the Communist Party had been actively campaigning for positive aid for the Spanish workers, as they were later to be primarily responsible for organizing the British contingent to the International Brigade. At Edinburgh the Communist Party's application for affiliation to the Labour Party was rejected for the umpteenth time, but the renewed prescription did nothing to gainsay the appeal of the communists' ongoing campaign for the creation of a united front against fascism – least of all to Cripps and Laski and the Socialist League.

Disheartened by the trade union bias of the *Daily Herald* and its subordination to the party machine, a handful of left-wingers, including Laski, Cripps, Bevan and William Mellor (one-time editor of the *Herald*) launched the weekly *Tribune* in January 1937. Cripps wrote in the first issue:

> We are often urged to make good resolutions on the first of January. They seldom last long, if made, because so often they are about small things that concern our private welfare. Today I ask you to write this resolution: I pledge to my fellow workers throughout the world my faith to strive increasingly to work for unity as a step to power, by which power the workers shall control their lives in peace and security.

Cripps's resolution mocked the unity that he solicited. *Tribune*, quickly dubbed 'Cripps's Chronicle', represented a direct challenge to the Labour establishment and provided a powerful plat-form for the launch of a Unity Campaign at the end of January. The essence of the campaign was that the Communist Party, the Socialist League and the remnants of the ILP should collaborate in 'the struggle against fascism, reaction and war, and against the National government' and in the process seek 'the return of a Labour government as the next stage in the advance of working-class power'. It was not so much the ambition that the Labour Party leadership anathematized, more the method of achieving it. Once again, it seemed that the Communist Party was bent on infiltrating the movement, but since Labour had spent almost two decades demonizing the party's very existence there could be no compromising with it now.

As the Unity Campaign took to the road Labour's National Executive Committee moved swiftly to stamp out this new apos-tasy. On 27 January, while Cripps and Bevan were sharing the same platform with the communist leaders Harry Pollitt and Willie Gallagher in calling for a 'United Front of the Working Class to Fight Fascism and War', the Executive disaffiliated the Socialist League and declared that membership of the league was incompatible with membership of the Labour Party. The dissi-dents' choice was clear, and in May the league was formally dis-solved. The National Executive was still not satisfied. Laski might reflect that the Labour leadership was 'more anxious to attack their own left than to fight the government. There is no thinking in the party, and no conviction', but he was wrong. Whatever he might think of their convictions there was no questioning the party's determination to expunge all evidence of left-wing heresy from its ranks.

In February the National Executive announced that any mem-ber of the party who appeared on a public platform with either communists or members of the ILP would be expelled and seri-ously considered applying the sanction to Cripps, Bevan and Laski. In reply to a letter from Laski against taking such a dra-conian step, Attlee wrote: 'I fight all the time against heresy hunting, but the heretics seem to seek martyrdom.' Not that it was martyrdom that the dissidents were seeking, rather what they regarded as political realism, a recruit to their cause, G. D. H. Cole, recapitulating on their position in *The People's Front*:

> I have worked for nearly thirty years in the hope of a Labour majority, and I want to see a Labour majority very earnestly indeed . . . But I do not propose, whatever the Executive Committee of the Labour Party may say, to give up doing my best to bring about these two things which it greatly dislikes – a 'United Front' for the entire working class movement, and a 'Popular Front' or, as I prefer to call it, a 'People's Front', wide enough to include everyone who can be persuaded to accept a democratic and immediate programme in national and international politics, even if they cannot yet be got to accept the full Socialist creed.

As a member of the National Executive, Cole's testament was a direct challenge to its authority. The committee temporarily backed away from any further confrontation with the left, however, for it was facing troubles enough of its own. Again the issue was defence; and again Labour was divided. The issue of whether or not the party should support rearmament was bitterly fought out in mid-July. Whereas Attlee, Morrison and the party's deputy leader Arthur Greenwood all opposed such a volte-face, Dalton first succeeded in persuading the parliamentary party to reverse its previous policy and then, by abstaining from voting on the defence estimates, to support, albeit tacitly, the government's rearmament programme. While Michael Foot was to reflect later that this was 'as skilful a piece of backstage intrigue as Dalton ever executed', the *Daily Express* was to highlight the significance of Dalton's coup immediately after the debate:

> Old Etonian ex-Foreign Under-Secretary Dr Dalton and his powerful group of 'intellectuals' contend that, while they are asking the government to stand by 'collective security', it is illogical to deny

the country the forces with which to carry out that policy . . . And trade-union leaders add their weight to the arguments of Dr Dalton by making it plain that they are on the side of rearmament.

The *Express* was quick to point out, however, that the new-found rapport between Dalton's 'intellectuals' and the unions was likely to be short-lived. The paper's political editor, Guy Eden, was right in one respect, but it was with Cripps's coterie rather than Dalton's intellectuals that the unions were to clash at the party conference three months later. Although the party had resolved its differences on rearmament, the United Front continued to challenge its diktat.

Echoing Cripps, Bevan was to rail against all talk of rearmament ('The people of this country must be made to realise that the danger of war arises from this Government's refusal to mobilise the peace forces of the world'), but it was Cripps rather than his protégé who was the unions' main target, as Bevin made clear in a letter to Laski: 'You talk about driving Cripps out. Cripps is driving himself out . . . joining up with the Communists who are out to destroy the trade unions and then asking us, who have done nothing at all to warrant the attacks on us, to stand it for ever and to never hit back, you are asking too much.'

Secure in the knowledge of where power in the party ultimately lay, Bevin added: 'I do not think that Cripps will have a very big following.' At Bournemouth Bevan argued the United Front's case, declaring that collaborating with the government would lead 'to a voluntary totalitarian state with ourselves creating the barbed wire around', for it to be rubbished by the unions and go down to defeat by 2,670,000 to 228,000 votes. As Laski was to write later: 'The big battalions attacked us with fury', but for Bevin it proved to be a pyrrhic victory. Before conference ended a proposal by Dalton to increase the constituency's representation on the National Executive by two seats was carried against the vote of the unions – and Cripps and Laski were returned to the committee, to Bevin's barely concealed annoyance.

If Dalton was 'looking forward to a great cooperative venture by this new executive of all the talents' he was soon to be disappointed. As Cripps campaigned for a United Front, Laski questioned the basis of Labour's assumption that 'respectable behaviour on their part will eventually bring them to power', detecting in Bevin 'a liberal reformer whose principles are not really distinguishable from those of Lord Baldwin or Mr Lloyd George'. Laski was playing the old tunes over and over again, a nostalgic number in which socialism danced to the slow-slow-quick-quick-slow tempo of its union partners.

Seemingly, it had always been thus, and the more the unions appeared to dominate Labour policy (in January 1938 the National Executive rejected a proposal by Laski to boycott Japanese shipping on the grounds that this was union business) the harder Laski pushed to the left, to refine his previous critique of capitalism: 'The survival of political democracy today is definitely impossible unless it can conquer the central citadel economic power . . .' and to reassert his political faith: 'There cannot, in a word, be democracy unless there is socialism', and to warn of socialism's vulnerability to fascism: 'It is not improbable that civilisation may have to pass through an age of dictatorships which . . . will seek to inhibit the emergence of egalitarian institutions for the benefit of invested interests.'

By the spring of 1938 it appeared that Laski's age of dictatorships had arrived. Although the civil war was still raging in Spain, Franco formed his first government in January, provoking Cripps to mount one of his most ferocious attacks on the government's policy of appeasing the fascists:

> Whenever any restraint has nominally been put on both sides it has been effective against the Government of Spain but never been effective against the Rebels. . . . We are not ashamed to say that we urgently desire the Spanish Government to be victorious. It is only the other side who are ashamed to say what is a fact, that they anxiously desire to see the victory of General Franco.

Neville Chamberlain was unmoved. Since he had replaced Baldwin as Prime Minister in 1937 the government's policy of appeasement had become increasingly pronounced, and in April it was to turn a diplomatic blind eye to the German's annexation of Austria and to counsel the Czechs to adopt a concessionary policy towards German demands on their Sudetan province. What hopes the Labour had vested in the League of Nations were in ruins, and while Bevan was to charge the government with conniving 'to satisfy Germany's ambition at the expense of her near neighbours', the party issued a statement calling for 'a positive and unmistakable lead for collective defence against aggression and to safeguard peace'.

By then it was too late. On 30 September Chamberlain returned from a meeting with Hitler where he and the French Prime Minister, Daladier, had accepted Germany's demands for the annexation of the Sudetanland. A crowd had gathered outside Number 10 to sing 'For He's a Jolly Good Fellow' when Chamberlain appeared at a second-floor window and to applaud when he declared: 'My friends, this is the second time in our history that there has come back from Germany to Downing Street peace with honour. I believe it is peace in our time.' The following day German troops crossed the border into Czechoslovakia. Having tested their nerve, Hitler knew that he had little to fear from the appeasers of Britain and France.

And if it was too late to check Hitler's territorial ambitions, it was also too late to revive any thought of collective security. In March 1938 the Soviet Union had proposed a conference of powers to seek a means to check German aggression. Chamberlain dismissed the idea peremptorily; this may have encouraged the German Ambassador to report to Berlin the deep understanding shown by the British government for one essential aspect of German policy: 'namely to prevent the Soviet Union from deciding the destinies of Europe'. Perhaps Cripps's suspicion of the government's proto-fascist tendencies was right after all. Perhaps there was some substance to Bevan's charge that

Britain and France were employing Germany as a counterweight to the Soviet Union. All this is speculation, for the Ambassador's dispatch was only made public after the war.

Not that the government was alone in making a bogy of communism. Largely through pressure from the trade unions the party repudiated any suggestion of collaborating with the Soviet Union and was equally quick to anathematize the activities of the Popular Front aimed at mobilizing the forces of anti-fascism. Since 1936 the Communist Party of Great Britain had been campaigning on a similar platform, a dangerously subversive activity as far as Dalton and Bevin were concerned. The left disagreed. The time for political faction fighting had passed, and as crisis succeeded crisis in 1938 Cripps, Laski and Bevan abandoned their support for the United Front to campaign for a Popular Front embracing partners of all political persuasions, Liberals such as Lloyd George as well as disaffected Tories such as Churchill and Eden.

The Labour leadership was outraged, and Attlee scathing:

> The shift from the advocacy of a rigid and exclusive unity of the working classes to a demand for an alliance with the capitalists, and from the insistence on the need for a government to carry out a socialist policy to an appeal to put socialism in cold storage for the duration of the international crisis, is a remarkable phenomenon.

It was a phenomenon that was not be denied, however. In April Laski argued that such an alliance was essential to overthrow the government, even if 'Mr Lloyd George and Mr Churchill, notably, are simply British imperialists whose anti-fascism is much more a recognition that the dictators are a threat to the British empire than a recognition of the bankruptcy of capitalism'. On May Day Bevan was to call for 'the establishment of a Popular Front . . . under the leadership of the Labour Party', and five days later four members of the National Executive – Cripps, Laski, the barrister D. N. Pritt and the MP Ellen Wilkinson – submitted a memorandum to the committee commending the creation of the Popular Front. Only four votes were cast in its favour. The party was as leery of what it regarded as a front orga- nization for communism as it was hostile to any thought of power- sharing should Chamberlain's government fall.

Whether the National Executive's suspicions were justified, or its hopes of Labour being returned to power well founded, its reservations made little difference. Through the summer and into the autumn the Popular Front movement gained momentum, for one of its candidates, backed by the local Labour Party in defiance of the National Executive Committee, to be returned as MP for Bridgwater in November 1938. As the contest within the party intensified, Cripps maintained pressure on the Executive to reverse its original decision, mailing what was to become known as the 'Cripps Memorandum' to the Secretary of the party on 9 January 1939. His case was as persuasive – that Labour should 'come out boldly as the leader of a combined opposition to the National Government' – as his proposal was precise, that a Popu- lar Front should be created by:

> The party issuing a manifesto inviting the co-operation of every genuine anti-Goverment Party or group of individuals who would be willing to give support to:

> (1) The effective protection of the democratic rights, liberties and freedom of the British people from internal or external attack.

> (2) A positive policy of peace by collective action with France, Russia, the United States and other democratic countries for the strengthening of democracy against aggression.

Herbert Morrison was dismissive: the notion was so much moonshine. Dalton was contemptuous: Cripps had 'gone over- board'. Offered the chance of recanting his heresy at a meeting of the National Executive on 25 January 1939 Cripps refused and was expelled from the party by an eighteen-to-one vote. The decision tore the party apart. It had happened not once but many times before, and like some well-rehearsed and timeless ritual the party turned on itself in a public display of ideological blood-letting, as vicious as it was destructive.

Careless of what remained of party unity Cripps stomped the country promoting his newly launched Peace Petition ('In view of the evils that confront us, we urge you to combine to drive the National Government from office'), while Bevan rounded on the National Executive with all the eloquence at his command:

> If Sir Stafford Cripps is expelled for wanting to unite the forces of freedom and democracy, they can go on expelling others. They can expel me. His crime is my crime . . . He insisted that his constituents should be informed of his views. The Executive insisted that only their views should be heard. This is tantamount to a complete suppression of any opinion in the party which does not agree with that held by the Executive.

It was a view that was widely shared, among others by such supporters of his petition as Lloyd George, J. B. Priestley and J. M. Keynes, and not least by George Bernard Shaw, who was to fulminate in the *Daily Herald*:

> Sir Stafford Cripps proposed a Holy Alliance to get rid of the present Government as Napoleon was got rid of at Waterloo, by a mixed force of British, Belgiums and Prussians under an Irish General. If a Labour Member may not propose this he may not propose anything. But the Labour Party Executive, taking a leaf out of Herr Hitler's book, promptly expels Sir Stafford who, whether right or wrong, will presently wipe the floor with it for being so silly.

As the conflict intensified it became increasingly personal. Carefully orchestrated or not, the impression was created that Cripps was a simulacrum of Mosley, an egomaniac bent on power, Morrison declaring that Cripps was 'an indelicate manifestation of egotism' and a union member of the National Executive writing: 'By accident of birth, and a privileged capacity to earn a fabulous income, a privately controlled political machine is being created that gravely menaces the authority of the party.'

Certainly Cripps's behaviour did nothing to allay such suspicions, the *News Chronicle* reporting on his triumphal appearance at a meeting on 22 March: 'Rolling drums, four white spotlights across the darkened hall, and tremendous applause as he ascended to the white, solitary rostrum made the setting for Sir Stafford Cripps's speech at the petition rally in the Empress Hall, Earls Court last night.'

Four days later Mrs Edith Johnson was to write in *Labour Women*: 'I went to Cripps's meeting . . . It was one's worst Nazi nightmare come true.'

As the *Daily Sketch* commented: 'A strange madness has infected the Labour Party. It appears to be hellbent on blowing its brains out.' The madness was, indeed, infectious. By the end of March the National Executive had expelled Bevan, Sir Charles Trevelyan, George Strauss and two other rebels from the party, their application for readmission receiving the gnomic reply that it could not be considered for some considerable time in view of the gravity of the international situation. It was a puny excuse. At times it seemed that, as the storm clouds gathered over Europe, Cripps and the party preferred to feud amongst themselves rather than to confront the menace that each professed to abhor.

At the party conference in May the Popular Front motion was debated, to be defeated by 2,360,000 votes to 248,000, and on 10 June Cripps announced his intention of disbanding the movement. Less than three months later Britain was at war. The long weekend was over. For almost two decades the Labour Party had been at odds with itself. On 4 September 1939 it suspended hostilities for the duration of the war.

9
1945: Walking with Destiny

WINSTON CHURCHILL: There was a Parliamentary democracy in this country before the Labour Party was born.

ANEURIN BEVAN: There wasn't. There was a Parliament, but not a democracy. Your people were here, mine were not.

– House of Commons, 1949

The war in Europe ended on 7 May 1945, and three months later the Japanese sued for peace. The mood in Britain was euphoric, and the crowd that burned Hitler's effigy on a pile of ration books in Trafalgar Square were celebrating the future they had been promised as much as the victory they had won. This time there would be no mistakes, the war would not be allowed to win for a second time in a generation. Indeed memories of the flawed peace of 1919 and the bitter decades that followed had so radicalized Britain that the khaki election of July 1945 led to the outright rejection of Churchill's wartime coalition and the return of a Labour government with an overall majority of 148 seats.

But while the *Daily Herald* reflected on the prospects for a brave new world and Dalton noted in his diary: 'We felt exalted, dedicated, walking on air, walking with destiny', Clement Attlee was altogether more cautious, warning of 'the difficult days ahead'. Few, however, cared to listen. As early as 1940 *The Times* had modified its politics to such an extent that it could declare: 'If we speak of equality we do not speak of political equality nullified by social and economic privilege', while in 1942 the Beveridge report had not only targeted the 'Five Great Evils' of 'Want, Disease, Ignorance, Squalor and Idleness' but had advanced a comprehensive programme for their elimination.

Although fashioned by a Liberal it was a vision that Labour espoused – of building 'not for the glory of rulers or races but for the common man'. Their problem was to realize it. Converts as the party members were, to Keynesian economics, Keynes's theories provided few clues as to how to balance public expectations against the reality of a near-bankrupt economy. For the war had been won at punishing cost, more than £1,000 million of Britain's overseas assets having being sold, and over £13,000 million of external liabilities having been incurred (figures at 1945 prices). And this was not all. Almost half of Britain's merchant fleet had been lost through enemy action, while the country's exports were running at less than a third of the pre-war total.

This was the crisis of the peace, that Britain could ill afford the price of the victory she had helped to win. Yet within two years of taking office the Attlee government had succeeded in redeeming many, if not all, of its far-reaching election pledges. Indeed the pressure on the legislature was so intense that Mannie Shinwell at the Ministry of Fuel and Power wondered that it did not crack under the strain: 'We're working a twenty-five-hour day, but sure as hell, we're getting there.' And 1946 proved to be Labour's *Annus Mirabilis*: the year in which the foundations of the Welfare State were laid with the passage of the Industrial Injuries Act, the National Insurance Act and the National Health Service Act and the first tranche of its nationalization programme (involving the Bank of England, public transport and the mines) was ratified. Even Tories such as Walter Monckton were impressed, describing Labour's programme as 'a triumph of political will over economic adversity'. If 1946 proved to be Labour's *Annus Mirabilis*, however, Dalton was to describe 1947 as its *Annus Horrendus*.

Clement Attlee remains an enigma. How was it that a man once scorned by Dalton as the 'little mouse' and dismissed by Beatrice Webb as 'irreproachable and colourless' succeeded in imposing his authority on the talented but always fractious group of individuals who formed his post-war Cabinet: the union grandee Ernest Bevin, translated to the Foreign Office; the Tammany boss Herbert Morrison, Lord President of the Council; the narcissistic 'Daddy' Dalton, Chancellor of the Excheque, and the ascetic Stafford Cripps, President of the Board of Trade? Together with Attlee they were the Big Five of government. Driven men, jealous of their consequence, what they shared in common disguised their often rancorous personal differences, yet in little more than eighteen months they were the figures who transformed Britain's political landscape.

Possibly, it was their commitment to the goal they had set themselves of 'building the future' that momentarily tempered their enmities; possibly it was the magnitude of their undertaking that left them with little time for feuding among themselves; or, again, it may have been that Attlee was much more than 'the modest man' of Churchill's description – for he certainly had little to be modest about. Indeed, as Bevin was to say of him: 'Clement's never put forward a single constructive idea, but by God, he's the only man who could have kept us together.' The enigma remains, for Attlee's memoirs reveal little of the man himself and even less about the growing tensions that marked the closing years of his premiership.

In 1945 a newly elected MP Hugh Gaitskell wrote that if the government could last out its full term the underlying forces in its favour would be very strong but 'that things would be just about at their very worst' in 1947. Even he can hardly have imagined how percipient he was to be proved.

Dalton's *Annus Horrendus* opened with one of the worst winters on record. Heavy snowfalls blanketed the country, chilled by Arctic winds; temperatures plummeted, bringing road and rail transport to a virtual standstill. On 28 January Big Ben struck once for midnight and then fell silent. For the next month Britain was all but frozen in. Deprived of fuel, factories shut down and domestic consumers learned to live without electricity for long periods of the day. Even this, however, was only the outward manifestation of a more fundamental crisis, a former head of the Economic Section of the Treasury, Lionel Robbins, cautioning that 'The gravest aspect of the fuel shortage is not its bearing on domestic comfort but its effects on the external balance. If we do not succeed in increasing our overseas exports by at least 75 per cent before the dollar credits run out we shall be faced with external bankruptcy.'

These were ominous words, although not new. Since 1945, when the government opened negotiations for a US loan to cover a balance of payments deficit, critics such as G. D. H. Cole had been warning of the dangers of the convertability clause within the agreement. Careless even then of any 'special relationship', the US negotiators had made it clear that without the inclusion of such a clause – under which sterling would be made freely convertible for all current transactions – the deal would be called off. President Truman finally approved the loan in July 1946, and on 15 July 1947 the convertability clause came into effect. Its impact on the British economy was catastrophic. Within a month, with Britain's gold and dollar reserves being drained at an unprecedented rate, Dalton announced details of a series of austerity measures – cuts in food imports and the petrol ration, the suspension of foreign travel, an increase in the length of the miners' working day – which exacerbated the divide that already existed in the government.

With much of the government's legislative programme in place, the evangelical fervour which had inspired it in 1945 had given place to growing doubts about the way ahead, and in the summer of 1947 an 'Attlee Must Go' movement surfaced in the Parliamentary Labour Party. It was not the first time that such a coup had been attempted. Two years before, on the day that Attlee presented the credentials of his new government to George VI, Morrison had proposed that the parliamentary party should be allowed a free vote on the leadership issue, holding with Laski that Attlee lacked 'a sense of the dramatic, the power to give a lead, the ability to reach out to the masses'. Bevin was quick to scotch the plot, as he was its successor in 1947.

As brilliant as he was occasionally naive, Cripps was the arch-conspirator. Convinced that Bevin was agreeable to the move, and on being told that Dalton's reaction had been that 'If Herbert's in, I'll think about', he called on Attlee and told him that the time had come for him to go. Only the creative gossip of Westminster accounts for what followed. On being asked by Attlee who was to replace him, Cripps replied that Bevin had agreed to take office. Picking up his scrambler phone Attlee asked to be put through to Bevin at the Foreign Office: 'Oh, Ernie, Stafford's here and says you want my job.' The reply was unprintable, but Attlee relayed the gist of it on replacing the phone: 'Ernie says he knows nothing about it.' Momentarily there was silence, then Attlee added that, having been impressed by arguments put forward for the appointment of a Minister of Economic Affairs, he was wondering whether Cripps would care to take on the job.

Attlee's success in foiling the putsch failed to check the growing restiveness in the party, however. Nothing, it seemed, failed like success. In fact, Labour's achievements encouraged the left wing to raise its own demands, the more so as it appeared that the government was losing momentum with the completion of the first phase of its programme. Bevan was fond of saying that 'there was no immaculate conception of socialism', but for back-bench critics there was more to the party's agenda than the adoption of the prescriptions of Keynes and Beveridge. Their nostrums were all very well, but they did not go far enough, and even during the *Annus Mirabilis* there were growing suspicions abut the nature of Attlee's agenda. There could be no question about Labour's achievement in humanizing capitalism; none the less, capitalism itself remained intact.

Twenty per cent of the economy may have been collectivized, but four-fifths still remained in private hands. The mines may have been taken under state control, but an alliance between

Morrison, the essential corporatist, and the unions had scotched
any idea that the industry should be worker-controlled, and
Cripps was to remind his Bristol constituents: 'Labour is not a syndicalist party.' The Bank of England may have been nationalized,
but the distribution of wealth and power remained virtually
unchanged. While Britain struggled to meet the conditions of
the US loan, there was growing concern that Bevin had become
what the left-winger Konni Zilliacus was to call 'the lackey of our
Washington paymasters'.

In 1945, the party manifesto, *Let Us Face the Future*, had
prompted the public's memory not only of Britain's wartime debt
to the Soviet Union but of the failure of British foreign policy in
the twilight years of the peace: 'Let it not be forgotten that in the
years leading up to the war the Tories were so scared of Russia that
they missed the chance to establish a partnership which might
well have prevented the war.'

Bevin can hardly have taken kindly to the stricture, for the
Tories had not been alone in rejecting Moscow's call for an anti-
fascist crusade. Obsessed by the bogy of communism, he had
spent two decades waging an unremitting campaign against the
British Communist Party and its political satellites, most notably
the United Front. It was an experience that was to condition
Britain's foreign policy in the immediate post-war years when, as
Foreign Secretary, Bevin was to become an archetypal Cold War
warrior. Indeed his hatred of communism was matched only by
his contempt for intellectuals, and at the party's 1947 conference in Margate he gave vent to both his prejudices. All the
resentment was there (true, he had 'been at Eton one night and
Harrow one afternoon', but 'he had left school when he was
ten'), compounded by his loathing for those left-wingers who
had dared to question his pro-American and anti-Zionist
policies.

It was a rhetorical *tour de force*, Richard Crossman recalling
how, during the final wind-up, Bevin's voice rose: 'to a hoarse roar
of righteous indignation. No man is so skilful at handling a work-

ing-class audience, mixing the brutal hammer blow with senti-
mental appeal . . . He did not smash his critics, he pulverised them
into applauding him.'

Together with Michael Foot and Ian Mikardo, Crossman was
one of Bevin's targets. Founders of the Keep Left group, they had
attacked his foreign policy and campaigned for cuts in the defence
budget to safeguard the government's welfare programme for
almost a year before the financial crisis of 1947. And in this they
were not alone. At the Treasury Dalton had some sympathy for
their views, regarding it as absurd that Britain's socialist experiment should be sacrificed in pursuit of the uncertain benefits of a
US alliance. If Bevan was right when he had remarked that 'The
language of priorities is the religion of socialism', then it seemed
to Dalton that as the Cold War intensified, the priorities of socialism were being seriously compromised. Either the party could
honour its domestic commitments or it could become an agent of
US power. It could not afford both.

It was a dilemma that was to convulse the party. In January
1947 Bevin had been the key figure among the six ministers who
had taken the decision that Britain should build its own A-
bomb, the £100 million cost of the project being laundered in a
secret budget. The news that Britain had entered the nuclear
arms race was only made public in May 1948, eleven months
before she became a founder member of North Atlantic Treaty
Organization, the 'alliance for democracy' of which Bevin was
one of the main architects. And as Britain 'armed for peace', the
costs escalated. By 1949 Britain was spending 10 per cent of its
national income on defence, while in the five years to 1950
Britain spent a higher proportion of its income on defence than
the USA.

To meet such commitments sacrifices had to be made, and
Cripps and Gaitskell were the men to impose them. Late in 1947
Cripps succeeded Dalton as Chancellor of the Exchequer, to
become known as the Economic Dictator of Britain for the
severity of his austerity programme. Unpopular as the regime

was, Gaitskell, as Minister of Economic Affairs, was convinced of its necessity, and in the spring of 1950 he advanced his own proposal that 'there should be a definite limit placed on the total National Health Service expenditure' to curb rising costs. Jealous of the service he had created, Bevan's response was incandescent – 'The Government's abandonment of a free and comprehensive health service would be a shock to their supporters in this country . . . and a grave disappointment to Socialist opinion throughout the world' – and in March he threatened to resign if the service's budget was cut or if health charges were imposed.

Momentarily there was a stand-off – the proposal was dropped, the threat of resignation withdrawn. Neither Gaitskell nor Bevan was appeased, however, and within months the issue resurfaced, to mark the opening of a bitter personal feud that came close to destroying the Labour Party as a credible political force in the years immediately ahead. Different as Bevan and Gaitskell were in virtually every other respect – one the Valleys boy, largely self-educated, the other the public school grandee and Oxford graduate; one the charismatic radical, the other the austere rationalist – they shared one feature in common: their appetite for power. Once hooked, the condition is addictive, and it was Bevan himself who provided an insight into its progress during a debate in the Commons in 1943:

> I started my career in public affairs in a small colliery town in South Wales. When I was quite a young boy my father took me down the street and showed me one or two portly and complacent-looking gentlemen standing at a shop door, and pointing to one he said: 'Very important man. That's Councillor Jackson. He's a very important man in this town.'

> 'I said: 'What's a Council?'

> 'Oh, that's the place that governs the affairs of this town,' said

my father. 'Very important place indeed, and they are very important men.'

When I grow older, I said to myself, The place to get to is the Council. That's where the power is. So I worked very hard, and in association with my fellows, when I was about twenty years of age, I got on to the Council, but I discovered when I got there that the power had been there, but it had just gone.

And so the pursuit began, Bevan recounting how he had chased the 'will o' the wisp of power' first to the County Council and then to the Commons: 'And sure enough I found that it had been here, but I just saw its coat tails around the corner.'

A parable of power and its illusory qualities, Gaitskell and Bevan were to make a vocation of it. There was more to their rivalry, however, than the issue of health service charges, for which Gaitskell continued to campaign on replacing Cripps as Chancellor in the autumn of 1950. Bevan himself was as bitter at being passed over as he was contemptuous of the tyro Gaitskell – 'He is nothing, nothing, nothing.' It was to prove a fatal misjudgement. Damned by the same goat-footed, Celtic demon of antiquity that Keynes had found in Lloyd George, Bevan failed to recognize that Gaitskell's quietly spoken opinions disguised the passion with which he held his beliefs; that contrary to there being 'nothing, nothing, nothing' to the upstart, he was the politician who was first to better Bevan in the protracted and often savage contest for the hearts and minds of the party and then to recruit Bevan to his own cause.

Not that this was evident when Gaitskell moved into Number 11. Four months had passed since the outbreak of the Korean War, yet even after the government announced an accelerated defence programme of £3,600 million in August 1950 there were critics in Washington who maintained that Britain was not 'fighting her weight'. Indifferent to the impact of any further increases in defence expenditure on Britain's domestic economy, Congress demanded more. Attlee was quick to recognize the danger, expressing fears that if Britain did not increase her already over-stretched defence budget the USA would reappraise its commitments to the defence of the West – not least since there was a school of thought in the USA which held that it would be better for Europe to be overrun and then 'liberated' by US A-bombs than to keep American troops in the front line of the Cold War.

In January 1951 the Cabinet agreed to raise defence expenditure to £4,700 million to cover a three-year period, a concession that Washington still regarded as inadequate but which Bevan regarded as a concession too far. It was not until March, however, that Gaitskell won approval to levy charges on false teeth and spectacles to help cover the cost of the new commitment and, while the saving to the Treasury was small (amounting to £13 million), it was the principle rather than the practice that triggered Bevan's anger. At a rowdy meeting at Bermondsey Town Hall on 3 April he staked out his position: 'I will never be a member of a Government that makes charges on the National Health Service for the patient.'

The implication was clear. Which did the government value more: Aneurin Bevan or £13 million? In his Budget speech on 13 April Gaitskell provided the answer, imposing charges on both teeth and spectacles. As the *News Chronicle* reported: 'It seems that the whole of the Labour Party is holding its breath to see what Bevan will do', but while feverish behind-the-scenes efforts were made to cobble together a compromise agreement, Bevan was in an uncompromising mood. The government was establishing a precedent that could unravel the whole of the NHS, and as far as he was concerned Gaitskell was 'a second Snowden . . . trying to please his friends in the Treasury'. The most damaging charge in the Labour canon, it was to be repeated within days in *Tribune*. Written by Michael Foot, the lead story mocked the delight of *The Times* that 'Mr Gaitskell seems to have resisted most of the temptations that beset a Socialist Chancellor', to deny that Gaitskell was a socialist, rather an apostate in the Snowden mould.

Twenty years had passed since the charge had first been laid, to divide Labour. Now the party was to divide again. In castigating Gaitskell's budget in his letter of resignation to Attlee, Bevan raised the tortured question of the future direction of the party. It was no longer simply a matter of personal animosity, or even the issue of health charges, more of Labour's ideological motivation, of whether the party was committed to a socialist programme of reconstruction or whether, once again, it was compromising its principles 'for the purpose of upholding . . . society in a somewhat shorn condition but a safe one'. As Bevan was to remark to Dalton, 'It is really a fight for the soul of the Labour Party', which led Dalton to reflect that if Bevan should win 'I'm afraid we shall be out of power for years and years.'

Two other Ministers resigned with Bevan, the President of the Board of Trade, Harold Wilson, and John Freeman, a Junior Minister at the Ministry of Supply, to join the Keep Left group which had been playing the devil's advocate on the back benches for the previous four years. Talented as its membership was, however, the group had lacked a leader of commanding stature or ministerial experience. Bevan was to provide it. Only recently Attlee had considered that at some future date he could well lead the party, while even Gaitskell had once been an admirer of Bevan's Celtic *élan* ('I thought he would almost certainly be PM some time'), but in the spring of 1951 it momentarily appeared that he had marginalized himself in the contest for power. With a shrinking majority in the Commons, and a General Election in prospect, the party had no patience for rebels. Unity was at a premium, and at the party conference in October Bevan played a cynical exercise on the prevailing mood:

> No matter what the differences, we must never allow the British Labour movement to become schismatic – we must never carry

doctrinaire differences to the point of schism – nothing must prevent us from uniting our forces to destroy the challenge now made
to the Socialist Movement.

As quick to forget as to forgive, conference applauded,
oblivious to Bevan's hypocrisy. His call for unity did little to
avert the election defeat. On 25 October Britain went to the
polls, for the Conservatives under Churchill to be returned to
power with an overall majority of seventeen seats and for
Bevan's critics to suggest that his rebellion had helped cost
Labour the election. If Bevan had forsworn schism in the
autumn, he had forgotten his undertaking by the spring. In
March the Bevanites divided the party, fifty-seven Labour MPs
defying a three-line whip to abstain from voting following a
debate on the government's Defence White Paper, a revolt
which prompted Gaitskell to consider 'the prospect of Bevan
and some others having to go out of the party altogether. Indeed
there would have been some advantage, for it would have left
us much freer to attack him.'

All the rancour is there, all the bitterness at what Gaitskell
regarded as Bevan's recusancy. The hostility was reciprocated,
although more on ideological than on personal grounds. To the
Bevanites it seemed that the party was losing both its drive and its
vision, Crossman reflecting that 'Labour is in danger of becoming
a party not of change, but the defender of the post-war status
quo.'

What the left needed was not only a new leader but a new
lead, and while Bevan provided the one he singularly failed to
provide the other. In April 1952 he published *In Place of Fear*. Far
from providing what it promised – 'A plan for the future which
nobody can ignore' – the book offered the left little more than a
garbled account of the history of socialism, punctuated by the sort
of gnomic utterances that would have been the envy of Ramsay
MacDonald: 'Democratic socialism is a child of modern society
and so of relativist philosophy . . . It must know how to enjoy the

struggle, whilst recognising that progress is not the elimination of struggle but rather a change in its terms.'

The critics were contemptuous, the *News Chronicle* dismissing the book as 'the maunderings of a disappointed prophet', but it made little difference to Bevan's standing amongst his confidants. Although lacking a constructive agenda, the Tribune Brains Trust, which on any one occasion might include Ian Mikardo, Barbara Castle and Richard Crossman, toured the constituencies canvassing support for what Michael Foot had described as 'the dynamics of free discussion', while in the Commons the Bevanites continued their piecemeal campaign against their own front bench. In all but declaration Labour was at war with itself, Crossman writing before the House rose for the summer recess in 1952 that the divide in the party was 'quite grotesquely obvious to anyone looking down from the Gallery. It really does look like two parties.'

The media was riveted. This was the everyday story of a party that appeared hellbent on dismembering itself. To Labour's Chief Whip, Willie Whiteley, only the expulsion of the Bevanite ringleaders would suffice, but the louder the calls for the rebels' expulsion became, the more they resisted and the more they resisted the louder the calls for their expulsion became.

Bevin, longtime hammer of the left, was dead, but a new generation of union leaders were quick to conjure up the bogy of 'a party within a party', which led Arthur Deakin, Bevin's successor at the Transport and General Workers' Union, to demand the dissolution of 'this subversive faction' at the party conference in Morecambe: 'Let them get rid of their whips, dismiss their business and campaign managers and conform to the party constitution. Let them cease the vicious attacks they have launched on those with whom they disagree, abandon their vituperation and the carping criticism which appears regularly in *Tribune*.'

Dalton was to describe Morecambe as 'the worst Conference for bad temper and general hatred since 1926'. In paranoid mood,

each side suspected the other of betraying the principles of socialism, and at times the debates degenerated into little better than
brawls, the miners' leader Will Lawther raging at one heckler:
'Shut your gob.' He could as well have been talking to himself for
all the difference it made, for as the conference progressed the left
succeeded in forcing through a range of motions against the platform (on health charges, defence and nationalization), culminating in the return of six Bevanites (Bevan, Castle, Mikardo,
Crossman, Wilson, and Tom Driberg) to the National Executive
Committee to replace, among others, such long-standing members as Morrison and Dalton.

Two days after the conference ended Gaitskell was to deplore
'the stream of grossly misleading propaganda, poisonous innuendo
and malicious attacks' directed against the party leadership and
orchestrated by *Tribune*, maintaining that 'its [*Tribune*'s] very existence, so long as its pages are devoted to so much vitriolic abuse
of party leaders, is an invitation to disloyalty and disunity. It is
time to end the attempt of mob rule by a group of frustrated jour-
nalists and restore the authority and leadership of a sound and
sensible majority of the movement.'

He misjudged the temper of the constituencies that had
voted virtually *en bloc* for the Bevanite candidates, as the
Bevanites were to misjudge the extent of their influence on the
NEC. Twelve of the twenty-five members of the committee were
statutorily returned by the unions, and as Charles Geddes,
leader of the Post Office Workers, made clear, it was a power
they employed for their own particular ends: 'The trade unions'
influence upon the party is due to two reasons: (1) money, lots
of it, and (2) votes, many of them. This money will be spent and
these votes will be cast in the direction which will further trade
union policy.'

The reality of where power lay in the party was as blatant as
that. As conservative in their own interests as their predecessors,
and as suspicious of political abstractions as they were of the intellectuals who peddled them, the union grandees wanted nothing

of the Bevanites, and under intensifying pressure the Parliamentary Labour Party called for 'the immediate abandonment of all group organisations within the party other than those officially recognised'. As *The Economist* noted, the ban marked the imposition 'of a far more rigid discipline than ever before experienced in British politics'. None the less the Bevanites complied. The group was disbanded, and in November 1952 Bevan joined the Shadow Cabinet.

The right had not done with the dissidents, however. While they might conform to authority in the Commons, their conduct elsewhere mocked their compliance, *Tribune* and the Brains Trust providing the rebels with a platform to attack what they regarded as the leadership's revanchist agenda. By the spring of 1953 eighteen months had passed since Labour had gone down to electoral defeat, yet the party seemed becalmed in the past. The future was out there, waiting, but, rather than address it, it appeared to its critics that the National Executive preferred to conduct a witch-hunt against its own members or, more precisely, the unreconstructed Bevanites. Accused of fellow travelling, they defended the right of free speech, but careless of such dialectical niceties a ban was imposed on the Brains Trust as 'being contrary to the spirit and intention of recent decisions of the PLP'.

Cancer-like, the bigotry turned inwards, to poison the body itself, prompting John Strachey, one-time Minister of Food in the Attlee government, to wonder: 'What country is this anyway – the birthplace of political liberty or some totalitarian state?' Barbara Castle was to provide a part answer at conference in 1953: 'The Labour Party is in danger of dying a death of three million cuts – the block votes of four men.' Slowly yet inexorably dissent was being crushed, and where the block vote failed to stifle apostasy the unions had no hesitation about employing the Cold War psychosis to reinforce their authority.

Incapable of recognizing that their dominance within the TUC contradicted their own assertions, the right sedulously fostered the impression that the unions were in imminent danger of becoming the agents of a communist conspiracy engineered by Moscow aimed at subverting the movement, a charge encapsulated in Arthur Deakin's denunciation of the dockers as 'a moronic crowd of irresponsible adventurers who are being exploited by foreign elements for purposes they do not see or understand'. Unquestionably, the communists did form a small and abrasive faction within the unions, but the facts of the case belied the extent of their influence, for neither the number of stoppages nor the total number of working days lost through strikes increased significantly during the early 1950s.

Yet the stigma of fellow travelling remained, the miners' leader, Will Lawther, accusing the Bevanites of being 'a group of people with anarchistic tendencies and highly inflated egos who are playing into Communist hands' – a charge that Lawther's successor, Ernest Jones, was to echo at the party conference of 1954, to earn himself a savage rebuke from Bevan: 'We are not going to be bullied, we are not going to be intimidated by individual trade union leaders going to the rostrum and talking about us being Communists and fellow travellers. I say to Ernest Jones: "Drop it."'

Only that morning Bevan had learned that, owing in large part to the deployment of the block vote, he had been overwhelmingly defeated by Gaitskell in the contest for the post of Treasurer of the party, and it was in a bitter mood that he excoriated first the unions and then the party leadership:

> I know now that the right kind of leader for the Labour Party is a desiccated calculating machine who must not in any way permit himself to be swayed by indignation . . . He must speak in calm and objective accents and talk about a dying child in the same way as he would about pieces inside an internal combustion engine.

Although this was directed at Attlee, the audience took Gaitskell to be Bevan's target, for the hurt of his rejection had gone deep. Always mercurial, the victim of his Celtic temperament, it may well have seemed to Bevan that at the age of fifty-seven he was already a yesterday's man, while Gaitskell represented a new generation of Fabian gradualists (the Samurai of Wells's description) who regarded his brand of Welsh *hwyl* as a throwback to a past they preferred to forget. Indeed Attlee himself had appealed to conference to refrain from indulging in 'emotionalism', as if the reason could exorcize memory when discussing the question of German rearmament.

Only nine years had passed since peace had broken out and now, under US pressure, it seemed as if it could be on the march again. The left's alarm at what *Tribune* called 'the Rebirth of the German Reichswehr' was as inflated as the right's fear of communism was exaggerated.

Forty years on, the mood of the times is hard to imagine. Then it was very different. During the 1950s there was an ever-present fear that the Cold War would one day turn hot, and if John Le Carré's novels caught something of the paranoid mood of the times, then Stanley Kubrick's *Dr Strangelove* captured the essence of that madness. Behind the closing shots of Slim Pickens riding an H-bomb to eternity, to the backing of Vera Lynn singing 'We'll Meet Again', lay the very real fear that this was what the future could hold, the madness of a policy of Mutually Assured Destruction (MAD) that prompted one eminent psychiatrist to reflect that Washington and Moscow were both manipulating the public mind for their own subversive ends – in Washington's case to induce its European allies to accept German rearmament to reinforce the NATO shield.

A recrudescence of the long-running dispute over Britain's subordination to Washington's diktat, the issue of 'guns to the Huns', as Dalton described it, was to divide the party from the first day it was raised in February 1954. Although neither a communist nor a fellow traveller, Bevan was none the less leery of US intentions, fearing that Washington's policy of 'containment' was leading to the institutionalization of the Cold War itself – a fear that was reinforced in April 1954 when the Foreign Secretary, Anthony Eden, informed the Commons of American plans to create a South East Asia treaty organization on the model of NATO.

Even Attlee was concerned that such a development should not lead to the revival of 'obsolete colonialism', but Eden's reassurances did nothing to satisfy Bevan. On 14 April he left the Shadow Cabinet in protest at its tacit support for the government's pro-US stance, to launch a scathing attack on US foreign policy in *Tribune* the following week:

> The alliance with America was forged with the hope of preventing war. It was not intended as opposition to Communism as such. If America wishes this, the Alliance is distorted beyond its original purpose. We should tell America so in the plainest possible terms. If after that she persists, she must do so alone.

Gaitskell, Morrison and the right were incensed. Once again Bevan had broken ranks with the party. Once again he had threatened Labour unity. The man was a liability. He would have to go, and the Big Three of the unions (Deakin, Lawther and Tom Williamson of the General and Municipal Workers) agreed. In the previous eighteen months they had succeeded in marginalizing the Bevanites on the NEC, but it was Bevan who they loved to hate, Deakin declaring emotively: 'We've thrown the sprats back in the water. There's no point in keeping them while the mackerel's still swimming about.'

Bevan's philippic at the party conference of 1955 was to confirm the right wing's belief that as long as he remained in the party Labour would remain unelectable. The growing momentum for Bevan's expulsion was not only powered by his factious nature, however. There were deeper, more personal forces at work. Gaitskell and Morrison both had ambitions regarding the party leadership, and as Attlee confided: 'Each of them thought that one day he might succeed me as leader, and he wanted to inherit a disciplined Party. Both wanted Bevan brought well to heel in advance.' Their concern to secure unity was appreciable, although for much of the party, and not only the left, the word 'discipline' had ominous overtones, smacking of the communist conception of democratic centralism. Failing to recognize the irony, Tom Williamson was to declare that factionalism 'can have no place in our democratic organisation' and that in pursuit of unity the party was willing to forgo its fears of authoritarianism.

Cavalier as always with discipline, Bevan continued to enrage his critics. In February 1955 he raised a new rebellion on the left, calling for talks with the Soviet government pending the ratification of the treaty permitting German rearmament. Although the parliamentary party voted down his proposal, the left succeeded in collecting more than a hundred signatures rejecting the PLP's decision, while in March Bevan led a back-bench attack on the party's support for the government's decision to build an H-bomb. To his friends, it seemed that Bevan was the victim of a political death wish. To his critics, a memorandum prepared by Gaitskell was enough to convince them that they had tolerated his recalcitrance for too long. With ruthless precision, Gaitskell listed the charges against him, to assert in a subsequent conversation with Crossman that 'Bevanism is and only is a conspiracy to seize the leadership for Aneurin Bevan . . . There are extraordinary parallels between Nye and Adolf Hitler. They are demagogues of exactly the same sort.'

As careless of the principles that motivated Bevan as he was of his own conspiratorial practices, Gaitskell suggested that Bevan should be expelled from the party for six months. As far as Morrison was concerned, the sentence was too lenient. As far as Attlee was concerned, it was too severe. In considering Bevan's standing with constituency parties, Attlee was quick to grasp that to banish Bevan would be to open a major rift in the party in the run-up to the forthcoming election, and at a meeting of the NEC he succeeded by a single vote in quashing the right's proposal for his expulsion.

Effectively, the Bevanite revolt was over. For five years he had tried the conscience of the party and, with it, the patience of the right. Brilliant, passionate, headstrong, it appeared at times as if Bevan was as careless of his own reputation as he was of the reputation of his critics. Following his *rapprochement* with Gaitskell, who succeeded Attlee as leader of the party, he was to remark dismissively of Labour's 1959 manifesto that it was little better than 'pre-style Liberalism brought up to date'. An historic charge in Labour's vocabulary, it was none the less potent for all that. Although a key player in implementing the ameliorative policies of the post-war Labour administration, Bevan never abandoned his belief that socialism meant more than tinkering with the outworks of capitalism or in the imperatives of the class struggle.

Sixty years had passed since Morris had entered the lists against Shaw. In Bevan and Gaitskell they found their political legatees. The times and the circumstances may have changed, but the central questions that divided them remained much the same: not just a matter of defining the meaning of socialism but of determining how it could best be achieved. For Bevan the fundamentalist, there could be no compromising with the society of inequality. For Gaitskell the rationalist, there could be no alternative to the inevitability of gradualism.

Crossman, among the most penetrating commentators on the ferocious wrangling that racked the period, once confided to his diary that 'The definition of the Left is a group of people who will never be happy unless they convince themselves that they are about to be betrayed by their leaders.' In Aneurin Bevan's case he was wrong. Ultimately it was Bevan who betrayed himself for, by failing to provide the left with a coherent policy, he deprived them of the leadership needed to address the future of socialism. It was a mistake that Gaitskell was not to repeat.

The week after Gaitskell was elected leader of the Labour Party in December 1955 *The Economist* reflected that his role was 'to turn his back on the age of Keir Hardie'. In different forms it had been said not once but many times before, by Richard Crossman: 'What was achieved by the first Labour Government was the climax of a long process, in the course of which capitalism has been civilised' , and, most notably, by Anthony Crosland: 'In the course of achieving statism, British Labour has put into effect a very large part of its traditional programme . . . Thus capitalism, with no hope of abortion, is forced to give birth to a new society.' The question was, what form would this new society take?

As early as 1951, with the return of a Conservative government, evidence had been accumulating of growing affluence. Real incomes were rising and unemployment was running at 1.5 per cent, a million permanent new homes had been built in the previous five years, and the demand for consumer durables had reached take-off point. This was the paradox of socialism, that Labour had been too successful for its own electoral good. Indeed, for all the deprivations of the immediate post-war years, the party had not only succeeded in implementing much of its programme but had also laid the foundations for a consumer society that was to transform the British way of life.

But if the evidence of embourgeoisement was already there when Bevan published *In Place of Fear*, he preferred to ignore it. Gaitskell and his lieutenant Anthony Crosland were more perceptive. In a letter to a friend Crosland had anticipated his own agenda, declaring that he wished to work in the revisionist tradition, and in a New Fabian essay of 1951 he was to address what he termed the 'the socialist dilemma' to conclude: 'It is now quite clear that capitalism has not the strength to resist the metamorphosis into a qualitatively different kind of society.' Five years later he had worked out the details of what this qualitative difference might mean. A seminal work, *The Future of Socialism* was to provide the Gaitskellites with what the Bevanites lacked – a closely reasoned blueprint for what Crosland regarded as a new post-capitalist order.

Asserting that 'the economic power of the capitalist (i.e.

229

industrial property-owning) class is enormously less than a generation ago', Crosland rejected the Marxist assumption that 'the inner contradictions of capitalism would lead . . . to the collapse of the whole system', to insist that 'the much thumbed guidebooks of the past must now be thrown away'. But if the left was to reject its history, what was to be put in its place? Precisely what alternatives were on offer to those ' indolent-minded people on the Left' who, being unable to mould the familiar categories of socialism to the contemporary scene, were 'inclined to seek refuge in the slogans and ideas of 50 years ago'? If Keir Hardie was dead, what was 'the right focus to capture the reality of the mid twentieth-century world'?

An iconoclast, Crosland was as headstrong in challenging the central tenet of socialism ('I at least do not want a steadily extending chain of State monopolies, believing this to be bad for liberty. State ownership of all industrial capital is not now a condition of creating a socialist society') as he was confident in his own prescription for the future:

> The ideal is a society with a diverse, diffused, pluralist and heterogeneous pattern of ownership, with the State, the nationalised industries, the Co-operatives, the Unions, Government financial institutions, pension funds, foundations, and millions of private families all participating.

Only when such a mixed economy was realized would it be possible to achieve the socialist ideal of 'democratic equality'. An admirer of Tawney, the 'magisterial authority' of ethical socialism, Crosland's ideal was based on a society in which the distribution of status and rewards were 'egalitarian enough to minimise social resentment, to secure justice between individuals, and to equalise opportunities'.

An optimistic scenario, Crosland's assumptions were flawed in two respects: on the one hand, that economic growth was sustainable, thus providing increased wealth for redistribution; on the other, that unfettered capitalism would never regain its lost self-confidence.

Writing in the 1930s, Laski had foreshadowed Crosland's thesis, contending that as long as capitalist economies continued to expand capitalism could afford to extend political and civil liberties and, consequently, the power of workers to seek higher wages and improved working conditions. Laski, however, added one critical proviso: that if capitalism should contract, the capitalist class would emasculate democracy in order to safeguard its privileged status. Although far removed from the conditions that gave rise to fascism, and singularly different from the monetarist experiment of the 1980s, the decade of Thatcherism was foreseen by Laski rather than Crosland.

While Crosland did not live long enough to see his ideas put to the test during the 1980s, they were to be tested to the point of near destruction during his own lifetime. To the left wing of the party, Crosland's thesis was little less than heretical. Since conference had called for the 'socialisation of the means of production, distribution and exchange' in 1906, a formula refined by Sidney Webb and Arthur Henderson in 1918, Clause IV had been the keystone of the socialist credo. Yet now Crosland was not simply questioning its relevance to the socialist agenda but implying that it had no place in the future of socialism.

Even before Crosland published his work Bevan was castigating the revisionists on their loss of faith: 'Are we seriously as Socialists going to be told that in 1952 we have discovered some royal road, some ingenious way of trying to reach our socialist purposes which would not lead us through the old, hard agony of public ownership? There is no royal road.'

As the right grouped around Gaitskell, the left intensified its attack on the revisionist policies he pursued. On this issue no quarter was asked and none given. Apparently the soul of socialism itself was at stake.

The electoral defeat of 1955, and Gaitskell's subsequent appointment to the leadership, was to concentrate the party's mind on the question. In making a bogy of Labour's traditional agenda, and not least its 'shopping list' of industries yet to be nationalized, it seemed that the Conservatives were consolidating their hold on the political centre ground. The catchphrase had yet to be devised, but for large sections of the electorate the era of never-having-it-so-good had already arrived – an era that rejected what Crosland termed the certainties and simplicities of public ownership. In 1956 Gaitskell published a Fabian pamphlet in which he repudiated the notion of nationalization being a universal economic panacea, prompting Crossman to write that he was 'making people think that the Labour Party is a party to be taken seriously, that it is thinking, that it is beginning to get a policy and there can be such a thing as a second stage of socialism'.

As Crossman noted, the contrast with the left was marked: 'The fact is that Nye and Harold [Wilson] are not interested in rethinking policy at all.' Of course it is possible that in Bevan's case he was no longer interested in trying to best-guess the future, or it may simply have been that having tired of playing the hellraiser for a quarter of a century he settled for what he hoped, mistakenly, would be a quieter life. Whatever the case, Bevan's *détente* with Gaitskell, and his subsequent appointment as Shadow Foreign Secretary, were to convince the left of his betrayal, the full extent of which was to be revealed at the party conference in 1957. The issue was unilateralism and, having declared that to adopt such a policy would be to send a British Foreign Secretary 'naked into the conference chamber', Bevan turned on hecklers to accuse them of indulging in 'an emotional spasm'.

What followed was chaos. James Cameron was to write in the *News Chronicle* the following day of 'Aneurin Bevan insisting on the hydrogen bomb; Aneurin Bevan writhing on the twin hooks of conscience and expediency, passionately defending the American alliance; Aneurin Bevan, his face vermilion, hearing for the first time the jeers of the Left, producing what one had not expected from Bevan: Casuistry.' Seemingly, 'the star of Aneurin Bevan had skipped its course'.

There could be no disguising the left's sense of betrayal. This was the man who had once condemned Britain's subservience to US authority. This was the rebel who, not long before, had urged Labour 'to call the people out on to the streets against the Bomb'. And, finally, this was the Judas who had discovered the royal road to socialism, having endorsed the party's policy document *Industry and Society* which substituted state shareholding within a mixed economy for large-scale public ownership.

For the updating of Clause IV was the touchstone of the revisionists' agenda, the more so after Labour's election defeat of 1959. Apparently the Gaitskellites had been right. The party was losing touch with the electorate, its share of the poll having fallen for a third time within the decade. And if its analysis of the problem was radical, its solution was iconoclastic: that what Douglas Jay termed 'the myth of nationalisation' should be disposed of for once and for always. Like the mythical albatross, it had hung around the neck of the party for too long. For the left, however, Clause IV remained equally symbolic. While not subscribing to the state control of the economy, public ownership remained their test of ideological purity.

The terms of the contest may have changed, but in essence it remained much the same, of right ranged against left, gradualist against fundamentalist, and while Gaitskell advocated pragmatism ('While we shall certainly wish to extend social ownership . . . as circumstances warrant, our goal is not 100 per cent state ownership'), Harold Wilson invoked memories of a more evangelical past: 'We are being asked to take Genesis out of the Bible. You don't have to be a fundamentalist to say that Genesis is part of the Bible.' Significantly, Frank Cousins, who had succeeded Deakin as General Secretary of the Transport and General Workers' Union, agreed ('We can have nationalisation without socialism, we cannot have socialism without nationalisation'), significantly in so far as it was the unions in alliance with the constituency parties that were to sabotage Gaitskell's attempt to jettison Clause IV.

Since 1955 there had been a radical shift in the balance of power within the Labour Party as the unions moved to the left in defence of the constitutional status quo. Innately conservative, they wanted no part of revisionism and the harder the Gaitskellites pressed their case the more intransigent the unions became. Once again it seemed that a conspiracy of intellectuals, this time members of a Hampstead set grouped around Gaitskell, were bent on imposing their will on the party with their proposals to rewrite Labour's constitution and to loosen the party's ties with the unions. And when, within days of the election defeat of 1959, one of Gaitskell's closest allies, Douglas Jay, published an article in which he purported to have identified the two 'fatal handicaps' that had led to the defeat – of the party's cloth cap image, allied to its commitment to public ownership – it reinforced the unions' suspicions that this was not only a conspiracy against the constitution of 1918 but also against themselves. Indeed, as Dalton was to say, Jay's article 'struck the tuning fork for all the Gregorian Chants of the Old Believers'.

As quick to distance himself from the more extravagant proposals of the revisionists (among them, that the party should change its name) as he was to assert that public ownership 'was not end in itself, but a means . . . to certain ends', Gaitskell had no hesitation about calling up the past to justify his own position at the party conference in 1959: 'I am sure that the Webbs and Arthur Henderson who largely drafted the Constitution would have been amazed and horrified had they thought that their words would be treated as sacrosanct 40 years later in utterly changed conditions.'

Circumspect as he was, Gaitskell's appeal for the Labour to rethink its founding principles incensed rather than assuaged his audience. Ironically, it was Bevan who, in giving qualified support for Gaitskell's proposals, 'soothed the explosive passions which were simmering not far below the surface'. The speech, Bevan's last to conference, was a masterly exercise in circumlocution. For all his casuist skills, however, the passions remained. By mid-1960 it was clear to Gaitskell that the unions were not to be denied, and on 13 July the NEC decided 'not to proceed with any amendment or addition to Clause IV', which prompted him to reflect that the clause was 'never an issue of principle; it was an issue of presentation'.

Aneurin Bevan died on 6 July 1960, leading the political editor of the *Daily Mail*, Walter Terry, to write of 'the roistering, excitable crusader who more than once split the party that had become Labour's great unifying force'. The irony must have entertained Gaitskell. For three decades Bevan had made a cockshy of unity, yet now it was to serve as his political epitaph. But if Gaitskell was entertained, he did not begrudge Bevan the posthumous tribute, recognizing that for all their differences they had complemented one another in their efforts to define the future of socialism. Neither, however, could escape the past – while Gaitskell could not escape the future. Defeated both on unilateralism and Clause IV, he was quick to recognize that a third defeat at conference would destroy his credibility as leader.

The issue was Europe and whether or not Britain should enter the Common Market. The majority of Gaitskellites, led by Roy Jenkins and Bill Rodgers, were Euro-enthusiasts and cautiously optimistic that Gaitskell shared their views. At Brighton in 1961 they were to be disabused.

In a speech commending Britain's 'thousand years of history', Gaitskell betrayed the Gaitskellites' hopes to reject all talk of Britain entering Europe. The response was ecstatic, but as Jenkins was to write in his memoirs: 'Unlike Bill Rodgers . . . who more courageously remained seated with his arms folded, I did stand but did not applaud. Probably only afterwards I worked out a sophistical theory that standing was a tribute to the man, whereas clapping would have been a tribute to the speech.'

The Gaitskellites were bitter, but Gaitskell's leadership was safe. It was to prove short-lived. After a short illness, Gaitskell died on 18 January 1963. In thirty months the Labour Party had lost two of its bestriding figures. But while Bevan and Gaitskell had ultimately come to terms, the debate as to the future of socialism remained to be resolved.

10

In Place of Strife

'The plural of conscience is conspiracy.' – Arthur Henderson, Chairman of the Labour Party, 1931

In the two years before Gaitskell's death, an eerie calm enveloped the Labour Party. Exhausted by internecine feuding, it momentarily appeared that the party had come to terms with itself. Indeed, as Peter Shore was later to write, there was widespread agreement on the need for the combatants 'to get out of the trenches of the battles of the 40s and 50s'. The appearance was illusory, an ideological truce during which revisionists and fundamentalists regrouped their forces, but as co-author of the party's 1960 policy document *Labour in the Sixties*, Shore himself played a key role in mediating between left and right by devising a formula which, while reaffirming the party's commitment to Clause IV, captured something of the revisionists' mood:

Our Socialist beliefs will be vindicated in the 1960s, as it is ever more clearly seen that the new, post-war capitalism is creating its own insuperable problems and that, in the epoch of scientific revolution, democracy, if it is to survive, must plan its resources for the common good.

Gaitskell's successor, Harold Wilson, was to make a talisman of the phrase during the early years of his leadership, to echo and re-echo his belief that 'socialism must be harnessed to science, and science to socialism' during an 'epoch of revolutionary change'. The words captured something of the man himself – the brilliant scholar destined for an academic career (for a short period he worked as an assistant to Beveridge) with the consciously affected avuncular touch; the precocious radical (at the age of thirty-one he was appointed President of the Board of Trade), who came to regard Elizabeth II as one of his few confidants; the latter-day prophet of socialism who could write of his predecessor:

> What Hugh Gaitskell never recognised was that from the party's earliest days a great number of converts had joined Labour because they believed that socialism was a way of making a reality of Christian principles in everyday life.

A politician for all seasons, Wilson's elusive personality was well suited to the mood of compromise in the party that he inherited in February 1963 – the Bevanite revisionist whom Crossman regarded as the leadership candidate least likely to divide Labour; the political changeling to whom Randolph Churchill sent a pink tie on the eve of the 1964 election with the couplet

> The Leader's tie is the palest pink
> It's not as red as people think

and the 'diabolical enigma' of whom Denis Healey was later to write:

> His short-term opportunism, allied with a capacity for self-delusion which made Walter Mitty appear unimaginative, often plunged the government into chaos. Worse still, when things went wrong, he imagined everyone was conspiring against him. He believed in demons and saw most of his colleagues in this role at one time or another.

And with reason. Even during the leadership contest of 1963, the Gaitskellite faction, careless of the peccadilloes of their favourite, were busily peddling rumours of Wilson's relationship with his private secretary, Marcia Williams, whom they cast as the *femme fatale* of his entourage. Their whispering campaign had little foundation, although it may well have exacerbated Wilson's paranoid tendencies, which were to intensify during this time in office, fuelled by still unsubstantiated evidence that elements in the British intelligence services were bent on discrediting him as an agent, witting or otherwise, of the KGB.

It was neither the intrigues of the Gaitskellites nor the machinations of MI5 that concerned Wilson on taking office on October 1964, however; rather, the marginal nature of Labour's victory at the polls. The party had run an effective campaign under the slogan 'Forward With Labour', but a three-seat majority hardly provided the grounds for satisfying public expectations or realizing Wilson's ambition that Britain was going to be 'forged in the white heat of this [scientific] revolution' – the more so when it was revealed that Britain was running at trade deficit of £8000 million a year, twice the figure that had previously been forecast.

Within weeks the new administration was forced to raise a £2000 million loan from the US Federal Reserve, to impose a 15 per cent import surcharge and to raise interest rates to 7 per cent. In his post-election broadcast Wilson had promised a 'hundred days of dynamic action', although this was hardly what the electorate had expected. And this was only a beginning of the government's contest with the financial markets or what, in paranoid mood, Wilson regarded as 'the gnomes of Zurich'. In March 1966 Labour went to the country, to win an increased majority and to meet renewed pressures on the economy leading to a run on reserves culminating in November in what *The Economist* described as 'perhaps the biggest deflationary package that any industrial nation has imposed on itself since Keynesian economics began'.

Significantly, it was wage inflation that had played an important role in generating the crisis, and, of equal significance, it was the government's attempt to tackle the crisis that led to the precipitate resignation of Wilson's Minister of Science and Technology, Frank Cousins. The outspoken left-wing leader of the Transport and General Workers' Union, Cousins had been recruited by Wilson in 1964: 'I want you close to me, Frank. There is no one else I can trust as I can trust you. That is because

I know you are the one man who doesn't want my job.' If Wilson expected Cousins to act as his stalking horse in the unions, however, he was soon to be disappointed. By late 1965 the issue of imposing some control over prices and incomes was already poisoning the government's relationship with the left, and in July 1966 Cousins resigned following the publication of a Prices and Incomes Bill.

If any one event was to give notice of the troubles to come, it was Cousins's resignation. In arguing that while it was desirable to control prices it was wrong to curb union negotiating powers, he crystallized an issue that was to rack successive administrations, Labour and Conservative, and one that was eventually to play a major role in bringing down the Callaghan government. The débâcle of 1979, however, simply added injury to irony, for it was Callaghan's opposition to Barbara Castle's policy document *In Place of Strife* which in large part helped to undermine Labour's attempt to contain wage inflation by regulating the wage-bargaining process. In the first half of 1968, more than 3 million working days had been lost through strikes, as workers fought to shore up their incomes against rising prices. Acutely conscious of the damage that was being inflicted on the party Wilson asked his new Minister of Labour, Barbara Castle, to tackle the problem.

A former Bevanite, who had served her time both as Minister of Overseas Development and Minister of Transport, Castle had welcomed the challenge of government: 'This is the real morality, having to choose, not having to choose. Anyone can be on the side of the angels when there's never a devil around.' In the case of the trade unions, however, she was to learn that the devil had an unconscionably long memory, for her previous strictures on the employment of the block vote can hardly have endeared her to a new generation of union grandees. And what doubts they may have already harboured about her were seemingly confirmed when they were given a sight of the draft of *In Place of Strife*. The assertion that it was, indeed, a charter of trade union rights – among them, the right to belong to a union, for safeguards from unfair dismissal and protection for sympathy strikes – could not disguise the fact that it imposed responsibilities; the charter proposing that the government should be given power to order a ballot among strikers and that fines could be imposed on employers, unions or individual strikers in the case of certain disputes.

As far as the unions were concerned, the left-wing MP Eric Heffer's indictment of the charter as 'a spoonful of syrup in a barrel of tar' was notable only for its constraint. Once again it seemed that the party was on the verge of civil war; union leaders branded Wilson a class traitor and Wilson retorted: 'They're not so much barons, they're bloody Dukes.' With a third of all MPs sponsored by the unions, this was fighting talk, and both the right and left wings of the parliamentary party adopted the cause of the unions as their own – for the Gaitskellites to meet in conclave and decide that Wilson must go and for a fundamentalist such as Neil Kinnock later to consider the possibility of 'packing in Labour and forming a new Party, to be founded on the trade unions': its suggested title – the Social Democratic Party!

But while right and left jostled for position, it was Callaghan who sabotaged Castle's proposals. Brought up within a bos'n's whistle of the naval dockyards in Portsmouth, where he was quickly taught respect for the proper order of things ('My father had taken me aboard the *Victoria and Albert* [the royal yacht] when I was a toddler, but I did not suppose it ever crossed his mind that one day his son would be invited to return as Prime Minister of the United Kingdom'), Callaghan honed his political skills first as an official and then as Secretary of the Inland Revenue Federation. Largely self-educated, among the last of the breed to reach a leading position in the party, Callaghan was elected MP for South Cardiff in Labour's landslide victory in 1945. As politically friendly as his nickname Sunny Jim implied, but careful always to end up on the winning side, he had secured a powerful base for himself in the Parliamentary Labour Party by the late 1950s, a position reinforced by his standing with the unions.

The recurrent financial crises of the first years of Wilson's government, when Callaghan served as Chancellor, led to a Cabinet reshuffle in 1967, in which Callaghan was promoted sideways to the Home Office, the graveyard of so many political ambitions. Momentarily, it appeared as if he had a great future behind him, although not for long. His campaign against *In Place of Strife* was to provide him with the opportunity to rehabilitate his reputation, more especially with the unions. As a former Chancellor, Callaghan must have appreciated better than most the dangers of wage inflation, but through the spring and into the summer of 1969 he tirelessly championed the unions' case.

The mood in Cabinet was poisonous, and there could have been no mistaking the Foreign Secretary Michael Stewart's target when he passed a note to Barbara Castle: 'Anyone who lets you down at this stage is a prize shit.' And as tensions rose, so tempers frayed, fuelled by suspicions that Callaghan was exploiting the issue as much to further his own ambitions as to aid the union cause, Tony Benn noting after one Cabinet meeting that 'he [Callaghan] has more or less made an open challenge to Harold's leadership.' Wilson's reply was significant, that he had no intention of standing down as 'he was certain that no one else could form a government'. Even his most strident critics could not deny the claim. In their contest for power left and right had merely succeeded in neutralizing one another, leaving Wilson and Castle to strike a nugatory deal with the unions and Callaghan to reflect on the virtues of opportunism. It was to cost him dear.

Dubbed by the media 'Solomon Binding', the 'solemn and binding' agreement struck between Wilson and the unions was hardly worth the paper on which it was written. A cynical exercise in political legerdemain, both parties to the deal knew full well that the unions could never deliver on their undertaking to get their members back to work in the case of unofficial strikes. In celebrating their victory, however, the union leaders neglected Barbara Castle's warning that if they could not put their own affairs in order then someone would do it for them. It was to be another ten years before their prophecy was fulfilled.

With the fall of Wilson's government in June 1970 the Conservatives returned to power, pledged to curbing union powers, and on 3 December the Industrial Relations Bill was published. Edward Heath, his confidence fortified by surveys indicating that more than half the electorate believed the unions had too much power, placed his faith in the good sense of trade unionists to enforce the measure:

> Now when it is implemented, I don't believe for one moment that the trade unions leaders, let along the trade unions members, are going to challenge the verdict of the electorate in this democracy with a democratically elected Parliament in which a government is carrying through the policy on which it went to the electorate.

He was to be proved conclusively wrong, and for the next three years the government was engaged in a knock-down, drag-out contest with the unions, culminating in the election of February 1974, when Heath went to the country in a final throw against union militancy: 'Only one thing can threaten our future. That is our continued record of industrial strife. We can't afford the luxury of tearing ourselves apart any more. This time the strife has got to stop. Only you can stop it. It's time for you to speak with your vote.'

Heath's appeal was unavailing, however. On 28 February Labour was returned to power with a wafer-thin majority. Yet again expectations were high, and yet again they were to be disappointed. In the last quarter of 1973 oil prices had quadrupled, prompting Peter Shore to write: 'the whole post-war period, in a sense, came to an end on that day. In his first year he [Wilson] had to face a trade deficit of £3,500 to £4,000 million.' Added to this, inflation was running at 15 per cent in February 1974 and rising. The sense of *déjà vu* was inescapable. Ten years had passed since Wilson had first come to office to be faced with an economic crisis. In the spring of 1974 it must have seemed to him that history was repeating itself

– compounded, this time, by wage inflation.

In bullish mood, having rubbished *In Place of Strife* and helped to demolish the Tory government, the unions were in no mood to be placatory. In opposition, Labour had cobbled together a so-called Social Contract under which the unions agreed to impose voluntary restraint on wage demands in return for the introduction of a wider social and economic package. Even before the election, however, the leader of the Amalgamated Engineering Unions, Hugh Scanlon, denied that such an agreement had ever been struck. Temporarily, he was a lone voice of criticism, but not for long, the Chancellor, Denis Healey, writing later that 'if the unions had kept their promises, inflation would have been back to single figures by 1975. They did not.'

This was understandable. In the push-me-pull-you-through inflationary environment of the mid-1970s the unions had some justification for believing that they were being asked to do the government's dirty work for it. And in this they were not alone. Since *In Place of Strife* had been jettisoned, leading Healey to declare that the unions were emerging as 'an obstacle both to the election of a Labour government and to its success once it was in power', the left wing of the parliamentary party had discovered a new ally in their contest with the revisionists. Where once Barbara Castle had rued 'the complacency of her left-wing colleagues', the Tribune group were resurgent, provoking Labour's Chief Whip, Bob Mellish, to write to Wilson in late 1974: 'This Group is more arrogant than ever before . . . We have, as you know, always been a party that quarrels about almost everything, but my bonhomie, I think, is not sufficient today and I really do believe that you should get a replacement.'

Wilson rejected Mellish's appeal, but he was unable to ignore that growing rift in the party, provoked by Healey's counter-inflationary strategy and the left's suspicion that the Treasury favoured the introduction of a statutory incomes policy. For all the early hopes vested in the Social Contract, it could not contain wage inflation indefinitely. The pressures on the pound in the pocket were too great for that. By the summer of 1975, with inflation running at 26 per cent and wage settlements averaging 30 per cent, the Cabinet discussed plans to introduce a voluntary scheme under which there would be a £6 a week ceiling on all pay increases, with a fallback position that if the voluntary approach should fail a statutory incomes policy would be imposed.

Momentarily, it appeared that the problem had been resolved, though following an emotional broadcast on television in which Wilson asked viewers to 'Give a Year for Britain', Tony Benn was to write that 'although the message sounded reasonable, it was Ramsay MacDonald all over again' – a view echoed by Barbara Castle some months later, when Healey called for a £3.5 million cut in public expenditure: 'I can see no reason for the existence of a Labour government. We had adopted the Tory *mores*. The only difference is that we carry out Tory policies more efficiently than they do.'

As for Wilson, an increasingly isolated figure, disenchanted with the in-fighting that racked his administration, he was losing his zest for government. Shortly after the 1974 election he had confided to Marcia Williams that he meant to stay in office for no more than two years. Now that time was fast approaching. In January 1976 Barbara Castle noted that he was in one of his '"I'll get to hell out of it moods" (I personally think he is getting ready to chuck things up)', and at a little after 10:30 a.m. on Thursday 16 March Wilson announced his resignation to the Cabinet.

In his compelling study, *A Question of Leadership: From Gladstone to Thatcher*, Peter Clarke wrote: 'Wilson's departure in fact opened the era of clarification in Labour politics. His heritage of manipulative Labourism now faced a double challenge. On the left, the idiom of Marxism acquired a new cachet and a new militancy . . . Conversely on the right of the party there was a more self-conscious adoption of the language of social democracy.'

The challenge was not new. It had existed since the formation of the party, and like two ageing pugs, right and left chafed in their ideological corners as Callaghan succeeded Wilson. They were to have to wait for another two years before the call 'Seconds out', two years during which the crowd at the political ring-side grew increasingly fractious.

With a fine contempt for his former engagement with the unions, Callaghan staked out his own position at the party conference shortly after taking office:

> For too long . . . we have postponed facing up to fundamental choices and fundamental changes in our society and our economy. That is what I mean when I say we have been living on borrowed time . . . We used to think that we could spend our way out of recession, and increase employment by cutting taxes and boosting Government spending. I tell you in all candour that that option no longer exists.

In 1975 Healey had abandoned Keynesianism. A year later Callaghan followed suit. Seemingly the forward march of Labour had been halted in its tracks.

And as the government pursued a policy of squeezing inflation until 'the pips squeaked', so union militancy intensified. Always a temporary expedient, the policy of voluntary wage restraint was coming under growing pressure by the summer of 1978, fuelled by reports that the government was planning to bring wage settlements down to a 5 per cent norm the following year. Although previously discussed in Cabinet, the proposal only became public when it 'popped out' in an answer by Callaghan to an interviewer's question. Whether or not it was a deliberate leak, the issue was to divide the party and, while Callaghan's left-wing deputy Michael Foot called for realism ('If you have a Tory government, what sort of wages policy do you think you are going to have? You can have a wages policy imposed by mass unemployment, far worse unemployment than anything we have experience. That is the Keith Joseph–Thatcher policy.'), the party conference was to reject his appeal by a two-to-one majority.

If not poetic, there was a certain rough justice about the verdict. It was a decade since Callaghan had helped to subvert *In*

Place of Strife and what remained of the Social Contract was now in ruins. The Winter of Discontent started with unions demanding pay increases of between 20 and 30 per cent and the government being defeated by its own back benches when it attempted to continue sanctions against firms that agreed to pay increases above 5 per cent. The scene was set for the disaster that was to follow, a reprise of the *Annus Horrendus* of 1947, for as the weather deteriorated Britain was racked by a series of wildcat strikes of refuse collectors and hospital porters, lorry drivers and railwaymen, culminating in a widely publicized and bizarre stoppage in Liverpool where gravediggers refused to bury the dead.

For the Callaghan government it was the beginning of the end. Callaghan wrote: 'The serious and widespread industrial dislocation caused by the strikes of January 1979 . . . set the Government's fortunes cascading downhill, our loss of authority in one field leading to misfortunes in others just as an avalanche, gathering speed, sweeps all before it.'

Denis Healey was not so generous: 'This shambles was of course a triumph for Mrs Thatcher. The cowardice and irresponsibility of some union leaders in abdicating responsibility at this time guaranteed her election; it left them with no ground for complaining about her subsequent actions against them.'

On 3 May 1979 the Callaghan government went to the country, and the Conservatives were returned with an overall forty-three seat majority. Margaret Thatcher quoted St Francis of Assisi on the steps of 10 Downing Street: 'Where there is error, may we bring truth' – the error being Britain's long-standing dalliance with socialism; the truth being that she, too, had discovered a New Jerusalem, albeit little more than a recrudescence of Victorian *laissez-faire*. Quick to recognize that 'socialism is never defeated', Thatcher could never have imagined how successful she would be in neutralizing its vision and rewriting its agenda in the decade that lay ahead.

In their dance with dogma the Thatcherites were to expose the full extent of the breach within the Labour Party which, by 1981, prompted certain political aficionados to suggest that the party was on the point of disintegration. A century had passed since Morris and Shaw had first contested the meaning of socialism, and with the fall of the Callaghan government the question was reopened with renewed intensity. Abandoning what little pretence remained of unity, Labour indulged in a frenzy of ideological bloodletting, left and right each accusing the other not so much of having cost the party the election, more of betraying the principles of socialism itself. The left and right had once been dubbed by Crossman as 'the best of enemies'; the breakdown of the so-called 'post-war set-tlement', with its emphasis on the mixed economy, full employment and expanding welfare provision, appeared to confirm his assertion.

Indeed the leadership's contest with the unions had tended to disguise a more fundamental dispute which had been brewing up since the fall of Wilson's government in 1970. High hopes had been vested in his first two administrations, and twice they had been disappointed. It was all very well for revisionists to subscribe to Crosland's critique of fundamentalists (quixotic figures who continued to tilt at 'the outrageous giants of that detested race . . . capitalist barons, Wall Street, exploiting profiteers') and to respond, as Crosland did, to the question 'Is this still Capitalism? I would answer: No.' As far as the left were concerned, the experience of the 1960s gave the lie to his assertion, and the Conservatives' return to office in 1970 simply reinforced their scepticism. For all of the elegance of Crosland's thesis, the 'commanding heights of the economy' had not been scaled, the old enemy, capitalism, been not been vanquished.

Apparently Shaw and the Fabians had been wrong. Apparently the gradualism they had championed was not as inevitable as they had supposed, and under the twin pressures of electoral defeat and the hardline policy adopted by the incoming Heath administration Labour moved sharply to the left, to the growing alarm of the revisionists on the party's right flank. A mirror image each of the other, they were to rail at their own reflections in the decade that lay ahead, bitter at what they regarded as the betrayal of their other self. Subversively, the image mocked them, and the more they defied their own reflections, the more irreconcilable the image became – a schizophrenic condition, as inexorable as it was destructive.

As early as 1968, encouraged, on the one hand, by union militancy and disillusioned, on the other, by Labour's performance, a left-wing splinter group calling itself Socialist Charter had been established. Critical of the fact that in many cases Labour MPs sat for what, in effect, were pocket boroughs, the Chartists' aim was to bring constituency pressure to bear on the parliamentary party. Their modest ambition was to have radical consequences, although it was not until the late in 1971, with the deselection of Lincoln's sitting MP Dick Taverne, that the full implications of what this new generation of Labour activists were about dawned on the Labour establishment – not least on right-wingers such as Roy Jenkins.

Taverne, adopted as a candidate in 1961 on Hugh Gaitskell's say-so, had clashed with his local party first over his support for *In Place of Strife* and then over his support for Britain's entry into the European Economic Community in defiance both of the party's three-line whip and his constituency's instructions that every Labour MP should vote against entry. In November 1971 the Lincoln Constituency Labour Party passed a vote of no confidence in Taverne, a decision that was later to be confirmed by the NEC. For the first time in a decade a Labour MP had been sacked, although in his memoirs Jenkins was to put a sophist's spin on the turn of events:

> In a most extreme form this contradiction [of Jenkins's invidious position as Deputy Leader of a Party for which he had diminishing sympathy] expressed itself in the Lincoln by-election of 1 March 1973. Dick Taverne, goaded by the bandelliras of the Lincoln

Labour Party, decided to break free, resign, and fight the seat again at a by-election.

Under pressure from the Labour establishment, Jenkins refrained from canvassing for Taverne, who won the seat on a Democratic Labour ticket. Immediately there were few who read the seeds of time or foresaw the birth of the Social Democratic Party some eight years later. Their concern, rather, was with the increasing militancy of the party.

In 1973, the NEC, where the left now commanded a majority, rewrote the party's 1960s' manifesto, to assert: 'The experience of Labour Governments had made it increasingly evident that even the most comprehensive measures of fiscal and social reform can only succeed in masking the unacceptable and unpleasant face of capitalism, and cannot achieve any fundamental changes in the power relationships which dominate our society.'

This was much more than the 'bandelliras' of a handful of Lincoln activists. This was Labour restating what the left regarded as its founding principle: that compromising with capitalism would never provide a credible political alternative for socialists. When Wilson rejected *Labour's Programme, 1973*, he can hardly have imagined where his obduracy would lead or appreciated the significance of the National Executive's decision to scrap the old 'proscribed list' which banned members of certain groups – most notably communists and Trotskyites – from joining the party. In demonizing his own shadow spokesman for Trade and Industry, Tony Benn ('He immatures with age'), Wilson failed to recognize that Benn reflected the growing restiveness among grass-roots activists who felt, with some justification, disenfranchised by the party to which they belonged.

In fact, it was Wilson who was to summarize the authoritarian nature of the Labour establishment: 'We only take notice of Conference resolutions when it suits us' – an assertion which was later to provoke Ian Mikardo's charge that it was Wilson himself who had 'started changing the operations of both the Government and the party from democratic management to presidential rule'.

Mikardo knew better than that. Although entrenched in the party's federalist constitution, the notion of democratic control – of a balance of power between the PLP, the unions and the constituency parties – had always been illusory. For all the decisions of conference, Wilson had exposed the reality of where power in the party lay. And quite possibly it was this, a question as much of the structure of the party as of its differences over Europe, that provoked Roy Jenkins's resignation from the Shadow Cabinet in 1972. Quite possibly it was memories of the dissidents of Lincoln that offended his political sensibilities – their often inchoate but always pertinent call for the devolution as opposed to the concentration of power.

Never one to disappoint his critics, it seemed at times as if Jenkins played up to his role of Whig grandee, with all that the term implied. The appearance was deceptive. The son of a Welsh miner who had been sentenced to nine months' imprisonment for illicit assembly in the year of the General Strike, Jenkins graduated from Oxford and saw wartime service with the Royal Artillery before being elected to the Commons in 1948, where he was to succeed Callaghan as Chancellor for Exchequer in 1967. A *bon viveur*, satirized in *Private Eye* as 'Smoothychops', he kept good company with his socialist past – with Charles Broadhurst and Jimmy Thomas, and Ramsay MacDonald who flattered himself thinking about being kissed by all the duchesses in London.

It was the nature of this past that the activists rejected – and not only the activists. At the heart of the crisis that was to rack the party, its General Secretary, Ron Hayward, was to exclaim: 'We didn't work and spend to send an MP to the House of Commons to forget whence he came and whom he represents . . . In my forty-six years' membership of this party I've never yet seen it try Socialism in any sense.' That was in 1982, a decade after Roy Jenkins had resigned as Deputy Leader of the party and the party chairman, Tony Benn, had launched *Participation 1972*, a wide-ranging programme aimed, among other things, at democratizing the party:

> The problem of achieving greater party democracy is now the central internal problem facing the Movement. It is not just a question of considering constitutional amendments . . . It is not just a question of re-opening old arguments about the relationship of conference decisions to the Parliamentary Labour Party . . . It is not just about the merits or de-merits of the block vote . . . It involves all these things and it does so by making Party democracy a major political theme.

The radical content of Benn's appeal was to have far-reaching consequences, provoking a ferocious ideological dispute that was to culminate in the revision of the party's constitution and the creation of the Social Democratic Party. Few of the twelve activists who met at the Commons to form the Campaign for Labour Party Democracy (CLPD) in June 1973 could have envisaged where their initiative would lead when they drafted their statement of aims:

> We believe that policy decisions reached by annual conference should be binding on the Parliamentary Labour Party, and undertake to secure the implementation of this principle. We call on the National Executive Committee: (a) to carry out fully its responsibility as custodian of conference decisions; (b) to be responsive to rank and file opinions between conferences, and to extend the processes of consultation with constituency Labour parties . . . Finally, we urge the NEC to take firm action to ensure that Labour's election manifesto accurately reflects party policy as expressed by annual conference decisions.

The apparent reasonableness of the demands disguised their explosive potential. Modest as they may have appeared, they challenged the entire basis of establishment power and what the CLPD regarded as its innately conservative bias. Although never numbering more than a few hundred members, the campaign's lobbying – carefully orchestrated by its founders – not only reflected the mood of the constituencies but encouraged them to adopt a more radical approach to policy-making. The left's majority on the NEC, which was to serve as Tony Benn's power base, was to reinforce the emergent radicalism of the rank and file of the movement. While the one was to press for constitutional reform, the other was to table proposals for the nationalization of the shipbuilding and pharmaceutical industries and the creation of a National Enterprise Board that would take a stake in Britain's twenty-five largest companies.

Wilson was not alone in condemning the project: 'Who's going to tell me we should nationalise Marks and Spencer in the hope that it will be as efficient as the Co-op?' Tony Crosland was to dismiss the idea as 'half-baked' and 'idiotic', and *Tribune* was to remonstrate: 'Nothing could suit the Tories better than to confine the national debate about public ownership to the precise item of twenty-five companies . . . The inclusion of the phrase was likely to cause the maximum of alarm with the minimum of commitment'. Benn, however, was unrepentant: 'The party is now firmly launched on a left-wing policy . . . it is a remarkable development of views that we have achieved over three years of hard work.' The proposal was not debated by conference in 1973, but it did nothing to relieve the pressure for reform. Piecemeal but inexorably, the demands for change were gaining momentum, and in 1974 Ken Coates, author of *The Crisis of British Socialism* and a member of the Institute for Workers' Control, moved a resolution at conference calling for the mandatory reselection of Labour MPs.

Three years had passed since Dick Taverne had been deselected by the party. Now Ian Mikardo was to liken the process to divorce: 'It should not be easy; divorce should never be easy because divorce is a last resort. Divorce is a confession of failure by both parties, and when this happens it is a confession of failure both by MP and CLP, and therefore it is right that the process should take a little time and there should be some time for thought.'

Although the NEC opposed the resolution it none the less

won more than 2 million votes. And where the CLPD continued to attack what it regarded as the incestuous nature of the power structure within the party, the left-wing MP Stuart Holland was to provide the left with a coherent critique of revisionism.

Published in 1975, *The Socialist Challenge* argued that capitalism was not only irresponsible and inefficient but also perpetuated the inequities of the class structure. Focusing on the expanding power of a small number of large often multinational companies, with all that entailed in terms of their economic and political influence, Holland maintained that Crosland's thesis had been flawed and that traditional methods of regulating the power of monopoly capital were becoming increasingly ineffective. For all the detail of his analysis, his conclusion was straightforward, that such developments 'support the traditional socialist argument that without public ownership and control of the dominant means of production, distribution and exchange, the State will never manage the strategic features of the economy in the public interest'.

The party's legacy was not to be easily expunged, and as the debate within the party intensified, so the situation became increasingly anarchic. In effect, the Labour establishment was fighting its own troops on three fronts – with the unions over what remained of the Social Contract; with the CLPD and a motley of left-wing activists over the form of the party's constitution; and with the NEC over the future direction of socialism itself.

It was a situation that the right, especially Roy Jenkins's coterie, found increasingly intolerable. Recalled from exile to become Home Secretary in Wilson's third administration, Jenkins had already given rein to his disillusionment in a conversation with Wilson in the summer of 1974.

Asked by Wilson what points he intended to raise in a speech he was planning, Jenkins replied: 'That a Labour government should show absolute respect for the law, must explicitly accept the mixed economy, with enthusiasm and not merely toleration for the private sector, and must accept with equal enthusiasm our full membership of the Atlantic community, which had implications for economic policy (no siege economy) as well as for foreign and defence policy.'

If anything was to reinforce Jenkins's concern with the state of the party, it was the growing furore surrounding one of his closest Cabinet allies, the 'bravely accident prone' Reg Prentice. A former trade unionist and Wilson's Secretary of State for Education, Prentice's progressive shift to the right had culminated in a call for his deselection by the Newham Constituency Labour Party. In defence of what Jenkins regarded as a serious constitutional principle, he mustered a handful of colleagues, including Shirley Williams and Bill Rodgers, to campaign for Prentice at a meeting in East Ham Town Hall. The event degenerated into farce, Jenkins being bombarded with flour bags by protesters, and did little to help Prentice's case. In the autumn of 1975, he was deselected by the constituency, to begin a pilgrimage that was to end with him crossing the floor of the House and becoming a Minister in Thatcher's first administration.

Newham represented much more than a victory for the left wing, however. In microcosm, it symbolized the extent and the bitterness of the divide within the party. To the right, it seemed that the party was in the process of losing its senses. To the left, it seemed that it was in the process of recovering them, and while the activists paraded their banners outside East Ham Town Hall – 'Campaign for Labour Democracy – Labour MPs Must Be Chosen – by Labour Party' – Jenkins was left to reflect on what, precisely, they revealed for the future of socialism.

It was to be another twelve months before he gave the first tentative hint of his own conclusions – twelve months during which the CLPD extended its operations into the unions, anxious to secure the block vote in support of mandatory reselection; during which an economic crisis prompted one commentator to write that 'when the International Monetary Fund foreclosed on Britain, it foreclosed in Croslandism'; and during which the hard left pressed for the adoption of an Alternative Strategy reaffirming Labour's traditional commitment to public ownership. Seemingly, socialism was alive and well and personified in Tony Benn, whom Peter Shore came to regard as 'the architect and custodian of party policy' and of whom Marcia Williams was to write: 'he has become a cult hate figure in the way that Shirley Williams has become a cult love figure . . . Never before have I seen antagonism to a leading political figure so openly expressed within his own Party.'

Or at least by his critics, for Benn's unpopularity with the right was in direct proportion to his popularity with constituency activists, and while his critics claimed that he espoused the left to further his own ambitions, his admirers maintained that he articulated exactly what they represented – 'the born-again socialist' of Philip Whitehead's description who had been 'radicalised by his experience of the workers in struggle'. The son of a Labour peer, Benn renounced his title in favour of remaining in the Commons and in 1966 was appointed Minister of Technology by Wilson, who then regarded him as a potential leader of the party. By the mid-1970s Wilson had revised his views, as had Benn.

Disenchanted with what he regarded as the fudge-and-mudge of successive Labour administrations, he was moving progressively to the left, although, with hindsight, Kenneth Morgan's dismissive comment about his populism says more about the party's prejudices at that time than it does about Benn's politics: 'By the end of the 1970s, there seemed hardly a fashionable radical cause – that of the black activist, feminist, "gay lib" or Greenpeace environmentalist – with which he was not passionately identified.'

And it was this, not so much the causes Benn adopted as the passion with which he argued the left's case, that progressively alienated the right. It was a difference that Wilson could not afford, and in June 1975 he sidetracked Benn from the Department of Industry to the Department of Energy in an abortive attempt not only to pacify the pro-European lobby led by Jenkins but also to curb his burgeoning influence with the party's rank and file.

The mood in Cabinet was venomous, and in his diaries Benn provides a revealing insight into the machiavellian games being played in the corridors of power.

On 6 June Benn was summoned to Wilson's room in the Commons, where the two men first discussed the question of whether or not Benn would accept the new appointment and then the implementation of the industrial strategy incorporated in the party manifesto. Wilson was quick to declare his support for the policy, a declaration that Benn was as quick to deny: 'The Industry Bill is in chaos because you've taken me off it. With Eric Heffer [Minister of State at the Department of Trade] and myself gone there is nobody to run it. What you are doing is simply capitulating to the CBI, to the Tory press, and to the Tories themselves, all of whom have demanded my sacking.'

Although no mention was made of Jenkins, Wilson's retort was significant: 'Well, I am not taking Jenkins's advice.' In the cat's-cradle of intrigue that was a feature of the Cabinet during his last days in office Wilson exhausted what remained of his political finesse to hold the centre ground, but there could be no disguising the difference between the right and left and their respective champions – most notably Jenkins and Benn. Once friends, they were to point and counterpoint one another in the years immediately ahead – the one convinced of the need to redefine the meaning of socialism, the other convinced that socialism itself was being betrayed. Indeed all they shared in common was their disenchantment with the present state of the party and their commitment to reordering its future.

It was with some relief that Jenkins resigned from the Cabinet in September 1976 to take up the post of President of the European Commission in the following year. Before he left for Brussels, however, a small group of his friends held a farewell dinner in the Commons where, as Prentice later revealed, Jenkins voiced his growing misgivings about the party and hinted at the need for a realignment in British politics. In the four years that Jenkins was in Brussels, the conflict in the party intensified, for all the efforts of Callaghan and Foot to maintain a semblance of unity. The alliance was a surprising one, for they had neither been friends nor political allies, but there was no questioning Callaghan's sincerity when he declared at the conference in 1976 how much he appreciated the support of his deputy leader for putting aside his personal feelings: 'in the name of the unity of our movement . . . in order to help our party and our government.'

As incisive a journalist as he was a bestriding Parliamentarian – one of a handful of MPs who could pack the chamber of the Commons when he spoke – Foot had edited Beaverbrook's *Evening Standard* during the war but resigned when Beaverbrook refused to allow him to publish an exposé of the Tory right's links with Mussolini.. Elected MP for Devonport in 1945, he was to play the loyalist's role as editor of *Tribune* during the last years of Attlee's government. Foot's shift to the left in support of his political mentor Nye Bevan and the Bevanites, and his loose association with the Keep Left group during the 1950s, tended to disguise the fact that at heart he placed the interests of the party above those of faction. For all of his apostasy – as a leader of the unilateralist movement and a rebel over incomes policy and the Vietnam war – he was first and foremost a party man, but neither his reputation nor his polemical skills could save the party from itself during his time first as Callaghan's deputy and then as leader of the party. Labour, it seemed, was hellbent on self-destruction, and while the unions engaged the government on the industrial front the CLPD extended its demands for a revision of the party's constitution.

Where, initially, the Campaign group had limited its objective to the issue of mandatory reselection, by the late 1970s it was calling for rank-and-file involvement in the election of the party leader, previously in the gift of the Parliamentary Labour Party, and in the drafting of the party manifesto, previously the responsibility of the leader. And as the campaign gathered momentum, so it attracted new and foreboding allies – not least the Militant Tendency. It was to prove a damaging alliance, for where the CLPD was committed to parliamentary methods for achieving social and economic change, Militant had no such reservations.

Committed to Trotsky's vision of 'the permanent revolution', and born out of the congerie of far left factions that existed in the

1950s, Militant produced a paper in 1961 that summarized what was to become its creed: 'The Marxists do not accept the view that it is possible, within the framework of Parliament, or the existing structure of local government, to achieve socialism. The parliamentary system has to be replaced by the Soviet system. This applies on a local as well as a national level.'

A century and more had passed since Feargus O'Connor had stirred the Chartists with the call 'Peaceably if we may – forcibly if we must'; more than half a century since Tom Mann had invoked the Syndicalists 'to declare economic war on capitalism', and now that restless spirit was abroad again. In socialism's rites of passage it seems that there is no substitute for extra-parliamentary activity, and while Roy Hattersley was later to differentiate between the legitimate left and 'the [Trotskyite] cuckoo in the Labour nest', many were happy to exploit the confusion to anathematize dissent, careless of its political credentials.

The full extent of this purge had yet to be revealed when delegates met in Brighton for the conference of 1977 to debate the issue of mandatory reselection. While Callaghan pleaded for the party to reconsider the issue – 'I understand that they [the votes for mandatory reselection] are already in the bag . . . if any of you want to recall your delegations during lunchtime and think again, I shall feel that this speech has been worth while' – he was talking against the tide of opinion. That afternoon the resolution was carried by a million majority. After five years the CLPD had achieved its first objective. And that was not all. Although defeated, three different methods for the future selection of the party leader were tabled by the NEC, while a composite resolution recommending that in future the executive should draft the party's General Election manifesto ('after the widest possible consultation with all sections of the movement') was referred back to the 1980 conference.

Seemingly the whole carefully constructed edifice of power within the party – of top-down control that smacked of the sort of democratic centralism which was a feature of Soviet regimes – was under threat, to reinforce the right's growing alarm, especially that of the Jenkinsites. Committed to Europe and the dictates of the markets, their counter-attack on the left centred largely on constitutional issues. In fact, it is hardly coincidental that within three weeks of the end of the conference Jenkins gave the first hint of a possible break with the party in his Dimbleby Lecture of 22 November.

Earlier he had test-marketed the lecture's contents on Ian Gilmour, Thatcher's Lord Privy Seal and among the first of the 'wets' to leave her Cabinet. Considering his position, Gilmour's reaction was telling, for as Jenkins was to write later: 'He thought much of the end was too right wing. In particular, he objected to the phrase "the social market economy", saying that he thought it had gone out with Erhard [an avowed monetarist, who had served as German Chancellor for three years during the 1960s] until revived by Keith Joseph [Margaret Thatcher's monetarist guru].'

Jenkins's lecture, while circumspect, provided an insight into his thinking, particularly of the need to develop a new political force: 'I believe that . . . if [the electorate] saw a new grouping with cohesion and relevant policies it might be more attracted by this new reality than by old labels which have become increasingly irrelevant.' And again: 'The response to such a situation [of the ideological dogfight racking the Labour Party] in my view should not be to slog through an unending war of attrition . . . but to break out and mount a battle of movement for new and higher ground.'

Significantly, in light of what was to come, Jenkins concluded by calling for the strengthening of 'the radical centre'. An oxymoron defying exact definition, the phrase was to enter the political lexicon, although at the time few in the Labour Party appreciated the full implications of Jenkins's remark or what it would mean for the future.

In his biography *Time and Chance* Callaghan was to reflect that his last days in power were 'not a happy period' – an understatement of Olympian proportions. After a lifetime in Labour politics, it seemed that the party was on the verge of civil war. The left was rampant, and the greater their success the more they demanded, and the more they demanded the greater the reaction from the right. At a Wembley conference in mid-May 1980 delegates endorsed a manifesto advocating the extension of public ownership and calling for increased public expenditure and wide-ranging reforms of the European Community, while on 30 May Tony Benn was among those present at what he called 'a new left gathering' – a combination of radical groups including the CLPD, the Institute for Workers' Control and the Socialist Campaign for Labour Victory committed to implementing a programme of party democracy.

Jenkins's worst fears were being realized, and in a speech to the parliamentary press gallery on 10 June he deplored Labour's 'major lurch to the left' and reflected: 'The likelihood at the start of most adventures is that of failure. The experimental plane may well finish up a few fields from the end of the runway . . . But the reverse could occur, and the experimental plane soar into the sky. If that is so it could go further and more quickly than few now imagine, for it could carry with it great and now untapped reserves of political energy and commitment.'

The Westminster press corps had no difficulty in deciphering the message, coded as it was, and neither had Callaghan. The challenge from the left was being met with an altogether more ominous threat from the right: the prospect of the break-up of the party itself. Only five days after Jenkins's speech one of his closest confidants, David Owen, launched a savage attack on Callaghan at a meeting of the Shadow Cabinet, claiming that in giving his support to a proposal for the creation of an electoral college to choose the party leader he was betraying the parliamentary party. Callaghan gave as good as he got, accusing Owen of conspiring with Jenkins to form a new political party. He was right in everything but the time-scale involved.

The Jenkinsites might conspire among themselves, but in the summer of 1980 they were still unprepared to go it alone. There were too many imponderables in play for that: questions as to how long Callaghan would remain in office and who would replace him;

of the response of leading Shadow Cabinet figures such as Healey (with whom the Jenkinsites had already had long discussions), Gerard Kaufman and Ray Hattersley if a breakaway were to occur; and the Liberals' reaction to such a development. The stakes were as high as the risks involved, but as the left maintained its pressure it reinforced the nerve of Jenkins's confederates, the so-called Gang of Three (Owen, Bill Rodgers and Shirley Williams) to play their hand. On the first day of the party conference of 1980 Benn set the tone for much that was to follow, announcing from the platform that Labour would be required to introduce three major pieces of legislation within a month of being returned to office: an Industry Bill to extend public ownership, a bill to take Britain out of the EEC and a Bill to abolish the House of Lords – if necessary by the creation of a thousand new peers.

The left was ecstatic, the Shadow Cabinet appalled and Shirley Williams incensed. The party was living in a dream world, but reality was made of different stuff and, dismissing Benn's three pledges, she concluded: 'And all this would be done in a couple of weeks. I wonder why Tony was so unambitious. After all, it took God only six days to make the world.' For all the right's rearguard action in defence of what they regarded as political sanity, however, conference was in no mood to forgo its new-found radicalism. Motivated, in part, by the evidence emerging of Thatcher's reactionary agenda ('the distilled monetarist frenzy' as Gilmour was later to describe it), in part by memories of past disappointments, delegates voted by overwhelming majorities to campaign for unilateral nuclear disarmament, to reject any form of incomes policy and to hold a further conference in January 1981 to finalize plans for the composition of an electoral college under whose aegis future leadership contests would be decided.

For Williams it was a timely deadline, and in the last days of the conference she suggested that the Gang of Three would give the party until January to resolve its differences, after which . . . and the question hung in the Blackpool air like a storm cloud from off the Pennines. For Callaghan it was the deciding moment. Determined that his successor should not have to subjected to the hazards of the proposed new electoral procedures, he resigned as leader of the party on 15 October. Healey was quick to announce candidature ('I was obviously the front runner, and no one else from the right or the centre of the party challenged me'), as were Peter Shore and John Silkin, both standing on a moderate left platform. Momentarily it was a three-horse race, prompting Ian Mikardo to remark: 'My immediate reaction was to wonder how anyone could possibly imagine that Peter Shore or John Silkin had any chance whatsoever of beating Healey', and it was not until 20 October that Michael Foot was persuaded to allow his name to go forward.

Never happier than when harrying the government in power from the back benches, he had little inclination to enter the lists. The party, however, came before his personal preferences, not least the realization that if Healey were elected it could well split the party. The left had no truck either for the man or his policies – at Blackpool he had opposed virtually every major resolution passed by conference – and yet without a credible alternative it seemed to Foot that Healey could win by as many as thirty votes. In the event Foot was to win by ten votes on the second ballot, for one of his leading campaigners, Neil Kinnock, to 'let out a blood-curdling Indian war whoop' and for Foot himself to call up the words of his mentor Nye Bevan, 'Never underestimate the passion for unity in the party.'

Two months later, on 24 January 1981, the special conference called to decide the composition of the electoral college voted in favour of a forty–thirty–thirty balance between the unions, the parliamentary party and the constituencies. Before singing the 'Red Flag' David Owen left the platform, declaring that 'Four trade union barons meeting in a smoke-filled room was no way to elect a Prime Minister', and the following day the Gang of Four (with Jenkins now in the forefront) called a press conference where they issued their so-called Limehouse Declaration:

> The calamitous outcome of the Labour Party Wembley Conference
> demands a new start in British politics . . .We recognise that for
> those people who have given much of their lives to the Labour
> Party, the choice that lies ahead will be deeply painful. But we
> believe that the need for a realignment of British politics must now
> be faced.

For all of Michael Foot's heartfelt appeal the unthinkable had
finally occurred. After three-quarters of a century, the Labour
Party had divided against itself.

As far as Labour was concerned the Gang of Four had stood for
too long upon their going, and their departure was greeted with a
compound of delight, anger and bitterness in the party: the
delight of the radicals who regarded their defection as the legit-
imization of their policies; the anger of the moderates who were
never to forgive the defectors their act of treachery; and the bitterness of Michael Foot to whom the exercise of power had little
appeal yet who had become leader of a party which appeared to
be disintegrating about him. Within days of the publication of the
Limehouse Declaration twelve Labour MPs had resigned the
party whip, and when the Social Democratic Party was formally
launched on 26 March Foot could no longer contain his contempt
for its founders: 'Their Party starts with an act of dishonour. They
will never be able to wipe away the stain.'

During the civil war of the 1980s few can have foreseen what
the SDP presaged for the future of the Labour Party or envisaged
that sixteen years later one of David Owen's closest advisers, the
MP turned academic David Marquand, would write cautiously but
none the less appreciatively of the Blair government: 'Like the
Owenite SDP in the 1980s, New Labour in the 1990s has accepted
the central assumptions of the Thatcherite counter-revolution in
political economy: that is what makes New Labour new.'

Left and right, the grounds for the contest for the future of
socialism had been drawn, although in 1981 the Gang of Four's

defection, and the subsequent establishment of the SDP, fortified the left's confidence in its own agenda and reinforced its already powerful standing within the party.

Half the members of the NEC (including five trade unionists) were left-wingers, which led Foot to write later that in their disputes with the right the Committee: 'was transformed into a mock Parliament of the Labour movement in which every shade of difference was examined and broadcast, every division recorded and enflamed . . . Open government was interpreted to mean perpetual disagreements openly arrived at.'

Apparently the departure of the SDP had done nothing to assuage the differences within the party, and there could be no disguising them when, on April Fool's Day 1981 Benn announced that he intended to stand for the deputy leadership of the party against Foot's preferred choice, Denis Healey. A born fighter, who had fashioned a blunt instrument out of his native Yorkshire wit, Healey had been a member of the Communist Party while at Oxford, but on entering the Commons in 1952 he sided with Gaitskell in his contest with the Bevanites. Healey was a quintessential individualist whom Crossman once described as 'a very lone mover'. He had had extensive ministerial experience, having served as Minister of Defence under Wilson and Chancellor under Callaghan. None the less he was a somewhat reluctant candidate for a post he was later to compare with that of the Vice-President of the USA: 'If he is bad he can do much damage; if he is good, he can do nothing.' In the spring of 1981, however, he was convinced that there was one thing he could do – check Benn's bid for power in the belief that if he had become deputy leader 'there would have been a haemorrhage of defections to the SDP both in Parliament and in the country. I do not believe that the Labour Party could have recovered.'

Six years had passed since Marcia Williams had cast Benn as a bogy figure to be exorcized by the Labour establishment, six years during which Benn's demonization by certain of his colleagues had helped to establish him as leader of the party's left wing. Damned by some as a political maverick for his commitment to the democratization of the party, by others of promoting a leadership cult, Benn none the less represented the mood of much of the rank and file of the party. For all Michael Foot's protests that the idea of 'perpetual, non-stop elections' was 'the politics of the kindergarten', and that conference decisions were not absolute, there were sound grounds for the critics' charge of disenfranchisement and their consequent demands for constitutional reform.

The contest proved as poisonous as any in the history of the party, the tribes of left and right engaging one another in a spectacle of public bloodletting – not least because Benn's campaign attracted a brawl of Militants who harried Healey whenever he appeared in public and of whom Healey was to write in his biography: 'They gave the party a reputation for extremism, violence, hatred and division from which it has not yet recovered.' Few of Militant's revolutionary plans were ever stated explicitly, but it is unquestionable that its extremist tactics did irreparable damage to the cause it pretended to represent, not only by alienating moderate opinion but also by disguising the fact that there was a case to be made out for devolution of power within the party which, in Benn's opinion, was one reason why he entered the contest: to compel people to make choices:

> That's what's called polarization, divisiveness, and all the rest, but it's true. You can't go on for ever and ever pretending you're a socialist party when you're not, pretending to do something when you won't, confining yourself to attacks on the Tories when that's not enough. People want to know what the Labour Party will do and I think that this process is long overdue.

And the choice, when it came, was pathetically slim. At the party conference in Brighton in September the vote under the new forty–thirty–thirty electoral college rules split 50.4 per cent to 49.5 per cent in favour of Healey. Significantly a couple of left-wing unions voted for Healey, and two days later the right won an additional five seats on the National Executive. While Healey's campaign manager, Giles Radice, held that in beating Benn Healey had 'saved the Labour Party', and Healey considered that the results of the election for the NEC had finally broken 'the stranglehold of the left on the party', those on the right who thought they could now launch a counter-revolution were soon to be disillusioned. The balance of power in the party may have shifted, but Labour's commitments to the Alternative Economic Strategy, to withdrawing from the EEC and to unilateral nuclear disarmament remained unchanged.

At Brighton the right had won a battle, but the war had still to be won. In recognition of the differences that still rent the party, and in a further attempt to secure unity, Foot paid handsome tributes to both Healey and Benn in his conference speech: 'What I want to see is a new Labour Cabinet in which Denis Healey and Tony Benn and a few others . . . play leading and honourable parts . . .What we want to see is a proper tolerance established and sustained throughout the party as a whole.' Once again, his plea was in vain. The influence of the left may have been contained, but Benn remained the guardian of its interests on the NEC, while as far as such 'entryist' factions as Militant Tendency were concerned tolerance had no place in their vocabulary, as a young Australian, Peter Tatchell, revealed in an article in *London Labour Briefing*:

> Labour has lost the radical and defiant spirit of its early pioneers . . . Reliance on the present token and ineffectual parliamentary opposition will advance us nowhere. We must look to new, more militant forms of extra-parliamentary opposition which involve mass popular participation and challenge the government's right to rule.

Like the Commonwealth grandees of the civil war, it may have seemed to the Bennites that they had 'raised those spirits which they could not lay'.

Although not a member of Militant Tatchell was closely associated with the Tendency's views, and when he was selected to stand as Labour candidate for the Bermondsey by-election in November 1981 it precipitated a new crisis within the party. On 26 November Shirley Williams was on the way to winning a notable victory for the SDP in the Crosby by-election, while in the Commons Thatcher was taunting Foot with the charge that Tatchell was typical of the new, extremist Labour Party that he led. For a moment it must have seemed that he was in a no-win situation – that the unity he sought was indeed illusory – although only momentarily.

At a meeting of the NEC Foot instructed the retiring General Secretary of the party, Ron Hayward, to conduct a full-scale inquiry into Militant's activities. Although backed by the Executive Foot's decision provoked a bitter response from the left, not least from Chris Mullin, a committed Bennite and editor of *Tribune*. A quarter of a century had passed since Foot the Bevanite had edited the paper and used it as a platform to denounce witch-hunting and maintain that differences amongst socialists should be settled by free debates between them, yet now it seemed that he, too, had fallen victim to the authoritarian practices he had once anathematized.

The publication of Hayward's report, however, vindicated Foot's decision. As Peter Shore was to write, the report left no doubt that Militant was a disciplined organization: 'with political principles and a programme quite distinct from that of the Labour Party; a Trotskyist revolutionary party with a clear and central strategy of "entryism" with the purpose of capturing the weakly organised and frequently gullible institutions of the democratic socialist Labour Party'.

When the core members of Militant were finally expelled as a result of some subtle manoeuvring on the part of the NEC, the damage had already been done – and not only to the image of the party. In discrediting the legitimate left Militant undermined the campaign to democratize the party and provided a sanction for the increasingly authoritarian regimes that were to come. And even this was not all, for the hostility that their campaign generated did much to provoke the backlash that was to follow Labour's defeat in 1983 – and the consequent emergence of New Labour.

Michael Foot's acceptance of electoral defeat in the early hours of 9 June 1983 could not disguise his despair: 'It was the verdict of the electorate not only on our campaign but also on the whole period prior to it.' His wretchedness was understandable. Some months before, in answer to a suggestion that there was something rotten in the state of the Labour Party, he had replied with unusual acerbity: 'Cursed spite, that I was ever asked to put it right', and this is what it had come to – the loss of fifty-five Labour seats and Margaret Thatcher's return with a punishing 144-seat majority. While Foot was to lay much of the blame for Labour's defeat on the treachery of 'the defectors from our ranks', however, his deputy, Denis Healey, was to identify the party's image for 'crankiness, extremism, and general unfitness to govern' as the cause of the débâcle. This, in essence, was the tragedy of Michael Foot – the one-time rebel whose commitment to unifying the party he led was mocked by the differences that divided it.

Of course, they had always existed, but as the full extent of the disaster became clear one thing became obvious: that the party could never allow such a thing to happen again. This, in its turn, posed the question: on whose terms should Labour contest Thatcher's majority? What lessons, in fact, could be learned from the débâcle? The SDP had been decimated at the polls, and yet Gerald Kaufman was to describe the uncompromising tone of Labour's election manifesto as 'the longest suicide note in history'. Who was right? Should Labour shift towards the centre ground in pursuit of the fabled votes of Middle England and, in the process, revise, if not discard, its commitment to the party's founding principles, or should it refuse to compromise with revisionism?

They were questions that Foot left his successor to resolve. Less that forty-eight hours after the final results had been declared he resigned as leader of the party, to endorse Neil

Kinnock's nomination as his heir. Other candidates entered the contest (Roy Hattersley, Eric Heffer and Peter Shore), but at the party conference of 1983 Kinnock received an overwhelming 71 per cent of the votes cast by the electoral college. While the right may have had their suspicions about his political credentials, the left had no such doubts. At the age of forty-one Kinnock had already established his radical qualifications as a critic of the Wilson and Callaghan governments, as a paid-up member of the Tribune group and as a committed exponent of public ownership, unilateralism and Euroscepticism.

Only one question remained to be asked as far as Peter Shore was concerned. Kinnock might have 'a complete kit of then fashionable left-wing viewpoints', but did he have a settled conviction in any of them? The answers, when they came, were to devastate his former allies. Once in office Kinnock – 'the prophet from Tredegar' – was to adopt Barbara Castle's axiom that to govern is to choose and in making a choice of pragmatism adopted reality as the touchstone of his mandate: the reality of a party that had 'treated realism as treachery' and of its need to recognize 'the harsh electoral reality' that if Labour did not broaden its electoral base it could well be condemned to the political wilderness. During his early days in office Kinnock's commitment to pragmatism may have been little more than a damage limitation exercise, not least to limit the harm done to the party by what the media delighted in calling 'the loony left'. Allied to the fact that for all their poor showing in the number of MPs returned, the Liberals and the SDP had, between them, garnered 25.4 per cent of the vote, Kinnock's reflections on extremism undoubtedly played a significant role in conditioning his thinking when he came to appraise what the future held for the Labour Party.

The immediate need was to restore some semblance of discipline in the party, while recognizing that 'if you make the change at a speed which is not agreed or acceptable to the Labour movement, then you smash into the wall of the block vote or uproar in the constituencies'. As to the uproar, with the exception of Militant outposts such as Brighton, Kemptown and Liverpool, it was already muted as a result of the election débâcle. As to the block vote, it was the unions that were to provide Kinnock and his successors with their platform for the modernization of the party. Since the Conservatives' election victory in 1979 there had been growing evidence of the TUC's loss of nerve as the government tightened its grip on industrial relations. Frederick von Hayek, guru of the new right, had no hesitation about declaring that 'the whole basis of our free society is gravely threatened by the powers arrogated by the unions', and the Thatcherites had few qualms about applying his solution to the problem: 'to rescind every single privilege granted to the trade unions'.

In 1981 the Employment Secretary Jim Prior steered a Bill through the Commons which restricted picketing to a striker's place of work and a union's legal immunity for secondary action. As far as the Tory right was concerned, however, even this was not enough, and in September Prior was 'reshuffled' and Norman Tebbit appointed Secretary of State for Employment with orders from the Prime Minister to increase the pace of trade union reform. He needed no encouragement.

A hard-liner, Tebbit had already made plain his opinion of the unions: 'Today the cloth-capped Colonels of the TUC use their power for political ends . . . We can all see the evil, but the doctrine of appeasement is still to be heard. If the evil is so powerful that the faint hearts say it must be appeased, then there is all the more reason to deal with it before it becomes stronger still.'

Tebbit's conclusion was unequivocal. There was to be no appeasing what Thatcher came to call 'the enemy within', and shortly before the election of 1983 he laid down the provisions for the next tranche of industrial legislation, including measures to remove a union's legal immunity from any strike which had not been approved by its members in a secret ballot and requiring the governing bodies of all unions to be selected by secret ballot every five years. Only one hope of frustrating Tebbit's punitive package remained open to the unions, the return of a Labour government,

271

and with that hope gone the TUC lost what remaining appetite it had for militancy. If anything was to fortify its decision to carry moderation to extremes it was the collapse of the miners' strike in March 1985.

As early as 1977 the Conservatives had drawn up plans to confront and break the National Union of Mineworkers, long the praetorian guard of the labour movement. Seven years later it was to be employed with devastating effect. The strike, lasting 358 days, was the longest and bloodiest of the post-war years, yet it received only token support from the TUC, while the Labour leadership carefully distanced itself from any involvement in the dispute, an act of betrayal that prompted South Wales miners to fashion a banner in which Kinnock was caricatured as Ramsay MacKinnock. The legend said as much about Kinnock's dilemma as it did about the miners' sense of bitterness. The son of a miner, and raised in a mining community just over the hill from the Ebbw Vale constituency represented by Nye Bevan and Michael Foot, Kinnock's private sympathies may have been with the miners, but *realpolitik* demanded that the interests of the party came before his personal preferences.

It was a deciding moment in Kinnock's career, the moment when he rejected much of his own past in favour of an uncertain future. As for his political convictions, the indecisions remained. In an interview with the Marxist historian Eric Hobsbawn late in 1984 he insisted that 'we are committed to a process of re-nationalisation' as 'the only means to give coherence to the most efficient organisation of our resources'. Significantly he added the caveat that 'To pose stark alternatives between the public economy and the market economy is supreme folly.' Kinnock, it seemed, was locked in an ideological wrangle with himself, and it was only with the publication of the Fabian pamphlet *The Future of Socialism* in 1985 that the first clear signs of revisionism appeared. Rejecting 'the stale vanguardism of the ultra left and . . . the atavistic and timid premise of social democracy', Kinnock called for the party to adopt a 'third way' which, in recognizing the shift that had taken place in society, would allow it to realign itself. Faint as it was, there could be no escaping the echo of the SDP's call to break the mould of British politics, although Kinnock was careful to assert that his formula involved 'a shift in attitudes and presentation, not a change in principles'.

For all his protestations, Kinnock was indeed shifting his ideological position, to write approvingly in 1986 that 'the market is potentially a powerful force for good'. His critics maintained that there was no substance to Kinnock's rhetoric, but while the left railed at 'the Welsh windbag' there was little it could do to check his campaign to impose discipline on the party. With the support of the unions he had succeeded in isolating the left on the NEC, for the BBC's long-serving political editor, John Cole, to reflect that by 1987 Kinnock 'believed that he was about halfway through his efforts to put the Labour Party in good order again'. All that remained to be answered was what the other half of his project entailed.

Although scaled down, the party went to the country in the election of 1987 on much the same fundamentalist platform as it had fought the previous election – with much the same result. While the Conservative majority was reduced to a little over a hundred seats, Labour won only 30 per cent of the vote, against a 42 per cent share for the Tories. The left were completely demoralized by the outcome, and their disarray was compounded with the publication of the party's *Statement of Democratic Socialist Aims and Values* in 1988.

Echoing both the ideology and the tone of mid-nineteenth-century Utilitarians such as J. S. Mill, the *Statement* argued that socialism existed 'to provide – for the largest number of people – the ability to exercise effective liberty' and that such an goal could only be achieved by 'the more equal distribution of resources'. This was all very well as far as it went, but then it went too far for the purist tastes of the left, maintaining, as it did, that 'outside the area of natural monopoly, public utility and social services, markets are essential to any definition of socialism, which includes the encouragement of diversity and individual liberty and the economic autonomy (public or private) that goes with these essential conditions.'

Although the *Statement* was quick to deny any sympathy for an unregulated free market the left was quick to denounce it as 'socialism betrayed', remonstrating that Labour was now in the business of 'running capitalism better than the Tories'. At the conference of 1988, however, the left's attack on revisionism received little support, while the full extent of their loss of influence was revealed when Benn and Heffer's challenge for the leadership and deputy leadership were voted down by decisive majorities.

With his authority reinforced, Kinnock continued to pursue his reformist project. What little still remained of his past had no place in his political agenda and, confident that when push came to shove he would command the support of both the parliamentary party and the National Executive, he launched the next phase of his modernization programme, a policy review which, as it progressed, became increasingly revisionist. Nothing, it seemed, was sacrosanct, and when it was published in 1989 Ivor Crewe, Professor of Government at the University of Essex, was to describe *Meet the Challenge, Make the Change* as 'the least socialist policy statement ever to be published by the party'.

The whole world, or leastways, that part of it which had formerly subscribed to the manifold varieties of socialism, had been turned upside down. Indeed, there was a certain symmetry in the fact that at much the same time as the Cold War was ending and the Berlin Wall coming down – events which Francis Fukuyama described, albeit prematurely, as 'the end of history' – the Labour Party was in the process of rewriting its creed. If capitalism was triumphant, then it had no place for the remnants of socialism and, as Peter Shore was to write in *Leading the Left*, the party accepted the conversion with surprising ease: the commitment to a virtually unregulated market economy; the privatization of virtually the whole public sector; not only continued membership of the European Community but all the growing constraints that the

1986 Single European Act had imposed on state intervention in the economy; and acceptance of the major part of Thatcher's legislation on trade unions.

This was hardly Fabian socialism, let alone Fabian gradualism, rather a conscious effort to exorcize the party's past. Apparently Labour's founding principles were too strong for the new electorate, although as the architect of New Labour even Kinnock could not have foreseen where his commitment to modernization would eventually lead. Only five years had passed since he had pledged himself to safeguarding Labour's integrity, and now he was to be commended by the former SDP guru David Marquand as ' a better – or, at any rate, a more successful – revisionist than Gaitskell had ever been'. In the mid-1980s Thatcher had coined the catchphrase TINA – 'there is no alternative'. Now Labour was to adopt to it, maintaining that there was no feasible alternative to revanchism.

It had taken the party a quarter of a century to learn the lessons of embourgeoisement, and while continuing to pay lip-service to its traditional constituency it was significant that Marquand's analysis concluded that Labour's realignment had been opinion-survey driven rather that doctrine driven. It was to prove a powerful tool, the more so when added to the stress Kinnock had placed on 'a shift in attitudes and presentation' – a precept which may have done something to provoke Roy Hattersley's caustic remark that, having disposed of the *Statement of Democratic Socialist Aims and Values* before the coffee break at the 1988 conference, the delegates then turned their attention 'to the aspects of policy which we most enjoyed – not formulation but presentation'. The question was: presentation of what? Having jettisoned so many of its former commitments, what were to be put in their place? The party was long on rhetoric, but what of its political substance? What, precisely, did New Labour mean?

At best, the answers appeared elusive, at worst, the products of New Labour's image merchants. While successive polls in the early 1990s revealed that the party was becoming 'voter-friendly', the shift was insufficient to secure a Labour victory in the election of April 1992. In fact there was a certain irony in the fact that an element of Labour's failure at the polls was later attributed its new-found marketing skills, not least the premature triumphalism of the Sheffield conference stage-managed by Peter Mandelson. Apparently presentation was not all, although it was enough to encourage the leadership in its belief that image was important as essence in its pursuit of power.

Within seventy-two hours of the polls closing Neil Kinnock resigned as leader, to reflect later that part of the blame for the defeat lay with the savage media campaign that had been mounted against Labour, partly with his own personal image ('Some people say it's to do with Welshness'), but mainly because 'we still hadn't secured enough trust among the people . . . Our opponents were able to exploit ideas articulated by Mrs Thatcher and repeated by John Major that if they [the Labour Party] will move away from things that they have said to be fundamental parts of their conviction in order to get support, can't they move back again?'

It was a suspicion that John Smith did much to allay during his twenty-one months as party leader. An Edinburgh lawyer with impeccable right-wing credentials who had served for five years as Labour's Shadow Chancellor, Smith inherited a party in bullish mood. Although Labour had gone down to its fourth successive electoral defeat, the Tory majority had been slashed to twenty-one seats, and the conference of 1992 proved to be a buoyant, even self-congratulatory affair. After thirteen years in limbo it seemed that Labour was recovering confidence in the fact that it did indeed have a political future, and the delegates were as happy to confirm Smith's leadership as they were to endorse his brief policy document, *Agenda for Change*. As with Kinnock's revisionist agenda, Smith espoused the European Community and the mixed economy, while reinforcing the centralized control of the party with the establishment of a new joint policy committee to be made up of members of the NEC and the Shadow Cabinet and to include the chairman of the recently created National Policy

Forum – a foretaste of the focus groups yet to come.

Although his tenure in office was brief, no leader in Labour's history had exercised such authority over the party. Dissent had been all but crushed. The constituencies were relatively quiescent, while the unions – or at least their leaders – actively supported the leadership's revisionist programme. In fact Dennis Skinner, a veteran critic of the establishment and in 1997 one of the few remaining members of 'Old Labour' on the NEC, has no hesitation in laying the blame for Labour's loss of confidence in its socialist traditions squarely at the door of the TUC:

> Every single decision that has been taken since 1983 has been backed by a fairly substantial majority of conference votes, and that could not have been achieved without the trade unions and their block votes. I find it fanciful when I read headlines about union threats to the leadership here, there and everywhere when the truth is that they have backed virtually every decision taken by Neil Kinnock, John Smith and Tony Blair. A lot of people don't understand that revisionism, or whatever you call it, has actually been given life by the trade unions.

It was an arrangement that served New Labour well. For all its compromises the party continued to distance itself from the unions, insisting that there was no alternative to it becoming 'the party of business'. The break with the past was explicit, not that the role reversal appeared to trouble New Labour's conscience. On the contrary, following John Smith's death in May 1994 it was a platform that helped Blair to accelerate the process of reinventing the party, for Peter Mandelson (reinstated to power by Blair after being marginalized by Smith) and Roger Liddle (one-time member of the inner circle of the SDP) to write:

> Labour's current phase of reinvention was started by Neil Kinnock and continued by John Smith. But, essentially, they were engaged in a ground-clearing operation – first to rid the party of the

Bennite excesses that had led to the SDP split . . . and then to
restore its unity of purpose and democratise its internal procedures.

This was the base on which Blair was to build and which was to
allow him: 'to lead the party in the restatement of its values and the
wholesale modernisation of its policies'. The words sounded well,
but they disguised the intent. While the emphasis was on the need
to democratize the party, the process of concentrating power in the
hands of the leadership continued apace. Indeed, there was a certain irony in the fact that it was Tony Benn's long-standing rival,
Roy Hattersley, who not only questioned the nature of the democratization process but also the direction of the New Labour project:

Ideology is what keeps parties consistent and honest. In the long
term, the party's public esteem would be protected by a robust
statement of fundamental intention. Socialism – which is proclaimed in the new Clause IV – requires the bedrock of principle
to be the redistribution of power and wealth.

The revised clause offered neither, but its passage in 1995
became a test as much of New Labour's faith in itself as in its
capacity to manage dissent. After sixteen years, there could be no
question about the electorate's growing disenchantment with the
Conservative government and no question either of Labour's
anxiety to get their hands on the levers of power.

For Blair and the party modernizers the new clause was the
keystone of their project of reinventing Labour in their own
image. Abandoning any reference to the original version's commitments to 'the most equitable distribution of the fruits of industry' and to 'the best obtainable system of popular administration
of each industry or service' – part of a formulary that Mandelson
and Liddle regarded as 'infamous' – Blair himself was to read the
final rites over Labour's 'sacred text': 'The Labour Party is not a
preservation society. Those who seriously believed that we cannot
improve on words written for the world of 1908 when they are

now in 1995 are not learning from the past but living in it.'

A Christian Socialist, it seemed that Blair had no hesitation about rewriting his secular principles and, with them, much that was fundamental to Christian Socialism itself. John Ball's cry 'When Adam delved and Eve span, who was then the Gentleman?' was to be restated five centuries later when William Temple, later to be appointed Archbishop of Canterbury, declared:

> God wished the earth to be the common possession of all men, to produce its fruit for all men, but avarice created the rights of property . . . If Christianity is to be applied to the economic system, an organisation which rests primarily on the principle of competition must give way to one which rests primarily on co-operation.

An article of faith predating the publication of the original Clause IV, Temple's affirmation was to be replaced in 1995 by a formula (see Appendix 1) commended by Blair as speaking the people's language but which the *Independent* was to dismiss as showing 'no ambition to transform the fundamental contours of society' and which the *Guardian* was to catechize in the headline: 'Clause Four is dead. Long live – what?'

It was a question that defied an exact response, for while Blair was to declare that 'the old ideologies are dead' and that the new clause represented a defining moment in Labour's history, the exact definition of its meaning remained open to debate, provoking the radical QC Mike Mansfield to remark that 'it was an interesting reflection on modern times that it took Sidney and Beatrice Webb 60 words to spell out what is essential and it takes Tony Blair 300'. Like so much else, it appeared to their critics that the party leadership was spinning ideas like gossamer – now invoking visions of 'a stakeholder society', now of 'communitarianism', now 'of a new political settlement', now of 'one-nation socialism' – to make a web for the public mind.

For all the terminological spin, however, it seemed that, once begun, there was no end to the revisionist's project, that what had begun in response to Thatcher's dance with dogma was developing a momentum of its own in pursuit of a radical centre that its critics damned as a contradiction in terms and that even its admirers had trouble in locating. For Denis Healey the phrase is meaningless, to be dismissed with a single expletive and the afterthought 'an ideology with a hole in the middle'; while for Peter Shore the words disguise the reality that Labour is no longer what Harold Wilson regarded as a moral crusade:

> I'm not sure that a radical centre exists. New Labour is something quite distinct from the previous strands in the party and the debates that took place between them. It seems to me to be free of virtually all socialist philosophy and totally directed at the centre of British political opinion and that, having taken account of Middle England's preferences and prejudices, it has constructed itself around them. I regard this as a curiously passive approach to politics. Of course, Labour should be a listening party, but on the basis of its principles it should provide positive leadership as well.

As for Tony Wright, author of *Socialisms Old and New* and a leading player in Blair's New Labour team, all definitions of what the radical centre means lack precision simply because they reflect the uncertainties of the times:

> We are living in new political territory. The question is: How do we make a kind of politics which is different from what went before? I think that what the radical centre is trying to do is to put together things which for so long were thought to be opposites: faith and the markets; the collective and the individual; the public and the private. This is radical territory, and in trying to build on a shared starting point it is not at all clear what the implications are for many areas of policy.

However elusive the goal, it did nothing to discourage the revisionists, charismatics on the road to a New Jerusalem which its critics maintained was not so much a political mirage, more a recrudescence of neo-Thatcherism. And with some justification. Historically, progressive taxation to secure not only the redistribution of income, but also to finance the welfare state, had been the centrepiece of Labour's economic agenda. Now New Labour was to abandon it, for Blair to rubbish 'the nonsense' that social justice was measured by public spending and commit the party to a policy of low inflation and fiscal probity; while his Shadow Chancellor, Gordon Brown, was to reject any notion of a return to Labour's traditional, 'tax and spend policies', preferring to float the idea of tax cuts for middle-income voters, a proposal that provoked the *Guardian* to declare that 'To many traditional Labour supporters it will look quite bizarre that the historic party of redistribution is shelling it out in the reverse direction – to people earning between £26,000 and £30,000 a year.'

Brown's economic package undoubtedly appealed to the stakeholders of Middle England, careless of what his fiscal rectitude might mean for the future of the welfare state. As early as November 1995, however, there were already clear signs of what that future would hold, a leaked report revealing the outline of Brown's welfare-to-work proposals. Six months later, Chris Smith, the Shadow Social Security Secretary, was to reveal the full extent of Labour's policy shift when he published details of a new welfare system, under which private insurance would play a greater role:

> Surely it is time to get away from the sterile battle lines of public and private and, instead, look at how the two can best work to together in the interests of the citizen . . . How in every specific it [the new welfare system] is to be delivered is a matter of sensible judgement and rational analysis. It is not simply a matter of how much money is spent.

Committed to the free play of the markets, it appeared that New Labour's strategy was to dismember socialism piecemeal – a strategy that was to be reinforced by Blair's growing insistence that the party was pledged to ditching 'its traditional approach of intervening to control industry' – and was actively considering the privatization of utilities still in public control. In the run-up to the election of 1997, the message was fleshed out with growing precision: 'Blair woos industry with new contract' (*Guardian*, November 1994); 'Labour pledges hands-off industry policy' (*The Times*, June 1995); 'Blair shift on Europe to woo CBI' (*Guardian*, November 1995); 'More work rights rejected by Blair' (*Daily Telegraph*, June1996); 'Labour's capital road from socialism' (*Independent*, July 1996; 'Gordon Brown, veteran of the long march to economic respectability' (*The Times*, February 1997). And as Labour's relationship with industry and the City waxed, so its relationship with the unions waned – Blair making it clear that in future they would never be again be able to put 'an armlock' on Labour or its policies.

A century had passed since the unions had been among the founder members of the ILP, and in November 1996 Lord Callaghan was to remind New Labour that 'It is our heritage that we keep the link between the unions and the party. Only if you believe that can you understand the party.' As contemptuous of Labour's heritage as they were chary of the unions, the modernizers had no truck with Callaghan's warning. The past might be an interesting place to visit but was no place to stay, and in March 1997 at much the same time as Blair's aide, Geoff Hoon, the MP for Ashfield, was listing the converts to Labour among Britain's business establishment (although not the amounts they had contributed to the party's funds), Blair was reminding the media that 'After every change we are proposing, Britain will remain with a more restrictive trade union framework than any other country in the Western world.' New Labour, it seemed, demanded new friends.

As details of the New Labour project emerged it became increasingly clear that this was precisely the object of the exercise – whether by staging a reprise of a long distant past, although this time with the roles reversed, by engaging in 'full and frank discussions' with Paddy Ashdown and the Liberal democrats, or by sacrificing civil liberties in favour of 'zero tolerance' in an attempt to wrest the law and order vote from Tory control. Not that the policy was for public consumption only. Kinnock and Smith may have done much to ring-fence the left, but it was the modernizers who were to adopt a policy of zero tolerance towards any form of dissent. With the unions neutralized, and party headquarters having appropriated many of the constituencies' powers, new rules of conduct were drawn up for MPs, creating the open-ended offence of 'bringing the party into disrepute' which, in effect, would allow the whips to suspend dissenting Members at will.

During his disputes with the Gaitskellites in the 1950s Bevan had remarked: 'Either we restore the healthy vigour of Parliament which comes with independent discussion and criticism, or we submit to the corporate rule of big business and collaborationist Labour leaders.' If the modernizers recognized themselves in the description, it did nothing to check their pursuit of dissent, and in June 1996 the *Observer* reported that 'Labour MPs judged below standard or disloyal may be barred from standing as official candidates after the General Election', adding that, in future, constituencies would be urged to select candidates from a list drawn up by the party's National Executive. Slowly, yet inexorably, New Labour was tightening the leading strings of power, ensuring that criticism would become increasingly fragmented. Where independent discussion and criticism had once been the life force of the party, uniformity was now the rule, the silence of consent only being broken by the occasional despairing attack on the 'new Stalinists' in Blair's entourage, Richard Burden, the MP for Birmingham Northfield, writing in the *New Statesman*:

> Power is increasingly centralised on the leader's office, with immense pressure on everyone else to fall into line in the interests of unity . . . I am worried about the prospect of a party continually concerned to avoid the spread of negative images of itself, desperate to be elected as representative of mainstream opinion, and yet with its inner sanctum holding a virtual monopoly of what main-

stream opinion consists of. I thought that kind of approach to leadership went out of fashion when the Berlin Wall came down.

He was not alone in his concern. Outside the magic circle of
power there was growing criticism of what Old Labour, a pejora-
tive term in New Labour's vocabulary, regarded as the wholesale
abandonment of the party's principles. If the modernizers had
trouble in defining their principles, however, they had no doubts
about the reach of their authority.

In the countdown to the election of 1997 what little remained
of dissent was ruthlessly suppressed, awkward candidates being
deselected and replaced by Millbank nominees; veteran MPs
being subjected to what Ken Livingstone was to describe as
'bone-crunching pressure' to quit their seats and make way for
Blairite candidates; and one-time radicals such as Clare Short
being compelled to recant for her modest criticism of New
Labour's agenda. Indifferent to the charge that the party was in
the process of producing a generation of control freaks, the 'Millbank Tendency' – an epithet redolent of the repressive practices
of the once feared Militants – imposed its authority on the party
with military precision.

Modelled on the experience of President Clinton, whose wife
Hilary had suggested that he should establish 'a war room' to
manage his 1992 bid for the US Presidency, Millbank Tower was
to become the command centre in which 'the people in the dark'
packaged New Labour's image and of which Jay Rayner was to
write in the *Observer*: 'But what is most striking about the Labour
election operation is, perhaps ironically, the removal of politics
from the process.'

Kinnock's prescription had been well learned. Like marketing
pot noodles, presentation had come to substitute for substance.
On substantive issues such as Europe and constitutional reform
the party remained evasive, while even on such targeted topics
as employment and the welfare state the spinners of Millbank
ensured that they gave no hostages to media fortune, although

having cosseted much of the right-wing press there was little danger of that.

As far as New Labour's exact commitments were concerned, the party's five key pledges were encapsulated in a mini-manifesto published in July 1996: to cut class sizes to thirty or under for five- to seven-year-olds; to establish fast-track punishment for persistent young offenders; to cut NHS waiting lists by treating an extra 100,000 patients; to get 250,000 under-twenty-five-year-olds off benefit and into work; and to set tough rules for government spending and borrowing. To these were added the existing pledges to put an end to waiting for surgery for diagnosed cancer patients; to impose a ban on handguns and combat knives; to cut VAT on heating to 5 per cent and to begin a movement towards a starting rate of income tax of tenpence in the pound.

Save for the final clause, this was a victory for political minimalism, the product of sundry pollsters and the work of New Labour's focus groups, of whom Blair was to tell the *Sunday Telegraph* that 'there is no one more powerful in the world today than a member of a focus group' and of which Matthew D'Ancona was to write: 'The dictatorship of the focus group – replacing the dictatorship of the proletariat – has led the Labour Party to the point where it seems that its desire to please seems greater than its desire to lead, or to assert its core beliefs.'

And as the shadows of the Tories' years of rule lengthened, Labour had little difficulty in persuading not only its traditional supporters but also the voters of Middle England that there was indeed no alternative to the new millennium that Tony Blair proclaimed:

> We need to respond to the challenge of the new millennium by embarking on a journey of national renewal which creates a new, young Britain – a young, successful and self-confident country which uses the talents of all its citizens to give them a stake in the future.

> New Labour wants to give power to the people – to be a govern-
> ment working in partnership with the people, which gives them
> freedom, choice and responsibility, and where the country is more
> united, more open and more confident about the future than it has
> been for decades.

It was a vision that captivated the electorate. Like prestidigi-
tators, the leaders of New Labour had conjured up an image that
even they were unable to substantiate. Yet it worked. On 1 May
1997 Britain went to the polls to return New Labour to power
with an unprecedented 179-seat majority.

The modernizers' project had been realized, and in the euphoria that followed the silence of Old Labour was more eloquent
than words. Seemingly the long debate as to the meaning of
socialism had finally been resolved, although neither Morris or
Shaw could have recognized where their reflections would lead.
Indeed, the idea that after the party's first hundred days in office
three of Margaret Thatcher's most devoted admirers would be at
the forefront of the homage to New Labour would have beggared
even their beliefs. Surely there was more to their hopes than the
encomiums of the economist Madsen Pirie: 'Gordon Brown is
definitely to the right of Kenneth Clarke on markets'; the historian Andrew Roberts: 'Tony Blair is much more an instinctive
Tory than John Major was'; and the philosopher Roger Scruton:
'Labour have accepted that Mrs Thatcher was right.'

And while Old Labour was pondering the betrayal, and the
Tory right was applauding New Labour's conversion to 'the economics of common sense', it was left to Roy Hattersley, Kinnock's
deputy leader and a critic of Labour's impossibilists, to reflect: 'I
am not sure which depresses me the more: the Labour leadership's
rejection of redistribution or their refusal to face the arguments in
favour of equality.'

Perhaps Morris had been right. Perhaps 'the tremendous
organisation of civilised commercial society' had been playing cat-
and-mouse games with socialism after all.

Clause IV Revised

1. The Labour Party is a democratic socialist party. It believes that by the strength of our common endeavour, we achieve more than we achieve alone so as to create for each of us the means to realize our true potential and for all of us a community in which power, wealth and opportunity are in the hands of the many not the few, where the rights we enjoy reflect the duties we owe, and where we live together, freely, in a spirit of solidarity, tolerance and respect.

2. To these ends we work for:

– a dynamic economy serving the public interest, in which the enterprise of the market and the rigour of competition are joined with the forces of partnership and cooperation to produce the wealth the nation needs and the opportunity for all to work and prosper, with a thriving private sector and high quality public services, where those undertakings essential for the common good are either owned by the public or accountable to them;

– a just society, which judges its strength by the condition of the weak as much as the strong, provides security against fear, and justice at work; which nurtures families, promotes equality of opportunity, and delivers people from the tyranny of poverty, prejudice and the abuse of power;

– an open democracy, in which government is held to account by the people; decisions are taken as far as practicable by the communities they affect; and where fundamental human rights are guaranteed;

– a healthy environment which we protect, enhance and hold in trust for future generations;

3. Labour is committed to the defence and security of the British people, and to cooperating in European institutions, the United Nations, the Commonwealth and other international bodies to secure peace, freedom, democracy, economic security and environmental protection for all.

4. Labour will work in pursuit of these aims with trade unions, cooperative societies and other affiliated organisations, and also with voluntary organisations, consumer groups and other representative bodies.

5. On the basis of these principles, Labour seeks the trust of the people to govern.

Distribution of Wealth in the UK

Clearly there has been an enormous improvement in the standard of living in the UK since the foundation of the Labour Party in 1900, and in absolute terms the wealth and income of the majority of the working class has increased fairly steadily during that period. However, the shift in the actual distribution of wealth since the party first came to power in 1924 has been less marked:

Share of Total Wealth (%)

	1923	1971	1989
Top 10 per cent	89.1	65.0	53.0
Next 10 per cent	5.1	16.6.	
Next 15 per cent	NA	NA	22.0
Top 50 per cent	NA	97.0	94.0

Bibliography

R. Page Arnot, *The General Strike*, London: Labour Research Department, 1926.

C. R. Attlee, *The Labour Party in Perspective*, London: Left Book Club, 1937.

E. Belfort Bax, *Outspoken Essays*, London: William Reeves, 1897.

M. Beer, *History of British Socialism*, London: G. Bell and Sons, 1929.

Tony Benn, *The Benn Diaries*, London: Hutchinson, 1995.

Aneurin Bevan, *In Place of Fear*, London: Heinemann, 1952.

Robin Blackburn and Alexander Cockburn (Ed.), *The Incompatibles*, London: Penguin, 1967.

Tony Blair, *New Britain: My Vision of a Young Country*, London: Fourth Estate, 1996.

Robert Blatchford, *Merrie England*, London: Clarion Press, 1894.

George Brown, *In My Way*, London: Victor Gollancz, 1970.

Michael Barratt Brown and Ken Coates, *The Blair Revelation*, Nottingham: Spokesman, 1996.

Alan Bullock, *The Life and Times of Ernest Bevin*, London: Heinemann, 1960.

James Callaghan, *Time and Chance*, London: Collins, 1987.

John Campbell, *Nye Bevan and the Mirage of British Socialism*, London: Weidenfeld and Nicolson, 1987.

Barbara Castle, *The Castle Diaries, 1964-1970*, London: Weidenfeld and Nicolson, 1984.

Barbara Castle, *Fighting All the Way*, London: Macmillan, 1993.

Peter Clarke, *A Question of Leadership: From Gladstone to Thatcher*, London: Penguin, 1992.

Catherine Ann Cline, *Recruits to Labour, 1914–1931*, Syracuse, New York: Syracuse University Press, 1963.

Ken Coates, *The Crisis of British Socialism*, Nottingham: Spokesman Books, 1971.

John Cockburn, *Keir Hardie*, London: Jarrolds, 1956.

G. D. H Cole and Raymond Postgate, *The Common People*, London: Methuen, 1938.

G. D. H. Cole, *Fabian Socialism*, London: George Allen and Unwin, 1943.

G. D. H. Cole, *A History of the Labour Party from 1914*, London: Routledge and Kegan Paul, 1948.

G. D. H. Cole, *The People's Front*, London: Left Book Club, 1937.

Margaret Cole, *Beatrice Webb*, London: Longmans, Green and Co., 1945.

Margaret Cole, *Makers of the Labour Movement*, London: Longmans, Green and Co., 1948.

Margaret Cole, *The Story of Fabian Socialism*, London; Heinemann, 1961.

John Cole, *As It Seemed to Me*, London: Weidenfeld and Nicolson, 1995.

Ivor Crewe and Anthony King, *SDP, The Birth, Life and Death of the Social Democratic Party*, Oxford: Oxford University Press, 1995.

Michael Crick, *The March of the Militant*, London: Faber and Faber, 1986.

C. A. R. Crosland, *The Future of Socialism*, London: Jonathan Cape, 1956.

Hugh Dalton, *Memoirs, 1931-1945*, London: Frederick Muller, 1957.

George Dangerfield, *The Strange Death of Liberal England*, London: Random House, 1935.

A. J. Davies, *To Build a New Jerusalem*, London: Michael Joseph, 1992.

Mary Davies, *Comrade or Brother*, London: Pluto Press, 1993.

Gregory Elliott, *Labourism and the English Genius*, London: Verso, 1993.

Lord Elton, *The Life of Ramsay MacDonald*, London: Collins, 1939.

Eric Estorick, *Sir Stafford Cripps*, London: Heinemann, 1949.

Fabian Society, Fabian tracts, London: Fabian Society, 1884–98.

R. A. Florey, *The General Strike, 1926*, London: John Calder, 1980.

Michael Foot, *Aneurin Bevan, 1897-1945*, London: MacGibbon and Kee, 1962.

Michael Foot, *Aneurin Bevan, 1945-1960*, London: Davis Poynter, 1973.

Basil Fuller, *The Life Story of J. H. Thomas*, London: Stanley Paul, 1934.

J. K. Galbraith, *The Great Crash*, London: Pelican Books, 1961.

J. B. Glasier, *William Morris and the Early Days of the Socialist Movement*, Bristol: Thoemmes Press, 1994.

Peter Hain, *Ayes to the Left*, London: Lawrence and Wishart, 1995.

J. Keir Hardie, *From Serfdom to Socialism*, London: George Allen, 1907.

Brian Harrison, *The Transformation of British Politics*, Oxford: Oxford University Press, 1996.

Denis Healey, *The Time of My Life*, London: Michael Joseph, 1989.

Fred Henderson; *The Great Unrest*, Ipswich: Jarrold and Sons, 1912.

Eric Hobsbawm, *Labouring Men, Studies in the History of Labour*, London: Weidenfeld and Nicolson, 1964.

Eric Hobsbawm, *Politics for a Rational Left*, London: Verso, 1989.

Eric Hobsbawm, *Worlds of Labour*, London: Weidenfeld and Nicolson, 1984.

Michael Holroyd, *George Bernard Shaw: Volume 1, In Search of Love, 1856–1898*, London: Chatto, 1988; *Volume 2, The Pursuit of Power, 1898–1918*, London: Chatto, 1989.

Leslie Hunter, *The Road to Brighton Pier*, London: Arthur Barker, 1959

Alan Hutt, *British Trade Unionism*, London: Lawrence and Wishart, 1975.

H. M. Hyndman, *Historical Basis of Socialism in England*, London: Kegan Paul, Trench and Co, 1883.

Martin Jacques and Francis Mulhern (Eds); *The Forward March of Labour Halted*, London: Verso, 1981.

Roy Jenkins, *A Life at the Centre*, London: Macmillan, 1991.

Eileen Jones, *Neil Kinnock*, London: Robert Hale, 1994.

Tudor Jones, *Remaking the Labour Party: From Gaitskell to Blair*, London: Routledge, 1996.

Dennis Kavanagh (Ed.), *The Politics of the Labour Party*, Nottingham: University of Nottingham, 1982.

David and Maurice Kogan, *The Battle for the Labour Party*, London: Kogan Page, 1982.

Isaac Krammick and Barry Sheerman, *Harold Laski: A Life on the Left*, London: Hamish Hamilton, 1993.

Harold Laski, *Democracy in Crisis*, London: George Allen and Unwin, 1933.

Harold Laski, *What Are We to Do?*, London: Victor Gollancz, 1938.

Geoffrey Lee, *The People's Budget*, London: Henry George Foundation, 1996.

V. I. Lenin, *Lenin on Britain*, London: Lawrence and Wishart, 1934.

The Liberal Industrial Enquiry, *Britain's Industrial Future*, London: Benn, 1928.

Fiona MacCarthy, *William Morris*, London: Faber and Faber, 1994.

John McEwen, *The Riddell Diaries*, London: Athlone Press, 1986.

Alan McKinlay and R. J. Morris, *The Independent Labour Party on Clydeside, 1893–1932*, Manchester: Manchester University Press, 1991.

J. Ramsay MacDonald, *The Socialist Movement*, London: Williams and Norgate, 1911.

J. Ramsay MacDonald, *Socialism and Society*, London: Independent Labour Party, 1905.

Harold Macmillan, *The Past Masters*, London: Macmillan, 1975.

Tom Mann, *The Industrial Syndicalist*, Nottingham: Spokesman Books, 1974.

David Marquand, *The Progressive Dilemma*, London: Heinemann, 1991.

David Marquand, *Ramsay MacDonald*, London: Jonathan Cape, 1977.

David Marquand, *The Unprincipled Society*, London: Jonathan Cape, 1988.

David Marquand and Anthony Seldon, *Ideas That Shaped Post-War Britain*, London: Fontana Press, 1996.

Marx and Engels, *Selected Correspondence*, London: Lawrence and Wishart, 1934.

Roger Moore, *The Emergence of the Labour Party, 1880–1924*, London: Hodder and Stoughton, 1978.

Jane Morgan (Ed.), *Richard Crossman Diaries*, London: Hamish Hamilton, 1981.

Kenneth O. Morgan, *Keir Hardie*, London: Weidenfeld and Nicolson, 1975.

Kenneth O. Morgan, *Labour People: Hardie to Kinnock*, Oxford: Oxford University Press, 1992.

Kenneth O. Morgan, *Lloyd George*, London: Weidenfeld and Nicolson, 1974.,

William Morris, *Political Writings*, London: Thoemmes Press, 1994.

William Morris, *Signs of Change*, London: Reeves and Turner, 1888.

William Morris and Belfort Bax, *Socialism, Its Growth and Outcome*, London: Swan Sommerschein, 1893.

Herbert Morrison, *An Autobiography*, London: Odhams, 1960.

A. L. Morton, *A People's History of England*, London: Left Book Club, 1938.

David Owen, *Personally Speaking*, London: Pan, 1987.

Henry Pelling, *A History of British Trade Unionism*, London: Penguin, 1987.

Ben Pimlott, *Hugh Dalton*, London: Jonathan Cape, 1985.

Raymond Postgate, *The Life of George Lansbury*, London: Longmans, Green and Co., 1951.

Patrick Seyd, *The Rise and Fall of the Labour Left*, London: Macmillan, 1987.

Eric Shaw, *Discipline and Discord in the Labour Party*, Manchester: Manchester University Press, 1988.

G. B. Shaw (Ed.), *Fabian Essays*, London: Fabian Society, 1889.

Emmanuel Shinwell, *We Lived Through It All*, London: Gollancz, 1973.

William L. Shirer, *The Rise and Fall of the Third Reich*, London: Pan Books, 1964.

Peter Shore, *Leading the Left*, London: Weidenfeld and Nicolson, 1993.

Robert Skidelsky, *Politicians and the Slump*, London: Pelican Books, 1970.

Philip Snowden, *An Autobiography*, London: Ivor Nicholson and Watson, 1934.

Philip Snowden, *Socialism and Syndicalism*, London: Collins Clear Type, 1912.

John Strachey, *The Coming Struggle for Power*, London: Gollancz, 1934.

R. H. Tawney, *The Acquisitive Society*, London: G. Bell and Son, 1921.

R. H. Tawney, *Equality*, London: George Allen and Unwin, 1931.

Hugh Thomas, *The Spanish Civil War*, London: Penguin, 1965.

J. H. Thomas, *My Story*, London: Hutchinson, 1937.

E. P. Thompson, *Making History*, New York: The New Press, 1994.

E. P. Thompson, *The Making of the English Working Class*, London: Gollancz, 1963.

E. P. Thompson, *William Morris*, New York: Pantheon, 1976.

Willie Thompson, *The Long Death of British Labourism*, London: Pluto, 1993.

Malcolm Thomson, *David Lloyd George*, London: Hutchinson, 1944.

Dona Torr, *Tom Mann and His Times*, London: Lawrence and Wishart, 1956.

Hilary Wainwright, *Labour: A Tale of Two Parties*, London: Hogarth Press, 1987.

Beatrice Webb, *Diaries, 1924–1932*, London: Longmans, Green and Co., 1956.

Beatrice Webb, *Our Partnership*, London: Longmans, Green and Co., 1928.

H. G. Wells, *Experiment in Autobiography*, London: Gollancz, 1934.

H. G. Wells, *The New Machiavelli*, London: T. Fisher Unwin, 1911.

Anthony West, *H. G. Wells: Aspects of Life*, London: Hutchinson, 1984.

Trevor Wilson, *The Political Diaries of C.P. Scott*, Glasgow: Collins, 1970.

Francis Williams, *Fifty-Year March*, London: Odhams Press, 1950.

J. M. Winter, *Socialism and the Challenge of the War*, London: Routledge and Kegan Paul, 1974.

Tony Wright, *Socialisms Old and New*, London: Routledge, 1996.

Philip Ziegler, *Wilson*, London: Weidenfeld and Nicolson, 1993.

Index

What's Left?